BTEC Nationals – IT Practitioners

BTEC Nationals – IT Practitioners
Core Units for BTEC Nationals in IT and Computing

Sharon Yull and Howard Anderson

Newnes

OXFORD AMSTERDAM BOSTON LONDON NEW YORK PARIS
SAN DIEGO SAN FRANCISCO SINGAPORE SYDNEY TOKYO

Newnes
An imprint of Elsevier Science
Linacre House, Jordan Hill, Oxford OX2 8DP
225 Wildwood Avenue, Woburn MA 01801-2041

First published 2002

British Library Cataloguing in Publication Data
A catalogue record for this book is available from the British Library

ISBN 0 7506 56840

For information on all Newnes publications
visit our website at www.newnespress.com

Typeset at Replika Press Pvt Ltd, India
Printed and bound in Great Britain

Contents

Preface

This book has been written to help you achieve the learning outcomes of the core units of the new *BTEC Nationals – IT Practitioners* scheme from Edexcel. In covers the six core units common to all National Certificate and National Diploma courses. Three of these units form the compulsory core of the BTEC National Awards. The coverage is designed to cater for a General, ICT Systems Support, or Software Development course. The two authors have many years' experience of teaching computing students and have worked with BTEC to produce a modern course structure. In producing the book, the authors' principal aim has been that of capturing, within a single volume, the core knowledge required of all computing students at National level. The six core units covered in the book are:

1. Language and communications
2. Computer systems
3. Business information systems
4. Introduction to software development
5. Communications technology
6. Systems analysis and design.

The book has been organized on a logical basis with each chapter devoted to a single core unit. We have, however, attempted to reduce duplication, and some material is appropriate to more than one of the core units. Furthermore, to put supporting concepts into context, we have developed a number of topics within the individual chapters and in sections at the end of the book. You will also find that where difficult concepts are introduced, we have included notes in boxes under various headings. These will provide you with an alternative way of understanding them.

This book has been designed to provide you with a thorough introduction to each of the core units. Despite this, you are advised to make use of other reference books and materials wherever and whenever possible. You should also get into the habit of using all of the resources that are available to you. These include your tutor, your college library and computer centre, and other learning resources. Extensive use should be made of the Internet; to help you there are numerous universal resource identifiers (URIs) in the text. As this subject concerns perhaps the most rapidly changing of all technologies, the most up-to-date information is often only available from the Internet. You should also become familiar with selecting materials that are appropriate to the topics that you are studying. In particular, you may find it useful to refer to materials that will provide you with several different views of a particular topic.

Throughout the book we have provided worked examples that show how the ideas introduced in the text can be put into practice. We have also included problems and questions at various stages in the text. Depending on the nature of the topic, these questions take a variety of forms, from simple problems requiring short numerical answers to those that may require some additional research or that may require the use of an analytical software package in their solution. Your tutor may well ask you to provide answers to these questions as coursework or homework, but they can also be used to help you with revision for course assessments.

Language and communications are vital to any area of study, so form a very important part of the course. This book will help you develop clear communication skills and accurate language to suit a computing environment.

The **Computer systems** unit is concerned with the 'nuts and bolts' of small computer systems. The accent is on how it works without becoming too involved with technical details. The purpose is to develop sufficient knowledge to understand the performance and limitations of computer systems.

As well as providing some knowledge of writing program codes, the **Introduction to software development** unit will show how sound design ideas will enhance the process of software production to achieve reliable software that meets the user's needs.

Networks are covered in the **Communications technology** unit to a level required to communicate with network specialists.

Finally, the two units **Systems analysis and design** and **Business information systems** cover the ideas required to understand the use of computers in a business environment, how information flows in such organizations, and how best to use computers to aid efficient operation.

Support materials for Lecturers. Key skills mapping information is included in the resources on the companion website for this book: www.bh.com/companions/0750656840. A photocopiable tutor resource pack is also available from your usual supplier or direct from the publishers. BTEC Nationals – IT Practitioners Tutor Resource Pack 0750656875.

Sharon Yull and Howard Anderson

Unit 1　Language and communications

The aim of this unit is to provide students with knowledge and information that can be integrated into other units within the BTEC National for IT Practitioners qualification. This unit will also equip students with the skills to improve their own transferable skills and enable them to communicate more effectively. This unit focuses on a range of written, presentational, evaluative and research techniques. Students will be introduced to exercises and activities that will encourage independent learning and also group discussions, above all this unit will support and strengthen students' basic language and communication skills.

1.1 How do we communicate?

The tools and techniques of communication

Communication is a way of expressing thoughts and ideas from one person or party to another. To enable effective communication there need to be three main elements: a sender, a communication tool and a receiver, as shown in Figure 1.1.

Figure 1.1 *Elements to enable effective communication*

The sender of information is sometimes referred to as the source of information: all information will originate from a source of some description. The source generates or initiates the information that is to be sent. Sources of information can include:

- human resources (people)
- electronic resources (computer systems etc.).

Factors determining communication tool use

The type of communication tool that is required to transmit the information will vary, depending upon a number of factors. These factors are identified in Figure 1.2. Some communication tools may be more appropriate than others, because of their convenience and/or flexibility. For example, the quickest way to get a response to a question from a person sitting next to you is to ask, the communication tool being 'speech'. However, if this person has a hearing impediment the most effective form might be 'body language', 'sign language' or a form of written communication.

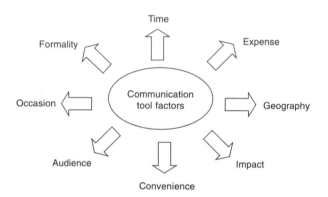

Figure 1.2 *Factors determining communication tool use*

A communication tool may be selected based on how long it takes to transmit the information. For example, it might be necessary to send a document by fax rather than post because of the urgency of the information.

Expense

Different communication tools have different costs: these could include the cost of a stamp or a telephone call.

Exercise 1.1

Identify the cost of the following communication services:

- first class stamp
- second class stamp
- sending a 1 kg parcel first class
- national phone call
- international phone calls from the UK to Australia, Hong Kong and the USA
- off-peak tariffs for two mobile phone companies.

Geography

The distance over which communication has to travel will influence the type of tool used. For example, it would not be feasible to shout over a distance of ten miles – it would be more practical to use the telephone, or send an e-mail.

Impact

The impression that you need to create will influence the choice of communication tool. You would not close a million-pound deal by sending an e-mail – you might deliver a presentation in person, face-to-face, or send a written confirmation. Similarly, you would not send an e-mail to a potential employee offering a contract of employment – this would be set out in a formal letter.

Convenience

Some communication tools are more convenient to use than others. Writing a letter can be quite time-consuming, especially if there is a lot to say in the content. Direct conversation, either face-to-face or using the telephone, may be more appropriate.

Audience

Your audience will influence the communication tool used to express information. Within an organization you might chat informally to a colleague, e-mail a team leader, and send a memorandum to the department.

Occasion

The occasion can determine the type of communication tool; for example, a birthday might trigger the sending of a card – a written format. A chance meeting with an old friend might develop into the use of physical communication such as a hug or a kiss.

Formality

There are some instances when a specific communication tool needs to be used to match the formality of the situation. Written communication provides the formality to make certain contracts and transactions legally binding, for example birth, marriage and death certificates, employment contracts, and guarantees offered by documents such as receipts.

The receiver

The final component required to enable effective communication is a receiver. The receiver, in conjunction with the sender, can be a human or electronic resource. Once information has been received, recipients can respond in a number of different ways. First, they themselves or the system can pass on this information, making them or the system both a receiver and a sender. Secondly, they or the system can carry out an action as a result of the information received, therefore activating a process. Finally, on receipt of the information they or the system can do nothing, retaining the information and storing it within their own memory bank as shown in Figure 1.3.

Information is sent to the receiver, who then passes it on to a third party. The receiver has thus a dual role of recipient and sender.

Information is sent to the receiver, who then carries out an action and processes the information received.

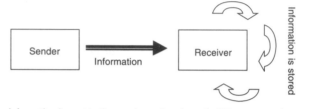

Information is sent to the receiver, who stores it within a personal memory bank

Figure 1.3   *Actions of a recipient of information*

Ways of communicating

It has been established that for effective communication to take place there need to be three components: the sender, use of a communication tool, and a receiver. However, another factor that influences the effectiveness of communication is the type of communication used.

Communication can broadly be categorized into four main areas:

- verbal
- written
- visual
- expressive.

Verbal communication

Verbal communication implies that information has been transmitted through speech or sound. Categories of verbal communication can include:

- chatting
- enquiring
- apologizing
- delegating
- directing
- advising
- informing
- challenging
- debating
- persuading.

Exercise 1.2

1. For each of the verbal categories of communication, identify a situation you have been in that reflects this category.
2. Choose five categories and identify how you influenced the situation through this category of verbal communication.
3. Identify another appropriate category of verbal communication that could have been used instead.
4. Are there any other categories of verbal communication that you can add to the list?
5. For each of the following scenarios, identify the most appropriate verbal communication category and state why; use a table template to complete the information.

Scenario	Verbal communication used	Why?
Attending an interview		
Buying a new computer game in a shop		
You have forgotten your friend's birthday		
Asking your parents to lend you some money		
Giving a talk in language and communications		

Speaking to somebody directly face-to-face is one of the most open forms of communication. Speech can be spontaneous, emotional and very influential, which is why you should have a licence to open your mouth – with a single word or sentence, you can change somebody's life for better or worse.

People communicate with each other every second of every day all over the world, and in each conversation a unique bond forms between the sender and the receiver. This bond can last a moment or a lifetime. People always say that first impressions count, and this is very true. From the moment that you open your mouth to welcome, enquire, dispute or confess, people lock on to what you are saying and react accordingly.

Thinking before you speak can sometimes be very difficult, especially if the circumstances are emotionally linked to love or hate situations. Arguments sometimes force people into a corner, boxing them into retaliating with words that are said in anger.

> ## Exercise 1.3
>
> 1. Think of a situation where you have been angry and have argued or said things that you didn't mean.
> 2. What triggered the argument?
> 3. What could you have done or said to stop the argument taking place?
> 4. What could you have said during the argument to make the situation better?

One of the ways to avoid an argument is to state that you would rather talk than argue. Talking can normally diffuse an argument because one of the reasons that an argument takes place is through lack of communication, either because people do not talk or through misinformation.

To ensure more open and positive verbal communication, follow and remember these guidelines:

T   Think before you speak
A   Analyse what is said before you respond
L   Listen to all aspects of the conversation
K   Kind words are free
I   Insults carry a price
N   Never seem distracted when somebody is talking
G   Give as much attention to the conversation as possible.

Advantages of verbal communication

Verbal communication has the advantages that it can be a very open format of communication, especially if it is face to face. Other advantages include that it:

- can be directed to a specific, and the correct, audience
- can generate an instant response or action
- can complete the communication cycle of controlling a situation and also providing feedback
- can address a single or a multiple audience
- is very expressive
- is inexpensive or free.

Disadvantages of verbal communication

One of the major disadvantages of verbal communication is that it is all too easy to say things in the heat of the moment that might not be expressed if another form of communication were used. It is easier to express anger verbally than it is to write it down in a letter. The spontaneity of verbal communication and the lack of control over emotions can then spill over into conversations or disputes.

Interviewing

The large majority of people will experience being interviewed or interviewing others. An interview may be required for a place in higher education or for a job. Interviews are a standard way of assessing how candidates present themselves, sometimes within a pressurized environment.

Interviews are conducted for a number of reasons; you may be interviewed:

- face to face, to assess how you look and how you present yourself
- to identify what you have done academically, socially and in your work life
- to clarify key areas as stipulated on an application form or curriculum vitae
- to assess your personality and interpersonal skills.

Interviews help to establish whether you are the right person for the position advertised.

There are a number of ways that interviews are conducted, including:

- telephone interviews
- one-to-one interviews
- panel or group interviews.

Telephone interviews are often the first stage in the selection process, especially if there are a number of applicants. You might be asked a set of questions that require you to draw upon your experiences in order to answer them. For example, 'Can you give me an example, based on your own experiences, where you have had to overcome a problem involving other people?' The telephone interview could also be set up purely to establish your skills and knowledge base in preparation for a second face-to-face interview.

One-to-one interviews are very common: this is where you are invited in for a set appointment with an admissions officer, course tutor, human resource manager or department manager. In a one-to-one interview you are being assessed against a number of criteria as identified in Figure 1.4.

How you look

How you present yourself (body language)

How well you answer questions

How well you sell yourself (skills and knowledge)

Your ability to communicate

Interpersonal skills and personality

Figure 1.4 *Interview criteria*

First impressions do indeed count in an interview situation, and therefore you should dress appropriately. If you are attending an interview for a job, smart formal dress such as a suit is appropriate. You may only have a short while to sell your skills and qualities and to convince the interviewer that you are the right applicant for the position. To aid in this process, remember the following eight-step interview procedure.

1. **Plan.** You may be competing with a number of other candidates and only get one chance to impress, so make sure that you plan in advance what you want to say and how you want to say it, given the opportunity.

2. **Research.** Research the background of the company or educational institute and find out additional information. For example, if applying for a job with an organization, find out about its structure, what it does, its financial situation, recent media coverage etc.

3. **Present.** Dress for the occasion and arrive relaxed and prepared. Ensure that you have a copy of your curriculum vitae, a copy of the job role/specification, evidence of your skills and knowledge (e.g. certificates, record of achievement), and letters of commendation, references etc. If appropriate, bring evidence of your skills that are appropriate to the job role. For example, if applying to be a web designer, bring a portfolio of your work and web page designs.

4. **Body language.** Always be aware of your body language in an interview situation. Some people do very strange things without realizing it – for example, tapping fingers, crunching teeth, looking down at the floor.

5. **Be alert and attentive.** Look enthusiastic and motivated, maintain eye contact (but do not constantly stare, as this can be off-putting), feel confident in the situation, respond to questions, do not be afraid to ask for a second to reflect upon an answer if you require it, or to ask the interviewer to repeat a question if you are not sure of it.

6. **Sell yourself.** You have reached the interview because you have the skills and knowledge, otherwise you would not have applied. You know this but the interviewer may not; all he or she has is an application form and a curriculum vitae. This is your chance to shine; tell your interviewer what you have done and what you are capable of doing, without being too arrogant or lying (see Figure 1.5). Convince the interviewer that you are the person required.

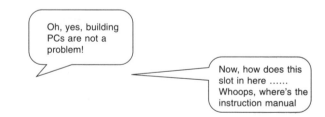

Figure 1.5   *Step 6 – Don't tell lies just to get the job*

7   **Listen.** Listening skills are very important, especially in an interview situation. Do not interrupt constantly; wait until you are prompted into giving a response. When listening, acknowledge what is being said by smiling or nodding occasionally. As you listen, reflect on what is being said and prepare your response.

8   **Questions.** If you can, always think of a question to ask at the end of the interview. This could be related to the research that you have carried out, for example: 'I understand that you have

six functional areas within the IT department; does this mean that the successful applicant will be able to gain experience in working in a range of these areas?'

Finally, always thank the interviewer for his or her time.

Panel or group interviews are usually set up to allows a range of people access to prospective candidates. In a panel interview, different skills and information can be recognized by different people on the panel, each member assessing different things such as technical knowledge, the ability to work in a team, academic skills, interpersonal skills etc.

Written communication

Written communication is of great importance because of the warranty or assurances that it provides. An application form, for example, identifies and provides assurances of the knowledge and skills of the applicant. A curriculum vitae (CV) provides written confirmation of ability and suitability for a particular task. A receipt is a warranty verifying the sale of an item. Certificates verify an achievement in a particular area (e.g. swimming or qualifications), or legal status (e.g. marriage). Birthday cards provide acknowledgement of a celebration.

Written communication can take a number of forms and serve a range of purposes for various audiences. Over recent years written communication has become even more popular due to the increasing interest in e-mail. E-mail provides the flexibility and convenience that traditional letter writing lacks. An e-mail sends information instantly, and is cheaper than traditional postal methods. Responses are faster and availability is 24 hour, with no restriction on postage times. As a result written communication has again become fashionable, especially amongst the younger generation, with the added bonus of convenience, flexibility and the ability to be interactive.

Written communication can be divided into two types; formal and informal. Formal written communication relates to official documents that provide guarantees and assurances; these document can be legally binding. Informal written communication includes letters to friends, memos, e-mails and greetings etc.

Exercise 1.4

For each of the following written documents, identify those that fall into the formal category and those that can be considered as informal.

Letter to a friend	Birth certificate	Receipt

Letter to a friend   Birth certificate   Receipt

Application form   Statement for a phone bill

Birthday card   Contract of employment

Booking confirmation for a holiday   Driving licence

Curriculum vitae   E-mail to a colleague   Memo

Agenda for a meeting   Newspaper

Letter of resignation

Different written documents have different styles and layouts, each with a set of essential criteria that make the document unique. By examining a range of formal and informal documents it is easy to identify various styles and this can be very useful when designing your own document templates.

Letters

The key characteristics of a letter can be broken down into four main areas:

- identifiers
- introduction
- content
- closure.

Identifiers include items such as the sender and recipient details (name and address), the date, any reference codes, and identification of who the letter is for (Figure 1.6).

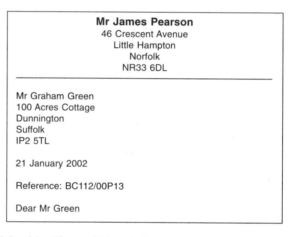

Mr James Pearson
46 Crescent Avenue
Little Hampton
Norfolk
NR33 6DL

Mr Graham Green
100 Acres Cottage
Dunnington
Suffolk
IP2 5TL

21 January 2002

Reference: BC112/00P13

Dear Mr Green

Figure 1.6   *Identifiers within a letter*

The introduction (Figure 1.7) should provide a short overview of the content and also set the tone for the remainder of the letter.

Application to join the East Anglia Interactive Computing Group

After reading the advertisement in 'Buzz Computing', I would like to subscribe for a twelve-month period to your interactive computing group.

Figure 1.7   *Introducing a letter*

The content of the letter (Figure 1.8) should contain the bulk of the information. The content should be set out clearly and specifically, ensuring that the subject matter is factual and relevant to the audience.

The closure section (Figure 1.9) focuses on signing off the letter, and informs the recipient of any other documents that are also being sent. The recipient will expect additional documents if Enc. (Enclosure) appears at the end of the letter. In this example, the enclosure will be the £85.00 cheque.

A complete letter template is given in Figure 1.10.

Your advertisement in Buzz Computing on Friday 17 January, Reference BC112/00P13, invited applications from keen gaming players to subscribe to a new computer interactive group being set up in East Anglia.

My interest in computers and games consoles has increased over the last year, with me acquiring a number of rare games consoles and software that can be considered as 'retro' items. I also enjoy interactive on-line adventure gaming sessions and role play scenarios.

I feel that I could contribute to your group in a number of ways. First, I have an extensive knowledge of hardware and software. I am a keen programmer and software enthusiast. I also submit regular on-line reviews of new games to the 'What's New in Computing' magazine.

I enclose a cheque for £85.00 in respect of twelve months' subscription to your computing group, and I hope that you accept my application.

I look forward to hearing from you in the near future.

Figure 1.8   *Contents of a letter*

Yours faithfully

James Pearson
Computing Enthusiast

Enc.

Figure 1.9   *Closing a letter*

Sender's information

Mr Mark James
56 Briers
Cranburn Road
Norwich
NR7 3DD

If there is no letterhead the address could go to the right-hand margin

Mrs Penelope Jordan
56 Briers
Cranburn Road
Norwich
NR7 3DD

Recipient information

SJ Archaeological Group
445 The Glades
Hingham Road
Norwich
NH3 3HD

Date

22 February 2002

Reference Number (if applicable)

Salutation   For the attention of Customer Enquiry Department

Introduction   Discovery of Roman Coin circa 66 AD

Content

_____

_____

_____

_____

_____

Closure

Yours faithfully

Mark James

Figure 1.10   *Complete letter template*

A letter can be considered as a formal or informal document depending upon the subject matter and audience. A letter can also be classified as being legally binding, for example an offer made with regard to a contract for employment.

Other documents

There are a range of other documents that are in frequent use, some of which are used specifically in organizations; these include memorandums, agendas, minutes and reports (see Figure 1.11).

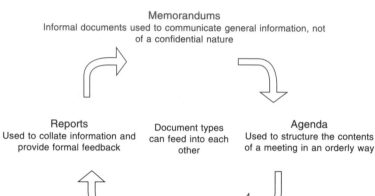

Figure 1.11   *Documents used within an organization*

Memorandums

Memorandums, or memos (Figure 1.12), are used internally within an organization. They are an informal way of communicating and documenting data and information.

Agendas

Agendas (Figure 1.13) are used within an organization to set out a timetable of activities or events in preparation for a meeting. Agendas provide the structure to a meeting, setting out individual actions to be addressed.

```
Memorandum

To:

From:

cc:

Date:

Re:

_____

[Body of text displayed here]
```

Figure 1.12   *Template for a memorandum*

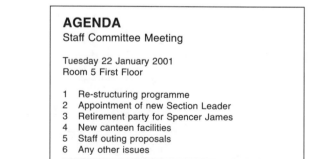

Figure 1.13   *Template for an agenda*

Minutes

Minutes are another form of written communication, and are taken during a meeting. The minutes document items discussed, and can also be used for action planning by nominating people to carry out certain tasks. Minutes also record who is in attendance at the current meeting.

Reports

Reports are used to collate and present information to a particular audience. A report might be generated as a result of a meeting where actions have to be researched in order to complete a task and feedback to a given audience. Formal written reports should follow a set structure that covers specific areas.

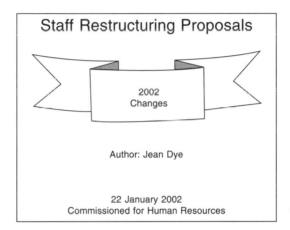

Figure 1.14 *Title page for a formal report*

Title page. This is the front sheet, identifying the report title, the author, the date, and who the report is commissioned for (see Figure 1.14).

Contents page. This references the information given on each page, and should follow the title page (see Figure 1.15).

Contents

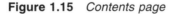

Introduction	.... Page 1
Statistical figures on department staffing levels	.... Page 2
Marketing resources	.... Page 4
Finance resources	.... Page 7
Staff training	.... Page 10

Figure 1.15 *Contents page*

Introduction. The introduction should provide a short summary of the overall focus and content of the report.

Procedures. Any procedures used to collect, collate, analyse and present information should be identified.

Main findings. The main findings section is where the bulk of the report content should be placed. It should be broken down into task, action and research areas. Each area of the findings section should put forward arguments or statements supported by research and analysis. The main findings section can be broken down further into sub-sections, for example:

3.1   Marketing resources

    3.1.1   Staffing levels
    3.1.2   ICT support
    3.1.3   Staff training

Conclusion. The conclusion section should bring together all the items discussed within the main findings section, and provide a summary of the key areas identified.

Recommendations. This section is solution-based, providing the subjects of the report with proposals as to how they can move forward with the report objective. For example, recommendations for staff training could include:

1. Provide residential management training to all supervisors and section managers
2. Offer in-house ICT training programmes to all data entry clerks within the marketing department
3. Set up staff training services on a rotary basis of three employees each week for eight weeks.

References. This section should identify and give credit for all information sources used, including books, magazines or journals, other documents or reports, the Internet etc.

Appendices. This section will provide supporting documentation to the report content. Appendices may include lists of facts and figures, leaflets, downloaded information, photocopied material etc.

Although the range of business documents can vary between organizations and even departments, each organization will have a standard set of documents that are common to all departments. These documents include standard logos and letterheads that appear as a corporate statement on every document in use.

Exercise 1.5

As a group, or in small groups of three or four, collect together a range of business documentation to include letters, invoices and statements etc.

Tasks:

1. Identify the common features of each business document.
2. Write down comments on the logo design and the letterhead.
3. Select the best logo and letterhead, and justify your choice.
4. Using suitable software, design a logo and a letterhead to go on a business letter.

Presentation of written information

The way in which written material is presented can affect how we interpret knowledge. Also our response to picking up a text and reading it can be based on how it is presented, including.

- quantity and volume
- language and style
- layout.

Quantity and volume

The number of pages in a book or other reading source can influence your response to and understanding of the text. Trying to master a thousand-page book on the uses and applications of software is unproductive if all you need is a couple of pages outlining how to set up a spreadsheet. Conversely, a few pages of medical text cannot teach you how to be a surgeon (Figure 1.16).

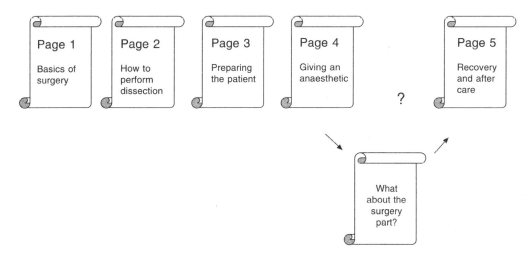

Figure 1.16 *Basics of surgery*

Language and style

The way in which a written document is expressed in terms of technical language and formality can also influence the reader. There are expectations that some reading materials will be presented in a particular way; examples include:

- exam papers
- instruction manuals
- course textbooks
- letters
- legal documents.

If you pick up a romance novel, you expect the language to be informal and familiar, set out within the context of telling a story. Therefore there are certain expectations about how written materials should be presented in terms of language and style.

Layout

The layout of a book can influence how you respond to the text. Layout includes a number of aspects, such as:

1. Size Of fonts

2. Font s*tyle*
3. Pictures, graphics or cartoons:

4. Photographic inserts:

5. Steps and instructions:

    - Fill the kettle
    - Press the switch
    - Pour out boiled water
    - Refill kettle

6. Tasks, case studies and exercises:

> Mr Smithers is the owner of a small organic health-food store. Although his business is quite successful and very profitable, it has been suggested that he could widen his target audience by setting up a web page.
>
> *Task:* Investigate the costs involved in setting up and maintaining a website for this purpose.

Visual communication

Visual communication provides a more expressive and colourful alternative to sending and receiving information in a written format. Visual communication is an important way of learning and absorbing data and information.

Visual communication incorporates a range of pictorial, graphical, design and interactive tools that enable a more effective understanding and conveyance of data and information. It is an integral part of everyday life, and we encounter examples wherever we go. Examples of visual communication tools are shown in Figure 1.17.

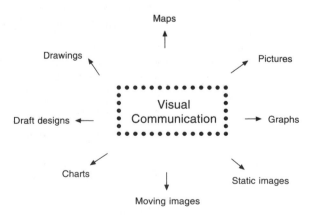

Figure 1.17   *Visual communication tools*

For each visual communication tool, further distinctions can be made to identify various sub-categories. For example, 'maps' includes

Underground maps, Ordnance survey maps, street maps, and mind maps. The purpose of each of these sub-categories is to provide a visual guide, or to aid direction to a certain point. Maps provide navigational information, which cannot be interpreted easily in a textual format.

Exercise 1.6

To emphasize the importance of visual communication, carry out the following exercise in teams of three.

1. One person within each group should draw up a set of written instructions of how to get from one familiar location to another, A–B.
2. The instructions should then be read out to enable the second team member to draw a map of how to get from A–B.
3. These team members should then present the two formats of instructions to the third team member, who can then identify which of the two formats is more appropriate and clearer to understand, giving reasons.

Pictures, drawings and static images are used for a number of different purposes, ranging from providing a general understanding (such as a picture of the human anatomy), to humour (such as cartoons and comic strips).

Graphs and charts

Graphs and charts are used to provide visual representation of data and tables, thus providing a clear breakdown of key data components.

Different graphs and charts are used to represent different types of information, and some of the more popular ones in use include pie charts, bar graphs, line graphs and scatter graphs.

Pie charts

In a pie chart (Figure 1.18), each segment represents a percentage – for example, of games consoles sold for each month from August

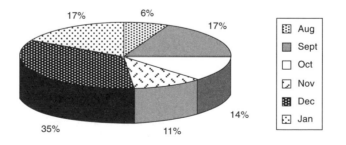

Figure 1.18 *Games consoles sales*

to January. The smallest segment is 6 per cent for August, and the largest is 35 per cent for December.

Bar graphs

Figure 1.19 is an example of a bar graph. The bars each represent a type of games console (types A–D). The bar graph identifies how many of each console was sold each month.

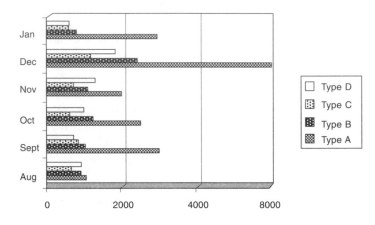

Figure 1.19   *Games consoles sales*

Line graphs

Figure 1.20 is a typical line graph. It clearly plots the sales of each console from August to January. It is very evident that Type A console is the best seller and Type C console is the worst seller. From this graph it is also clear that in August, September and January sales were very similar for Types B, C and D.

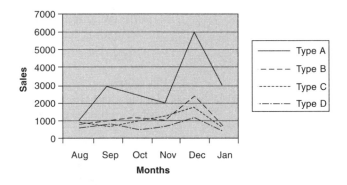

Figure 1.20   *Games consoles sales*

Scatter graphs

Scatter graphs (Figure 1.21) are best used when there are a lot of numerical data that require plotting to identify a correlation or pattern in the data. This particular scatter graph illustrates the pattern of sales for each month, 1–6. In August it clearly shows that all four games console types had similar sales figures; however, in December these are quite diverse.

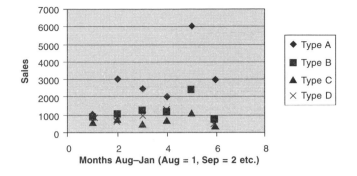

Figure 1.21 Games consoles sales

Exercise 1.7

Using the graph (Figure 1.22), identify four key elements of information that are shown.

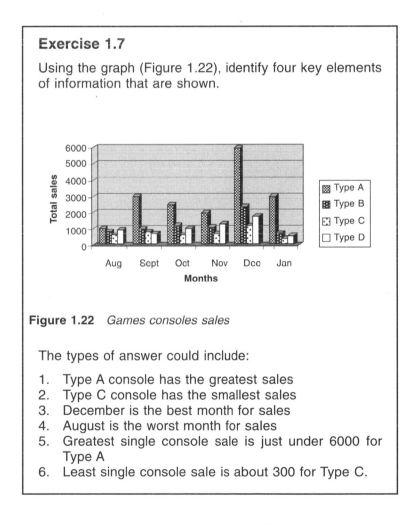

Figure 1.22 *Games consoles sales*

The types of answer could include:

1. Type A console has the greatest sales
2. Type C console has the smallest sales
3. December is the best month for sales
4. August is the worst month for sales
5. Greatest single console sale is just under 6000 for Type A
6. Least single console sale is about 300 for Type C.

Graphs alone can provide a great deal of information. However, visual communication by itself may not be sufficient. If the titles were removed the graph would not make any sense. Also, taking the above example, the total sales figures illustrated are only scaled as thousands, and therefore accuracy is limited.

For the purpose of gathering simple information this graph is adequate; however, to provide more detailed analysis the raw data also need to be included (Table 1.1). With this information more specific calculations, such as average sales, can be made.

Table 1.1   *Sales of games consoles 2001/2002*

	Aug	Sep	Oct	Nov	Dec	Jan
Type A	1000	3000	2500	2000	6000	3000
Type B	800	1000	1200	1100	2400	700
Type C	600	800	550	700	1200	400
Type D	900	700	1000	1300	1800	600

Exercise 1.8

Using Table 1.1, present the information in two different visual formats.

Moving images

Moving images have become one of the most important forms of communication, with the ever increasing popularity of television and movies. Moving images have been used to:

- advertise and sell
- entertain
- instruct and educate.

The new medium of communication is film and television, where actors, actresses, television personalities and soap stars seem to control what we wear, how we live, and what we say and do.

Draft designs

Drafts are used for a range of purposes, especially in engineering, construction and manufacturing. Draft designs provide the basis for fully implemented plans. Examples include car designs, house designs and architectural drawings (Figure 1.23).

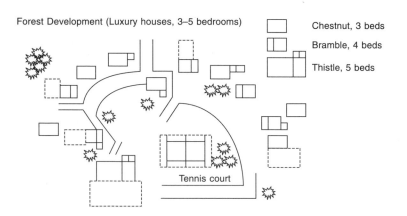

Figure 1.23   *Plans for a new housing development*

Expressive communication

Expressive communication includes body signs and language; BSL (British Sign Language), which is a language in its own right, also falls within this category.

Expressive communication can include a range of actions such as:

- smiling
- frowning
- hugging
- waving
- laughing
- crying
- kissing.

Each action communicates a specific thought or mood – for example, you might frown to express your discontent at a situation, or smile to welcome or show pleasure.

Exercise 1.9

1. Identify all the different body language actions that you used yesterday, and where, when and to whom you expressed these.
2. Would it have been more appropriate to have used an alternative expressive action?
3. Did you use another form of communication in conjunction with the expressive action?

For some people, such as those with severe hearing impairment, expressive communication may be the only way to communicate. These people may use British Sign Language.

1.2 Presentations, discussions and debates

Good presentation skills are essential for progression into higher education, training or employment. From the moment that you convey verbal or expressive communication, people will have expectations regarding your ability to present information clearly, cohesively, relevantly and knowledgeably. These expectations may in some cases be so high that your future depends upon the way you have presented yourself.

Presentations

Presentations can be formal and informal. Formal presentations include:

- interviews for a job/place at college or university
- providing feedback on a project at work
- representation at a meeting
- press releases
- awards ceremony speeches.

Informal presentations include:

- presentations on 'new film releases' as part of the language and communications unit
- feeding back events of a holiday to a friend
- thank you/congratulations speeches to friends or family.

At some point in your life you may be expected to deliver a presentation. This can be done in a number of ways:

- by reading from cards, sheets etc.
- freestyle
- by using presentation software
- by using aids such as flip charts, overhead transparencies (OHTs), whiteboard etc.

Some people find it quite difficult to recall large amounts of data and information from memory and therefore require a prompt to aid in the recall process. Prompts normally used in presentations are either small index cards containing a few bullet points, or a piece of paper. Although these presentation aids do help in the actual reciting of information, they can also be quite restrictive in terms of the delivery of the presentation. When you are delivering a presentation using cards or sheets, remember the following:

- the information recorded should be kept to a minimum, using bullet points only
- try only to glance at the aids – do not read from them
- ensure you place the aids discretely, for example on a desk or podium; if you need to hold them, ensure that they are not held high so they cover your face
- maintain a rapport with the audience by establishing eye contact and acknowledging their responses with a smile or a nod
- using your voice, control the presentation and captivate the audience; the problem with reading from an aid is that sometimes tone and expression is lost
- do not rush through each bullet point; use your own creativity to expand on it.

Freestyle presentations are usually given by people who:

- know their presentation topic inside out
- feel enthusiastic and motivated by the topic and therefore rely heavily on body language or another tool to demonstrate this
- feel very comfortable with their target audience
- draw heavily upon the participation and interactivity of the audience.

To deliver a freestyle presentation successfully takes a great deal of planning. You cannot stand up and deliver a fifteen-minute presentation on a subject that you have no or very little knowledge of; how would you remember everything? When you deliver a freestyle presentation, you should be very aware of what the rest of your body is doing and what signals are being given out when you are speaking. You might have a tendency to look down and admire your shoes, make artistic patterns on the floor with your feet, over use your hands, or generally fidget.

ICT now plays a big role in the overall quality of presentations. Software applications can be used for the specific purpose of delivering a professional presentation, and can provide a number of benefits (Figure 1.24).

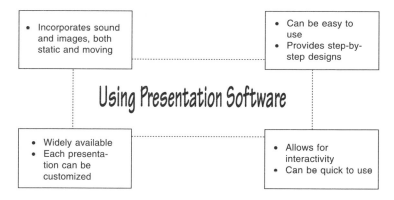

Figure 1.24 *Benefits of using presentation software*

Presentation software can provide a whole range of features that will enable you to:

- customize slide background/wallpaper
- control the speed of each slide
- determine the way in which the slide appears onto the screen (e.g. dissolving in)
- automatically time the length of each slide
- link to other applications or the Web.

Other aids, such as flip charts, boards and OHTs, can also assist in the delivery of a presentation. Flip charts are constantly used in the delivery of business presentations to portray sales figures, forecast charts and projection graphs. They are also useful if you want to encourage audience participation so that thoughts and ideas can be noted and discussed.

OHTs are commonly used to display facts and figures, and in some cases are preferred to using cards or reading from sheets.

Exercise 1.10

You must prepare two ten-minute presentations.

Presentation 1:
You have applied for a job in a large IT company and been successful in the first round of interviews. You have now been asked to attend a second round, and will be assessed on your ability to communicate to a group.

Tasks:
Prepare a ten-minute presentation based on one of the following topic areas:

- the need for team working
- the need to communicate at all levels in an organization
- the need to delegate
- the need to problem solve.

You have half an hour in which to prepare a presentation, using any resources available. You must deliver the presentation to your group.

Presentation 2:
This presentation is based on your own chosen topic area. Suggestions include:

- a hobby or pastime
- a holiday
- a special occasion
- sports
- pop music
- films or TV.

This presentation will last ten minutes, and must be delivered in a freestyle format with the use of no presentation resources. You can bring in any items to show as part of your presentation.

1.3 Reading and responding to written material

The ability to read and absorb information from written material can vary to a degree depending upon a number of factors. These include:

- subject matter
- objectives of reading
- level of material
- presentation of material.

Subject matter

Reading material (such as a book or magazine) that is of interest to you will increase the level of understanding and the will to absorb information. For example, reading a book that tells a story or portrays an event will usually stimulate the reader to continue to the end. Crime stories make an interesting read because the stimulus to identify the culprit is sustained throughout, the level of mystery and suspense encouraging the reader to continue.

Exercise 1.11

1. Think back to the last time you read a book, and answer the following:

   - what was the main story or theme of the book?
   - who or what was the main character?
   - what was the plot?
   - how did the story end?

2. Why do you think that you can remember so much about the book?
3. Think back to a book that you read last year and carry out the exercise again.
4. Think back to a book that you started to read and never completed:

   - why did you start reading the book?
   - how far into the book did you get?
   - why did you stop reading the book?

The more interesting the text the higher the chances of understanding the theme, which will improve the likelihood of reading to the end.

Objectives of reading

People read for different reasons, including:

- to investigate facts
- to understand and allow comprehension
- to consolidate prior learning
- to improve learning

Reading objectives fit together to form a cycle of continuous acquisition and improvement of learning skills, as shown in Figure 1.25.

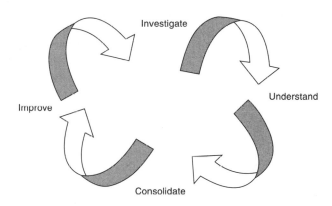

Figure 1.25 *Cycle of reading objectives*

Reading to investigate facts

The need to investigate facts and information could be self-directed or imposed. Self-directed learning requires the reader actively to seek out appropriate reading material for personal gain. Imposed investigation is a stipulated requirement from a third party, such as a teacher or lecturer of a course at college (Figure 1.26).

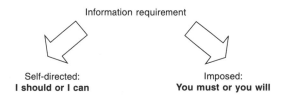

Figure 1.26 *Investigation of information*

Reading to understand information

Although the objective of reading six pages by a certain deadline through either self-directed or imposed requirement is the same, the way in which you understand and respond to such reading can be very different. Being told to do something can be seen as restrictive and the enjoyment factor reduced, thus minimizing the process of understanding. Taking the initiative to do a task for your own benefit is very different because the focus is more positive, and therefore the ability to understand information will increase.

Examples of reading purely to understand facts include:

- car manuals
- test logs
- computer guides
- maps.

You would not necessarily read an atlas from cover to cover; for easier and quicker understanding, you would identify the desired region or destination and source the appropriate page or pages.

Reading to consolide information

Reading to consolidate information again uses different techniques. For example, you might be re-visiting a piece of text that has previously been read, in preparation for a test. Revision reading is one way to consolidate the understanding process. Using this technique, a chapter of a book that may have been reviewed at the beginning of a course is examined again at the end to consolidate any additional information collected, or to serve as a refresher for new ideas (Figure 1.27).

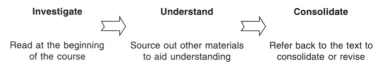
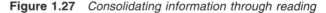

Investigate	**Understand**	**Consolidate**
Read at the beginning of the course	Source out other materials to aid understanding	Refer back to the text to consolidate or revise

Figure 1.27   *Consolidating information through reading*

If between the time of first reading the book at the investigation stage and the return to the book in the consolidation stage new information has been sourced, the re-visiting will act to consolide both existing information and new information sourced. Figure 1.28 illustrates this taking a car manual as an example.

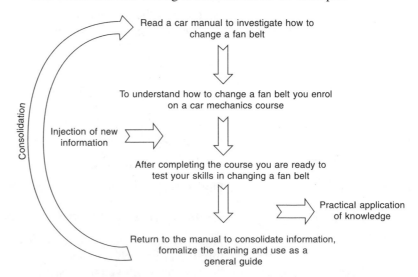
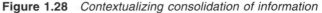

Figure 1.28   *Contextualizing consolidation of information*

The consolidation stage is cyclical because as learners we constantly refer back to resources and re-visit materials to aid with the transition into the final stage of 'improving' our own knowledge and skill base.

Reading to improve learning

Improving knowledge and skills through reading is an expectation on the majority of vocational and academic courses. Although we learn by 'doing', to aid us in this learning process we constantly refer to reading materials. Improving our learning through reading is also dependent upon a set of factors that include:

- the level of the reader and the reading material
- presentation of information
- the environment.

Level of the reader

The level at which you read can have an impact on how you read and understand, because everybody has certain boundaries when it comes to interpreting and comprehending written information.

Reading a degree-level textbook when studying a National Diploma course may be too difficult for some because of the expectations of existing knowledge of a typical degree student compared to those of a National Diploma student. Trying to read a book beyond your level of understanding can create a negative reaction to reading and stifle the learning experience. Conversely, you would be unlikely to read an intermediate text on the basics of programming if you had reached an advanced practitioner's level, because there would be very little stimulus with regard to learning new and exciting information.

Identifying the level of reading ability is not necessarily a science. Although at primary and secondary schools reading is tested to determine a particular level, this is not necessarily a true reflection of your overall ability. Reading in a controlled environment to meet a specific objective or requirement can pressurize a learner and again repress reading creativity. Even if a learner is assessed over the period of year, the final level of reading ability may not be a true representation. A child can struggle at school with literature texts or sheets of problem-solving exercises, but exceed expectations at home when reading a story or an article that is of interest.

To determine your own reading level, never judge a book by its cover, always venture into the first few pages, and try to figure out what the chain of thought is. If you can establish this, read on to the end of the chapter or book. One way of improving your reading level is to read a variety of texts, in a variety of styles, which serve a variety of purposes.

1.4 Reading and note-taking techniques

Reading techniques

People read in different ways as previously explored, some people skim read through chapters picking out key words and phrases, others might examine a piece of text from cover to cover. Some people read slowly constantly referring back to text in order to reflect on the information, others take notes to assist in their understanding. The ability to improve the speed at which you read and the ability to increase the level of understanding from what you have read can be improved by setting yourself targets and measuring the progress made in terms of your reading material, reading speed, and level of comprehension. Specific reading exercises have been developed by Tony Buzan which concentrate on:

- Muscle exercises
- Page turning
- Reducing fixations
- Speed reading
- Progressive acceleration

Note-taking techniques

Another vital skill is that of note taking. People take notes every day, jotting down facts, summarizing information such as a lesson, and recording data such as times and activities. Whatever method you use to take notes, it will probably fall into one of the categories, shown in Figure 1.29.

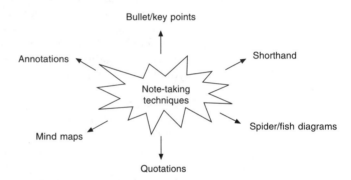

Figure 1.29   *Methods of note taking*

Bullet/key points

Taking notes using a bullet-point method is very common, especially with tools available on software packages to make the process easier. Using bullet points allows you to condense information into short sentences made up of the key elements of the information that you need to record. For example, in order to set up a website the following issues would need to be considered:

1. Costs
    - hardware
    - software
    - connection
    - call charges
    - ISP charges
    - maintenance and service charges
2. Security
    - passwords
    - firewall
    - hackers
    - unauthorized users.

Shorthand

Shorthand is a unique style of scribing complete words into short symbols to enable faster note taking. Shorthand is frequently used when documents are being dictated.

Spider or fish diagrams

Taking notes visually by using a spider, fish or other diagram is a very easy way of jotting down key points and relating them to a specific subject or set of criteria. In the example used in Figure 1.30, it is clear to see that the cost of setting up a website is the subject area, with each cost being identified around the body of the subject.

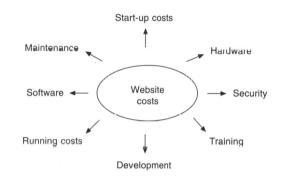

Figure 1.30 *Spider diagram of issues to consider for setting up a website*

Quotations

When you take notes, it is sometimes appropriate to jot down specific phrases or quotations from particular authors. These can then be used as references for future research or notes.

Mind maps

Tony Buzan (1989) developed a style of transferring notes into a diagrammatic format known as 'mind maps' or 'brain patterns'. In these, you start in the centre of a page with a word or phrase that represents the main theme, and from this branches extend outwards to incorporate links to that theme, and then again to sub-themes.

Annotations

Annotations are used to provide further expansion to thoughts and ideas. Annotations may be graphical or textual.

1.5 Punctuation, spelling and grammar

What use is it to have brilliant thoughts and ideas if we cannot communicate them effectively? Sometimes it is easy to explain or demonstrate then to somebody drawing upon verbal or visual skills. However, it is also important to be able to communicate these ideas in a written format. Throughout your life you will need to communicate via letters, memos, e-mails, reports and completing business or education documents. To do this effectively you need to ensure that what you are writing is correct in terms of grammar, spelling and punctuation.

It is all to easy to rely on tools such as a 'spell check' or 'grammar check' to correct our language mistakes, but, without these tools how well can we actually communicate in a written format?

Exercise 1.12

Read the following advertisement for a job and complete the tasks below.

> ## IT Solutions
> IT Support Administrator
> £15K plus benefits
>
> We are looking to recruit a dynamic young college leaver who has successfully completed a computing qualification. Must have experience of working within a team and good interpersonal skills. Should also have technical experience of computer hardware, software and networks. Web-based or programming skills are also desirable.
>
> Please send in a covering letter with your CV to:
> Mr Steven James, IT Manager
> IT Solutions, 11–13 Langston Road, Norwich,
> NR34 7DD
>
> Closing date: 2 November 2002

1. Hand write a covering letter in response to the advertisement for the job.
2. Once you have completed the letter, write down a list of things of which you were unsure – e.g. spelling, punctuation, grammar.
3. Pass your letter on to a friend and get the friend to write down a similar list based on your letter.
4. Get together to compare the lists and discuss any problems; you can then either check back with your tutor or type the letter into a word processing package to check your concerns.
5. Were the lists the same? Were there more mistakes than expected?

From Exercise 1.12 it is clear that there are sometimes difficulties with written communication; however, the way to overcome this is to create a better awareness of the English language.

Punctuation

Punctuation provides clarity, breaks and context in a sentence. It allows you to break down written extracts into manageable chunks (Table 1.2).

Table 1.2 *Punctuation*

Punctuation mark	Descriptor	Some examples of use
'	Apostrophe	Can state possession if used with the letter 's', e.g. the student's work
:	Colon	Indicates stops or breaks in clauses, usually used to introduce examples
,	Comma	Used to indicate breaks in a sentence between groups of words or a list of items
—	Dash	Denotes additionality to a sentence
" " ' '	Direct speech marks or inverted commas	Specifies what was spoken and by whom; also identifies a quotation or title
!	Exclamation mark	Denotes the feeling of surprise or other emotive expressions
.	Full stop	Represents the end of a sentence or an abbreviated word, such as e.g. or etc.
-	Hyphen	Links words or parts of words
( )	Parentheses	Separates primary and secondary ideas
?	Question mark	Represents the ending of a direct question
;	Semicolon	A pause that is longer than a comma but shorter than a full-stop, a dramatic pause

---

Exercise 1.13

1. Write down eleven sentences to incorporate each punctuation mark.
2. Identify which punctuation you found more difficult to use.
3. Why do you think this is?

Spelling

Spelling correctly has been made easier through the use of applications software and tools such as 'spell check'. However, spelling does not necessarily improve because of this. Some may argue that the level of literacy skills has declined because less of an effort is made to practise and learn how to spell, with increasing dependency on software.

There are a number of guidelines that can help to improve the general level of spelling, including:

- rules of thumb

- plurals
- prefixes and suffixes
- homophones.

Rules of thumb

These are general guidelines on what should happen under certain conditions with particular words and spelling.

- 'q' is always followed by a 'u'
- 'i' before 'e' accept after 'c'
- If a word ends in a single 'l' and the letter before was a vowel, the 'l' will need to be doubled before anything else (a suffix) can be added – for example, usual becomes usually, casual becomes casually.

Plurals

Plurals can be achieved by adding an 's' – for example, work becomes works, show becomes shows, eat becomes eats.

For some words adding an 's' is not enough, and 'es' is required – for example, tomato becomes tomatoes.

For some words ending in 'y', the plural becomes 'ies' – for example, personality becomes personalities, dolly becomes dollies, lorry becomes lorries.

For words that end in a 'y' and are preceded by a vowel, add 's' for the plural – for example, boy becomes boys, bay becomes bays, tray becomes trays.

Words ending in 'f' in the singular become 'ves' in the plural – for example, hoof becomes hooves, calf becomes calves, shelf becomes shelves.

Words ending in 's' 'x' 'z' 'ch' 'sh' and 'ss' in the singular become 'es' in the plural – for example, fizz becomes fizzes, lunch becomes lunches, push becomes pushes.

Some plurals are quite different to the original singular word – for example, die becomes dice, stimulus becomes stimuli.

Exercise 1.14

1. Identify four other examples of plurals with words ending in the following:
   - 'f'
   - 'ch'
   - 'y' with no vowel preceding it
   - 'ss'.
2. How many words can you identify that cannot be made plural?

Prefixes and suffixes

Adding a prefix or a suffix to a word does not necessarily alter the original word, but gives additionality. For example:

$$\text{disappear} \xleftarrow[\text{prefix}]{} \text{appear} \xrightarrow[\text{suffix}]{} \text{disappearing}$$

In some cases the word does change and a letter is dropped – in this example, the 'e'

$$\text{misbehave} \xleftarrow[\text{prefix}]{} \text{behave} \xrightarrow[\text{suffix}]{} \text{misbehaving}$$

Homophones

These are words that sound the same but are spelt differently, for example:

- fair, fare
- their, there
- horse, hoarse
- meet, meat
- flee, flea
- compliment, complement
- past, passed
- claws, clause.

Grammar

Using correct grammar will improve written communication skills. There are certain grammatical formats that are used to convey different aspects of a sentence; these include nouns and pronouns, verbs and adverbs, adjectives, articles, conjunctions, prepositions and interjections (Table 1.3).

Table 1.3 *Grammar*

Identifier	Description	Examples
Adjective	Describing word	Large, pretty, heavy, cold
Adverb	Extension to adjectives or verbs – how, where, when	Slowly, happily, cautiously
Article	Definite and indefinite	**The** assignment, **a** job
Conjunction	Linking word	And, next, when, if, after
Interjection	Feeling or emotion	Ouch, yippee, oh, wow
Noun	Naming word	Cat, car, computer, book
Preposition	Locator	Under, across, over, up
Pronoun	Naming or identifying words referring to people or things	**Who** did you invite?
Verb	Doing word	Writes, plays, jumps, shouts

Each sentence that is spoken or written will contain a variety of these grammatical formats.

1.6 Research skills

Effective communicator must be able to listen, read and write. Arguably, research skills are required to complete the package.

The ability to research a topic will provide greater depth and understanding of the subject matter, which can then be fed into a conversation or written piece of work.

To be an effective researcher you should follow a set plan (see Figure 1.31) to ensure that you have a good balance of resources and time. Every research plan will have a start and completion date, and these dates are important because they allow you to focus your research on a specific time period – e.g. one week, one month, six months.

University Application	
Start date: Early September 2002	Completion date: End November 2002

Objectives of the research

Tasks:

1. Identify universities in the North of England and Scotland.
2. Examine the entry requirements of universities in the North of England and Scotland.
3. Short-list four universities.
4. Collect information about the universities on the short-list.
5. Get a UCAS form.
6. Apply to universities.

Task dependencies

1&2, 3&4, 5, 6

Resources to be used

- books
- brochures/prospectuses
- magazines
- journals
- media
- Internet
- people (admissions officers, student advisors etc.)
- institutes (universities, Local Education Authority)

Allocation of time

1. ⎫
2. ⎬ Three days
3. ⎫
4. ⎬ Up to three weeks
5.   Up to one week
6.   Up to two weeks

Supporting information

October half term – able to visit short-listed universities

Figure 1.31   *Research plan*

The research plan

Objectives of research

The objectives of the research will be taken from the set tasks of the project or assignment. These could be quite broad (for example, 'identify universities in the North of England and Scotland') or quite specific ('get a UCAS form').

Task dependencies

Some of the tasks will depend on another task; these should be identified so that the research can be planned more effectively –

why use a particular resource for only one task when it could be used to gather information on two or three?

Resources

Identifying appropriate resources prior to the research will save time and also provide a structure to the research.

Allocation of time

Allocating time to each task is essential because this identifies how and when certain tasks need to be undertaken and whether they all fall within the allocated time.

Additional information

Any additional information will also aid the research plan; in the example used (Figure 1.31) the October half-term will provide the opportunity to research the short-listed universities by visiting the campuses, after which tasks five and six need to be completed before the end of November – which is feasible.

When carrying out research it is important to record what you have researched, where the information has come from and when it was collected. Comments about the research tool could also be beneficial. One way of doing this is to use research templates, such as those shown in Figures 1.32 and 1.33.

Book title	Author
Date of publication:	Publisher:
Edition:	ISBN:
Page(s) viewed:	
Information summary:	

Figure 1.32 *Book research template*

By using standard templates it is easier to collate the research information together and present the resources more professionally.

Exercise 1.15

You have been asked to carry out research on new developments in the area of 'games consoles'.

Using at least six different research sources, to include magazines and the Internet, record information on the topic of 'games consoles' using appropriate resource templates.

Search engine: (if applicable)	Web page address:
Website category: (academic, commercial, industrial)	Links used:
Summary of site information:	

Figure 1.33 *Internet research template*

Research tools

The Dewey decimal system

In order to locate reading material in a library, a system has been set up to provide easy identification and access to books. This system of categorizing information originates from Melvil Dewey (1851–1931), and is based on ten broad categories, each identified by a three-digit code number placed before a decimal point:

000. General books
100. Philosophy
200. Religion
300. Social sciences
400. Language
500. Science
600. Technology
700. Literature
800. Geography, history
900. Biography, autobiography.

Each category is further sub-divided into specialist categories, e.g.

600. Technology

    610. Medicine
    620. Engineering
    630. Agriculture

and again into discrete sections that focus on specialist subject areas within that category.

Exercise 1.16

Visit a library and find out the following information using the Dewey decimal system:

1. Where are the computer books referenced?
2. What numbers are used to categorize books on the following subject areas:
    - programming languages
    - networking
    - computer architecture.

The Internet

The Internet is one of the most dynamic research tools available. It provides a bank of information on a multitude of topics, however obscure or diverse. One of the major advantages of using the Internet to carry out research is the fact that everything can be accessed from a single computer – there is no need physically to visit different places to gather information, although this is what the Internet is doing on your behalf.

There are many advantages of using the Internet as a research tool, including the following:

- a diversity of topics and interests can be found
- it is a concentrated source of research – there is no need physically to collect information from different places
- it is relatively quick
- it can be a cheaper method of data collection than some other research tools
- it can be easy to use and to source information
- on-line help is provided to assist in the gathering of research
- you do not need to depend on a third party for the physical delivery of the information
- information can be presented in a variety of formats to aid understanding and learning
- you can receive up to the minute information
- information and ideas can easily be shared on-line through user groups.

Problems of using the Internet as a research tool can occur if users are not familiar with its use or how to search for information. It can be frustrating to use a search engine for information on a broad topic such as 'universities' because anything with 'universities' in the title will be displayed from all over the world, bringing up maybe 10 000 or more sites. A certain familiarity with the way in which search engines work, advanced features, Boolean operators, links and the basics of typing in a web address are also essential to get the most out of Internet research. This can cause problems in searching for appropriate and meaningful information if knowledge on search functions is limited.

Exercise 1.17

Using the Internet as a research tool, carry out searches on the following subjects and record the information using a template such as the one provided in Figure 1.32. You should include the use of four search engines to find out the following:

- information on the five latest cinema film releases
- information on an actor or actress of two new film releases
- details of which other films they have been in.

When the searches have been carried out, a summary of the information should be written up and presented to the group. The presentation of the information should also use an appropriate tool for delivery, such as presentation software.

1.7 Barriers to communication

There are many barriers that can constrain people from communicating with each other. One type of barrier can be categorized as physical, i.e. caused by the physical positioning of the sender and the receiver of the information. More specifically, the geography of the two can constrain the frequency or type of communication. For example, if the sender lives on a remote island and the receiver lives on the mainland, the only form of communication might be by letter. The frequency may depend on how the letter could be transported, for example by boat as and when it passes the island.

The actual physical terrain can also constrain the communication type, even in a heavily populated area on the mainland. Trying to get a mobile telephone signal from one county to another can sometimes be impossible due to the reception coverage. This is very apparent in the UK, especially in some areas of Scotland, Norfolk and Suffolk.

Cultural barriers can also limit communication, especially if you are trying to communicate with somebody who does not speak the same language. A general understanding and appreciation of different cultures can help in overcoming communication barriers – for example, different customs or gestures. An action considered acceptable in one culture might be deemed inappropriate and offensive in another.

Access to different types of communication tools can also constrain the way in which you communicate and how quickly. Access to ICT has certainly improved communication flow with tools such as e-mail and the Internet; however, if you are computer illiterate you may be disadvantaged and limited to using more conventional communication tools such as the telephone or mail.

Exercise 1.18

Considering six different ways of communicating, identify the following:

1. In order of preference, which would be the quickest to use over
    *   long distances
    *   short distances?
2. In order of preference, which would be the cheapest to use over
    *   long distances
    *   short distances?
3. What are the advantages and disadvantages of using the following communication tools:
    *   e-mail
    *   letters
    *   telephone
    *   fax?
4. How could you communicate with somebody from a different country if you did not know their language?
5. Identify four ways of expressing a sign of welcome or greeting to somebody who cannot speak your language.

1.8 The role of ICT in communications

The use of ICT can greatly improve the way in which we communicate. Software applications can be used to develop communication skills and provide tools that help us to present information clearly and professionally.

Different software applications serve different purposes (Table 1.4). The major benefits include professional and standard formatting, easy access and storage, automatic processing and interactivity of the communications tool.

Table 1.4 *Use of software applications as an aid to communication*

Software application	Function	Benefits
Word processor	Formats mainly textual information	• Provides standard formatting • Professional layout • Easy to use
Spreadsheet	Formats mainly numerical information	• Ability to process data easily and automatically (calculate, forecast and model) • Can display information graphically
Database	Stores information	• Easy access to information • Ability to search and sort information easily
Presentation	Assists with presentations	• Aid for displaying and delivering information • Professional delivery tool • Easy to use • Can incorporate different formats of data and information • Can be interactive
Drawing	Assists with designs, pictures and drawings	• Can be customized to own designs • Professional capabilities (e.g. CAD software) • Can be easy to use
Communication	Enhances communication	• Can be interactive • Fast • Cheaper than some other forms of communication • Easy to use

ICT has improved the way in which we communicate and the frequency with which we do so. Tools such as e-mail and the Internet have enabled synchronous communication and have promoted the sharing of skills, knowledge and information. Interactive gaming has developed a new culture of team building and group bonding, as quoted by a National Diploma student:

'Interactive gaming relieves stress and promotes good social behaviour, it also improves reflexes and general thinking skills.'

Unit 2 Computer systems

Most computers in the marketplace are binary. There are analogue machines that are quite different, and these will not be considered here.

Binary machines use logic circuits, and the purpose of this unit is to introduce binary logic, simple binary circuits and their assembly into devices. It is not the intention to look at the practical or economic issues involved in designing digital circuits.

2.1 Binary logic

Logic works with the idea of a **proposition**. A proposition is a statement that is either **true** or **false**; it can have no other value. The statement or proposition 'You are sitting down' may or may not be true as you read this book, so it has the value **true** or **false**. Notice it is not a question; it is not 'Are you sitting down?', which could have a range of answers such as yes, no, I will in a moment etc. For the purposes of logic, the proposition 'You are sitting down' is either true or it is not, there are no other possibilities.

It is usual to represent the value **true** as a '1' and the value **false** as a '0'. In an electronic circuit, this may mean 'on' or 'off', or it may mean 3 volts for true and 0 volts for false etc.

To save writing long statements to represent a proposition, it is normal to use the letters A, B, C etc. For example, the proposition 'You are sitting down' could therefore be represented as A, and the proposition 'You feel warm' by B. Both A and B could be true, which would mean you are sitting down and feeling warm. There are four possible combinations of true and false in this case:

1. You are not sitting down   AND   you are not feeling warm
2. You are not sitting down   AND   you are feeling warm
3. You are sitting down   AND   you are not feeling warm
4. You are sitting down   AND   You are feeling warm.

A more normal representation would be to write:

A = the proposition 'You are sitting down'
B = the proposition 'You are feeling warm'

and then to put them in a **truth table**:

A	B	R
0	0	0
0	1	0
1	0	0
1	1	1

where 1 = true, 0 = false. This table represents the same logic values as the list above. It is the truth table for the **logical AND function**, so named because the question being asked is: 'is A true AND is B true'. The column marked R is the resultant, i.e. the result of the logic. As you can see, only one line shows a 1, when A = 1 AND B = 1.

In more formal terms, the truth table here shows the AND logic function. As there are two propositions, there are $2^2 = 4$ lines in the truth table. If there were three propositions, there would be $2^3 = 8$ lines. The following table shows the resultants for the proposition 'A = true AND B = true AND C = true'; a three-input AND function:

A	B	C	R
0	0	0	0
0	0	1	0
0	1	0	0
0	1	1	0
1	0	0	0
1	0	1	0
1	1	0	0
1	1	1	1

This shows all the possible combinations of the propositions, A, B and C, and shows R = 1 only when all three propositions (A, B and C) are true.

Some of the assembly language files in this section can be downloaded from http://www.bh.com/companions/0750656840.

Question 2.1

How many lines would be in a truth table with eight propositions?

Answer

There would be $2^8 = 256$ lines, a fact that will be used a little later on.

Other logic functions

We could ask some different questions, for example: Is A true OR is B true?

This is represented in the truth table of the **logical OR function**:

A	B	R
0	0	0
0	1	1
1	0	1
1	1	1

This shows true when A = true OR B = true, or when they are both true.

Sometimes it is necessary to reverse or invert logic. In this case we could say NOT A – so if A = 1, NOT A will = 0, and vice versa. This is written as $\overline{A}$. The bar over the A means 'invert the value of A', and this is usually described as NOT A.

Table 2.1 shows a truth table with all the possible resultants of logical functions using two propositions. As there are four lines in the truth table, there are $2^4 = 16$ possible combinations. Some of these combinations have names such as AND or Exclusive OR. Notice that if you rotate the table 90° anticlockwise, the resultants appear to show binary numbers from the bottom, starting at 0000.

Table 2.1   *Truth table for two propositions*

A	B	NOT A $\overline{A}$	NOT B $\overline{B}$	A AND B $A \bullet B$					A XOR B $A \oplus B$	A OR B $A + B$	A NOR B $\overline{A+B}$						A NAND B $\overline{A \bullet B}$	
0	0	1	1	0	0	0	0	0	0	0	1	1	1	1	1		1	1
0	1	1	0	0	0	0	1	1	1	1	0	0	0	0	1	1	1	1
1	0	0	1	0	0	1	1	0	0	1	1	0	0	1	1	0	0	1	1
1	1	0	0	1	0	1	0	1	0	1	0	1	0	1	0	1	0	1

The actual functions in logic have some strange symbols. The OR function is often written as A + B (but the + sign does not mean addition!):

A + B is called A OR B
A • B is called A AND B

A ⊕ B is called A XOR B, which is short for A Exclusive OR B. This function is nearly the same as A OR B; it differs only when A = 1 and B = 1.

$\overline{A + B}$ is called NOR, short for NOT OR
$\overline{A \bullet B}$ is called NAND, short for NOT AND

Other columns can be generated using a combination of logic functions. For instance, one row shows the function A • $\overline{B}$; it is only true when A = 1 and $\overline{B}$ = 1. The row headed A NOR B can be generated from inverting the previous row, giving $\overline{A + B}$ or NOT(A OR B).

Care must be taken with NOT functions! You may have heard the London slang phrase 'I ain't done nothing', meaning 'I ain't done anything'. Since 'I ain't done nothing' contains a NOT function (ain't), the phrase actually means 'I have done **something**'. In logic terms, this is like writing NOT NOT A, which in fact is just A, $\overline{\overline{A}} = A$.

In a similar way, you can show that $A \bullet B = \overline{\overline{A} + \overline{B}}$, something that is called **DeMorgan's Law** which forms part of **Boolean algebra**. A detailed treatment of Boolean algebra is outside the requirements of this course.

George Boole

George Boole was the son of a shoemaker and was born in Lincoln, England, on 2 November 1815. He published *The Mathematical Analysis of Logic* in 1847, which introduced his early ideas on symbolic logic. In 1849 he was appointed Professor of Mathematics at Queen's College in Cork, Ireland, where he remained for the rest of his life. Boole published *An Investigation of the Laws of Thought, on Which Are Founded the Mathematical Theories of Logic and Probabilities* in 1854, which extended his previous work and contained much of what is now called Boolean Algebra.

2.2 Logic gates

Truth tables and Boolean algebra are mathematical descriptions of logic. To make a physical device that performs these logical functions, semiconductors are used to make logic gates. In computers these work on a low voltage, usually in the range of about 3–5 volts, and will perform at high speed with a low power consumption.

Circuits are then made using large numbers of logic gates to make useful devices. The next section will show in principle how this is done whilst ignoring some practical electronic details; it is not the intention of this book to provide practical electronic data.

In order to draw circuits, use is made of symbols to represent each gate. As is often the case in computing, there are several different 'standard' symbols. Table 2.2 shows the British Standard symbols to BS3939 and the more common American ones.

Using the more common American symbols, we can represent the function $A \bullet B$ (Figure 2.1). R is the resultant.

Useful devices can be made from several logic gates and the behaviour of the whole circuit described using a truth table. For example, Figure 2.2 shows a simple three-gate circuit.

Here we have three inputs, labelled A, B and C. To make filling in the truth table easier, the intermediate parts are labelled D and E.

To construct the truth table, first calculate the number of lines required. As there are three inputs, there will be $2^3 = 8$ lines. Now fill in all the possible combinations of A, B and C. The order from top to bottom is not important, but it is common to set them out counting in binary from the top as shown here:

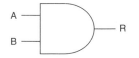

Figure 2.1 *Symbol for an AND gate*

A	B	C	D	E	R
0	0	0			
0	0	1			
0	1	0			
0	1	1			
1	0	0			
1	0	1			
1	1	0			
1	1	1			

Table 2.2   *British and US logic symbols*

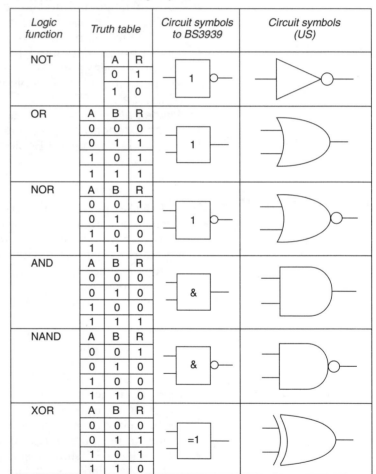

Logic function	Truth table			Circuit symbols to BS3939	Circuit symbols (US)
NOT		A	R		
		0	1		
		1	0		
OR	A	B	R		
	0	0	0		
	0	1	1		
	1	0	1		
	1	1	1		
NOR	A	B	R		
	0	0	1		
	0	1	0		
	1	0	0		
	1	1	0		
AND	A	B	R		
	0	0	0		
	0	1	0		
	1	0	0		
	1	1	1		
NAND	A	B	R		
	0	0	1		
	0	1	0		
	1	0	0		
	1	1	0		
XOR	A	B	R		
	0	0	0		
	0	1	1		
	1	0	1		
	1	1	0		

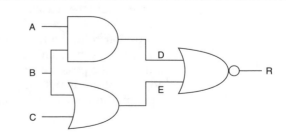

Figure 2.2   *Simple three-gate circuit (a)*

Next, fill the column for proposition D, which is given by A • B, i.e. there will only be a 1 when both A AND B are 1. At this stage, you need only to consider the AND gate with inputs A and B:

A	B	C	D	E	R
0	0	0	0		
0	0	1	0		
0	1	0	0		
0	1	1	0		
1	0	0	0		
1	0	1	0		
1	1	0	1		
1	1	1	1		

Now fill in the column for proposition E, which is given by B + C; again, you need only consider the OR gate with inputs B and C:

A	B	C	D	E	R
0	0	0	0	0	
0	0	1	0	1	
0	1	0	0	1	
0	1	1	0	1	
1	0	0	0	0	
1	0	1	0	1	
1	1	0	1	1	
1	1	1	1	1	

Finally, fill in the column for the resultant, given by D NOR E:

A	B	C	D	E	R
0	0	0	0	0	1
0	0	1	0	1	0
0	1	0	0	1	0
0	1	1	0	1	0
1	0	0	0	0	1
1	0	1	0	1	0
1	1	0	1	1	0
1	1	1	1	1	0

The resultant column, R, shows that when A = 1, B = 0 and C = 0, the circuit will output a 1 etc. We could now write the logic function for this circuit:

1. First, write down the logic for the 2 gates on the left: $(A \bullet B)$ $(B + C)$
2. Now connect them together with the NOR function, the gate on the right: $(A \bullet B)$ NOR $(B + C)$ written as $\overline{(A \bullet B) + (B + C)}$

Notice that neither D nor E appear in the completed function; their use was simply to make the truth table easier to write.

Figure 2.3 provides a further example.

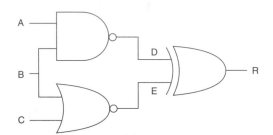

Figure 2.3   *Simple three-gate circuit (b)*

Write out the truth table and logic function for the circuit.

Now, construct the truth table in the same manner as above, column by column, to give:

A	B	C	D	E	R
0	0	0	1	1	0
0	0	1	1	0	1
0	1	0	0	0	0
0	1	1	0	0	0
1	0	0	0	1	1
1	0	1	0	0	0
1	1	0	0	0	0
1	1	1	0	0	0

The logic function = (A NAND B) XOR (B NOR C), written as $\overline{(A \bullet B)} \oplus \overline{(B + C)}$.

Exercise 2.1

Write the truth table and logic function for the circuits below. Remember, if a circuit has four inputs it will have $2^4 = 16$ lines in the table. The three-input OR gate gives an output of 1 if any of the three inputs are 1; otherwise it will output a 0 just like a two-input OR gate. The answers are in Appendix A to this unit.

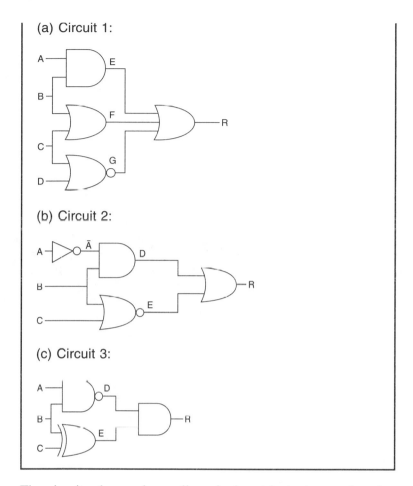

(a) Circuit 1:

(b) Circuit 2:

(c) Circuit 3:

2.3 Circuits with memory

The circuits shown above all work almost instantaneously – i.e. when a logic 1 is applied to the input, the output appears a very, very short time afterwards. Once the input is removed, the output changes as well; there is no 'memory'. Computers clearly need the ability to store values over time. This section will show some simple circuits that demonstrate this behaviour.

SR flip flop

Figure 2.4 shows a circuit that uses the output from one NAND gate to supply the input to the other one and vice versa; they 'keep

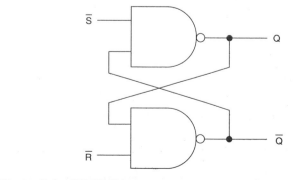

Figure 2.4 *SR flip flop*

each other going'. It is called a **Set–Reset Flip Flop** because it flips from one state to another.

The behaviour of the SR flip flop is shown on the **transition table** (Table 2.3) below (it is not really accurate to describe it as a truth table). When S = 1 and R = 0, the output Q goes to 0. When R = 1 and S = 0, the output Q changes to a 1. The interesting behaviour of this circuit is that when S and R both = 0, it remains in whatever state it was before; i.e. it has 'memory'. The S input is called **Set** and the R input is called **Reset** after their main purposes.

Table 2.3 *Transition table for SR flip flop*

S	R	Q	$\overline{Q}$	Q_{n+1}	$\overline{Q}_{n+1}$	Comments
0	0	0	1	0	1	No change in outputs
0	0	1	0	1	0	
1	0	0	1	1	0	SET action when S = 1 and R = 0
1	0	1	0	1	0	
0	1	0	1	0	1	RESET action when R = 1 and S = 0
0	1	1	0	0	1	
1	1	0	1	?	?	Outputs are indeterminate
1	1	1	0	?	?	

> The state where S = 1 and R = 1 may cause a **race condition**. In effect, this is where slight timing differences between the two NAND gates cause one gate to react sooner than the other so they 'race'. The result is an indeterminate output.

The circuit in Figure 2.5 has two extra gates on the left of the SR flip flop, and the input 'Clock' is used to control whether the circuit is to be changed or not. When Clock = 0, the inputs S and R have no effect (they can even have S = 1 and R = 1). Such a circuit is used to ensure changes occur at a certain time, the changeover being controlled by a **clock pulse**. This new circuit is called a **Clocked SR flip flop**.

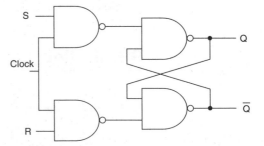

Figure 2.5 *Clocked SR flip flop*

> You should note that **clock** has no relation to the timepiece on the wall! In electronic terms a clock is a **pulse** that goes 010 or 101, i.e. changes state from 0 to 1 then back to 0 (or the other way round); see Figure 2.6.

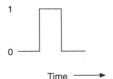

Figure 2.6 *Clock pulse*

D-type flip flop

The SR flip flop may not have S = 1 and R = 1, to avoid a race condition. The simplest way to avoid this is to place a NOT gate (also called an inverter) between S and R as shown in Figure 2.7, and to remove the external connection to the R input. When S = 0 R must = 1, and when S = 1, R must = 0. The outputs will only change when clock = 1, so this forms a very simple unit of **memory**.

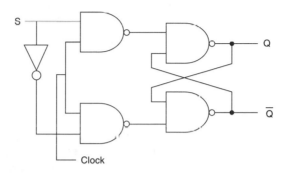

Figure 2.7 *D-type flip flop*

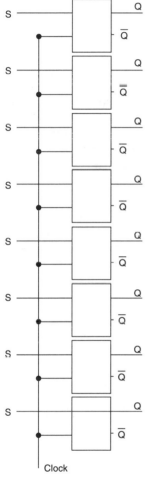

Figure 2.9 *Array of eight D-type flip flops*

Later in this unit a group of D-type flip flops will be used, and the symbol shown in Figure 2.8 will be used. Remember that a D-type flip flop is a clocked SR flip flop with an inverter, in this case represented by a simple rectangle. A D type has a very useful property; when the clock = 0 it 'remembers', and when the clock = 1 it takes on whatever value line S has.

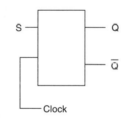

Figure 2.8 *Symbol for D-type flip flop*

Array of eight D-type flip flops

A byte is just eight binary bits. If eight D-type flip flops are arranged in parallel with a common clock signal, a circuit is created that will 'remember' a whole byte of information at once. Such an arrangement is shown in Figure 2.9. The eight wires connected to each of the eight D-type flip flops is called a **bus**.

2.4 Tri-state devices

It would be most useful if several of these devices could be connected together on a bus to store multiple bytes of information. A problem is caused when the inputs of two such devices are connected together, as the same logic level will be applied to both. To make a useful machine, some way must be found to isolate each device until is it needed – i.e. to 'disconnect it' until required. The arrangement in Figure 2.10 shows the problem.

If the left-hand array of D-type flip flops were all outputting a 1 and the right-hand array was outputting a 0, the state of the bus would be indeterminate because applying a 1 and a 0 would not give a satisfactory logic level.

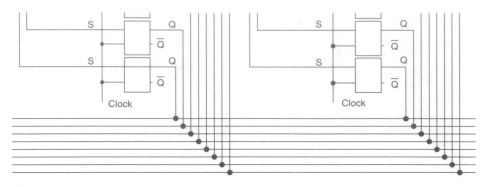

Figure 2.10   *Part of an impractical bus connection*

In a circuit, a logic level of 1 could be, say, 3.3 volts. In practical terms, this means that if the voltage is between about 3.0 and 3.5 volts a logic level of 1 exists, and if the voltage is between 0 and 0.5 volts there is a logic level of 0. If the voltage is some middle value like 1.6 volts, no clear logic level exists.

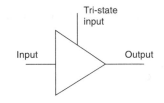

Figure 2.11   *Tri-state buffer symbol*

The solution to the problem is to use a **tri-state buffer**. This seems to go against the idea that computers are binary devices – i.e. their circuits have one of two states. A tri-state buffer has three states! These states are 0, 1, and high impedance. In place of the term 'high impedance' think 'disconnected', even though it is not quite true. When the tri-state buffer (Figure 2.11) is in its high impedance state, it really means that no logic level 0 or 1 exists on its output, and it is effectively disconnected from the circuit. This is summarized on the truth table, Table 2.4.

Table 2.4   *Truth table, tri-state buffer*

Input	Tri-state input (T)	Output
0	0	Not connected
1	0	Not connected
0	1	0, i.e. same as input
1	1	1, i.e. same as input

Use of tri-state buffers to make a useful byte storage – a register

If the array of D-type flip flops is connected to the bus via tri-state buffers, as shown in Figure 2.12, many such arrays can be connected to the same bus and the T line can be used to control which array of flip flops is in use. If the controlling circuits are arranged so that only one array of flip flops can output at a time, then the bus can be used to transmit data to other devices. As before, a symbol is used to represent the circuit (Figure 2.13). Notice that to make drawings clearer, the individual wires in a bus are not drawn.

This circuit, made of an array of D-type flip flops connected to a bus via tri-state buffers, is one way to implement a **register**.

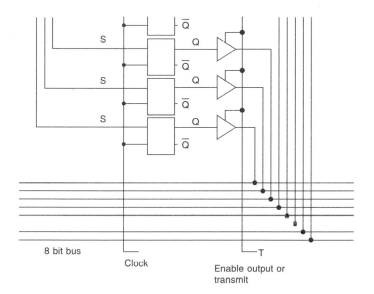

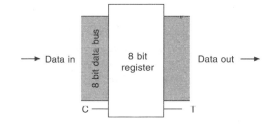

Figure 2.12 *Array of D-types connected via tri-state buffers*

Figure 2.13 *Symbol for a register*

Registers are used in many different components in a computer as a temporary store for data. Their properties are shown in Table 2.5.

Table 2.5 *Properties of a register*

Clock C	Input (T)	Output
0	0	Not connected
0	1	Stored value output to bus
1	0	Value on input bus 'written' to the register
1	1	Value on input bus written to the register and transmitted to the output bus at the same time

Array of registers

Several of these registers can now be used to build an array to store useful amounts of data. Figure 2.14 shows such an array. Note the following points:

1. The registers are numbered 0–3.
2. The control lines connected to each clock and T input are gathered together to form another bus called the **control bus**.
3. The data bus, 8 bits wide in this case, is connected to both

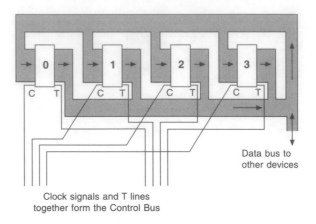

Clock signals and T lines
together form the Control Bus

Figure 2.14 *An array of four registers*

input and output sides of the registers. A common term to describe this is a **bi-directional bus**, implying that data 'travel' both ways, although this is not really the case.

Bi-directional bus

A bi-directional bus is both a source of data for a device and a way for the device to transmit that data elsewhere. The term 'bi-directional' is unfortunate, as it implies that data 'travel' along the wire when in fact they do no such thing. Imagine you are in Room 2 in a school or college, one of a set of four rooms connected via a straight corridor. Unusually, the rooms are numbered 0 to 3. It is one of those rather noisy buildings, and all the room doors are open. Someone in Room 3 shouts a message, and everyone in all the rooms can hear the message. Which direction did the **data** travel in as distinct from the sound waves? In fact, the data existed everywhere in the corridor (the bus) and the four rooms (the registers). The point is that when we consider a bi-directional bus, data move according to signals on the control lines; they are controlled in **time** rather than **direction**. A better term than bi-directional bus would be **common bus**, as the bus is common to the input and output sides of devices connected to it. Unfortunately, there are many parts of computers that have odd names!

Addressing an array of registers

Once an array of registers is connected via a common bus, a means must be provided to control them – i.e. to turn them on and off as required.

In the array, shown in Figure 2.14, it is not desirable to have more than one register 'on' at a time, so the control circuit must arrange for 0s on all the control lines except the one to be used addressing the register.

Table 2.6 is a truth table of this behaviour.

The truth table for all the variations of A • B is as follows:

Table 2.6 *Truth table for addressing an array of register*

T line to register 0	T line to register 1	T line to register 2	T line to register 3
0	0	0	1
0	0	1	0
0	1	0	0
1	0	0	0

A	B	$\overline{A}$	$\overline{B}$	A • B	A • $\overline{B}$	$\overline{A}$ • B	$\overline{A}$ • $\overline{B}$
0	0	1	1	0	0	0	1
0	1	1	0	0	0	1	0
1	0	0	1	0	1	0	0
1	1	0	0	1	0	0	0

The pattern of 1s in the right-hand four columns is the same as the pattern in Table 2.6, which shows that the functions A • B etc. can be used to make the required circuit. A circuit that has this behaviour is shown in Figure 2.15.

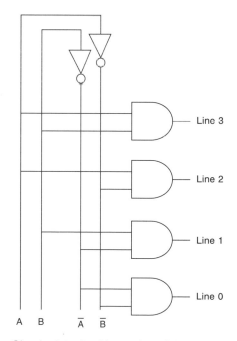

Figure 2.15 *Simple 2 to 4 address decoder*

Referring to the truth table above, the binary value of A and B combined corresponds to the register being 'turned on', so when A = 1 and B = 0, this 'turns on' register number 2, the binary value 10 = 2. In a similar way, when A = 1 and B = 1, register 3 is turned on as binary 11 = 3.

This is a very important idea in binary circuits, as the value applied to A and B is called an **address**, so when binary 11 or decimal 3 is applied to the inputs A and B it is said that register 3 is being **addressed**. If the idea is extended to eight inputs instead of two, the circuit could contain $2^8 = 256$ registers; if there were 24 input lines, there could be $2^{24} = 16.7$ million registers etc.

Extending this idea further, if the lines A and B are together considered as a bus, it is called the address bus. We now have three types of bus; the **data bus**, **control bus** and **address bus**. Remember, a **bus** is simply a collection of wires. If the data bus is eight wires (or 8 bits) wide, whole bytes can be transmitted at once, if it is 16 bits wide, 2 bytes can be transmitted at once. If the address bus is 16 bits wide, then $2^{16} = 65536$ addresses or storage locations can be addressed. Table 2.7 shows typical values for address bus width.

Table 2.7   *Typical address bus widths*

Address bus width	2^N	Number	Abbreviation
2	2^2	4	
8	2^8	256	
16	2^{16}	65536	64K
18	2^{18}	262144	256K
20	2^{20}	1048576	1M
24	2^{24}	16777216	16M
28	2^{28}	268435456	256M
30	2^{30}	1073741824	1G
32	2^{32}	4294967296	4G

Memory

Although logic circuits are shown here that have a 'memory' property, it should be noted that the main memory of a modern computer does not use these circuits because they would be too expensive to implement. Many different electronic effects are used to implement memory; all that is required is two stable states that can be modelled using a 1 or a 0. A common type of memory uses capacitance, i.e. tiny components that can be charged or not-charged are used to store 1s and 0s. For more information, look at http://xtronics.com/memory/how_memory-works.htm.

2.5 A simple microprocessor

In the last section, an array of registers was built up from simple binary logic. In this section, other components will be built into a simple microprocessor.

How to add

One of the functions that a microprocessor has to perform is addition. The easiest way to understand how to make a circuit that adds, an 'adder', is first to look at the arithmetic.

Consider an addition; in decimal, 1 + 1 = 2, but in binary, 1 + 1 = 10. If we set out this in columns we get

	1
+	1
1	0

where the 1 on the left is **carried** over to the next column. This is the notation normally used for addition etc.

If we were to write all the possible additions of two binary digits, we would get:

	1
+	1
1	0

	1
+	0
0	1

	0
+	1
0	1

	0
+	0
0	0

These can be summarized on a truth table like this:

Numbers to be added		Outputs	
A	B	Sum	Carry
0	0	0	0
0	1	1	0
1	0	1	0
1	1	0	1

As we are using binary numbers they can be treated as logical propositions, as they can only have values of 1 or 0. You should be able to see that the Sum output has the same truth table as the XOR function and the Carry output has the same truth table as the AND function. This means that we can draw a circuit that will add two binary digits and output the result, i.e. the sum and carry. The resulting circuit is called a **half adder** (Figure 2.16), and the outputs from this circuit will be those represented in the truth table.

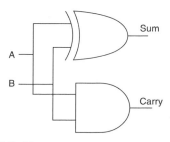

Half adder

Figure 2.16 *Half adder*

This circuit is fine if all we need to add is two binary digits, but if we need to add, say, 2 bytes together, we need a circuit that will cope with a carry from the previous column.

Consider the addition of 01 and 11:

1	1
0	1
Carry 1	
	0

The sum in the right-hand column is $1 + 1 = 0$, but we will need to **carry** 1 over to the next column. If we want a circuit that will add the next column, it will require **three** inputs, i.e. to add the 1 and 0 and the 1 carried over from the previous column. This can be done by using two half adders joined together as shown below. The result is called a **full adder** (Figure 2.17).

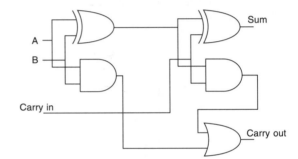

Figure 2.17   *Full adder*

We now have a circuit that takes three inputs (the two binary digits to be added and a previous carry) then outs the sum and the carry ready for the next column in the addition of a multiple bit binary number.

We can now use seven full adders and one half adder to add to 8 bit bytes to give an 8 bit result with a carry. In Figure 2.18, each full or half adder is shown as a square symbol:

These are connected as shown in Figure 2.19.

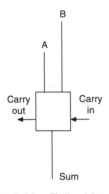

Figure 2.18   *Full adder symbol*

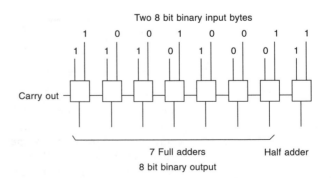

Figure 2.19   *8 bit adder (a)*

If we supply the values 147 and 235 as binary values 10010011 and 11101001, we should get the result 382. Eight bits will not hold the value 382, so the result will be 256 (represented as the carry bit) and 126 as the binary pattern 01111110. The carry out from each addition is connected to the carry in of the next adder. This is shown in Figure 2.20.

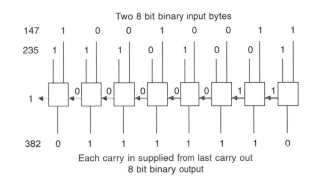

Figure 2.20 *8-bit adder (b)*

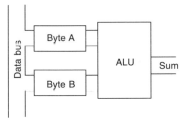

Figure 2.21 *Symbol for the arithmetic and logic unit*

This array of full adders can be incorporated into a more complex circuit that will perform subtraction, logic etc. This is represented as a symbol (Figure 2.21) ready to show in the diagram of a microprocessor. In this case it is called the Arithmetic and Logic Unit (ALU), its function is simply to add, subtract and perform AND, OR functions etc. on whole bytes of data.

A simple microprocessor (also called a CPU, or Central Processing Unit) is shown in Figure 2.22. It consists of simple parts.

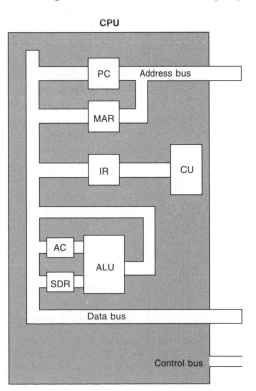

Figure 2.22 *Diagram of a simplified CPU*

The CPU

This is not a **real** microprocessor. It is a simplified version of the original microprocessors, and is presented to demonstrate the way that these devices work. Real microprocessors are more complex but share the same basic way of working.

Registers

The CPU contains **registers**. These are circuits that can remember individual numbers for a short time.

1. The AC register is traditionally known as the **Accumulator**; it is the register where the results of calculations are held.
2. The SDR register is called the **Store Data Register**, and is used to hold data ready for and instruction.
3. The IR is the **Instruction Register**, and is used to hold the latest instruction fetched from RAM.
4. The MAR is the **Memory Address Register**, and is used to hold addresses.
5. The PC is the **Program Counter**, and is used to store the location or address of the next instruction to be fetched.

Buses

The components of the CPU and those outside the CPU are connected together using **buses**. A bus is simply a collection of wires, so an 8-bit bus is just eight wires each carrying 1s or 0s. Remember that a byte is 8 bits, so an 8-bit bus could carry a single byte of information. For example, the information at one moment **could** be the letter G, which forms part of the data being processed by the CPU. ASCII for G is 64 + its position in the alphabet = 71 decimal or 47 hex. If you convert this to binary, you get 01000111. If each of the wires takes on the value 1 or 0 in this pattern, the bus could be said to be holding a letter G. There is no way of telling if the pattern 01000111 is a 'G' or not; the 'value' of a piece of data is only applied by the software that is using it.

In this simple microprocessor, the data bus is 8 bits wide so the largest number it can store is $2^8 - 1 = 255$. If it is required, you can write programs to handle larger numbers by breaking them down into 8-bit values. The older 8-bit microprocessors did this, which is one reason why they were much slower than modern microprocessors – arithmetic was laborious.

The address bus is also just 8 bits wide. This causes a much more severe restriction on operations than an 8-bit data bus, because you can only have 256 addresses. If some of the instructions need data (they usually do), you may have as few as 100 instructions in your program. When you consider that the main executable of Microsoft Word 97 comprises more than 5 **million** bytes and that this software needs even more support files to make it work, a 256-byte memory is very small!

The width of the data bus and the address bus are important considerations when specifying a microprocessor. The Pentium microprocessor has a 32-bit address bus and a 64-bit data bus. As $2^{32} = 4294967296$, a 32-bit address will allow 4 294 967 296 different addresses, or 4000 Mb or 4 Gb.

Question 2.2

(a) If a microprocessor has a 20-bit address bus, what is the maximum size of RAM this can address?

Answer

As $2^{20} = 1048576$, or 1 Mb, a 20-bit address bus will address 1 Mb of RAM.

(b) How many address lines are required to address 64 Mb of RAM?

Answer

$2^N = 64$ Mb. You could use a spreadsheet to find that $2^{26} = 67108864$, or 64 Mb, so it will need 26 address lines to address 64 Mb. Remember that 1 M = 1024 × 1024 = 1048576, not 1000 × 1000 = 1000000.

Control unit

The control unit is the 'heart' of the CPU. When fed with an instruction from the IR, the microprocessor responds with the correct action – i.e. the right registers are used and, if required, the ALU is brought into use.

Arithmetic and Logic Unit

The ALU is the **Arithmetic and Logic Unit** and, as its name suggests, is where the microprocessor actually performs additions and subtraction and logical operations such as AND and OR instructions.

What is a microprocessor?

A microprocessor is a complex circuit built from a large number of simple circuits that is made to perform logical instructions in **sequence** and thus make **decisions**.

The instructions to carry these out (the program) are separately stored outside the circuit in **memory** (Figure 2.23). The decisions or instructions are very modest in human terms; they usually take the form of something like: 'if number A is bigger than number B then execute instruction K else execute instruction X', or 'add 6 to number A'. The logical instructions are executed in sequence by the microprocessor; each is fetched from memory then executed, one at a time. (Complex modern microprocessors can execute several instructions at once.) No **single instruction** does anything really complex like 'move paragraph to the bottom of the document'; they all do relatively simple tasks. Complex tasks are built from hundreds or thousands of these simple tasks; just as a town is built from thousands of bricks, the town is complex, the bricks are simple.

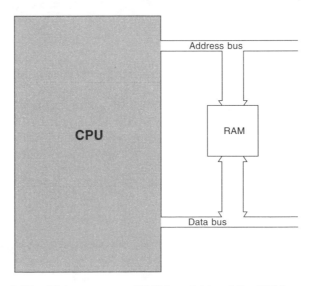

Figure 2.23 *The memory or RAM is outside of the CPU*

All the operations of the microprocessor are controlled by a **clock**, which means that a constant number of pulses or 1s and 0s are fed to the circuit and each instruction is executed on each pulse. A clock in this sense has nothing to do with telling the time! When you see that a Pentium processor has a clock speed of 600 MHz, it means that 600 000 000 clock pulses are supplied to the circuit per second. A quick thought is, if things are happening that fast, why is it that certain operations take some time to execute? The answer is simple; complex tasks are made from a large number of very simple tasks, and the simple tasks get executed at a speed hard to relate to human experience but there are **so** many to execute!

In Figure 2.23 there are two components, the CPU and the RAM. All the instructions are stored in the RAM and must be loaded one by one into the CPU. After a single instruction has been loaded, the CPU decides what it means, i.e. it **decodes** it, then **executes** the instruction. This is called the **Fetch–Execute cycle**. There is a clock input to the CPU, which supplies a series of timed 1s and 0s as a square wave.

In this example, the CPU will fetch an instruction on one pulse of the clock, decode it right away, and execute the instruction on 1, 2 or 3 of the next clock pulses. The reason it might use 1 or 2 or 3 clock pulses is because some instructions are a little more involved than others. The instructions are held in the RAM in a sequence of numbered locations, each of which is called an address. A possible sequence of instructions is shown in Table 2.8 below.

Table 2.8 *Program for the single CPU*

Address in RAM (numbered location)	Code for instruction or data held in RAM	Meaning
161	3A	Load the data at the next address into the AC register
162	23	Number to load, i.e. data not an instruction
163	3D	Load the data at the next address into the SDR register
164	12	Number to load, i.e. data not an instruction
165	8C	Add the numbers in the AC and SDR registers and store the result in the AC register
166	3E	Store the value in the AC register at the RAM address held at the next two addresses, low byte first
167	6E	Low byte of address
168	01	High byte of address
169	3A	Load the data at the next address into the AC register
16A	45	Number to load, i.e. data not an instruction

Fetch-execute cycle

Look carefully at Figure 2.24. You will see that the PC contains the value 161. The other registers have values that do not matter. Leaving

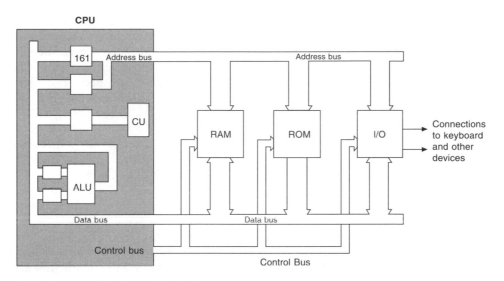

Figure 2.24 *The assembled microcomputer*

out quite a lot of detail, the fetch–execute sequence will proceed as follows.

In the fetch part of the fetch–execute sequence:

1. Instruct the RAM to give the contents of address 161 and place the number found there (3A) into the IR. This is done by putting the value 161 on the address bus and instructing the RAM to read; the value 3A will then appear on the data bus. The Control Unit provides all the signals for this to happen.
2. Allow the IR to feed its value into the Control Unit.
3. The Control Unit reacts by 'decoding' the instruction 3A, which in turn has the effect of putting 162 into the MAR, i.e. the address of the next address where the data is held. The microprocessor is now ready to execute the newly fetched instruction.

Once this is complete, the instruction **Load the data at the next address into the AC register** will be in the CPU, and so is the value of the next address, but note that it has **not** been executed – i.e. the AC register has not been loaded with the data.

In the execute part of the fetch–execute sequence:

1. Allow the contents of the MAR onto the address bus and instruct the RAM to read. This will result in the value 23 appearing on the data bus.
2. Load the contents of the data bus into the AC register.
3. Add 1 to the PC ready for the next fetch sequence.

The fetch–execute sequence is now complete and the next cycle can begin. Remembering this is not a real processor, we can safely ignore some practical details; in this example the fetch sequence took two 'ticks' of the CPU clock and the execute sequence took three ticks. If the clock was running at 1 MHz, i.e. 1 000 000 ticks per second (or, better, 1 000 000 1s and 0s), this would have taken 5/1 000 000 seconds, or 5-millionths of a second. This is quick in human terms, but all that has happened is that a number has been loaded into a register!

The next instruction in the program is **Load the data at the** next address into the SDR register, and this is fetched and executed in a similar way. The next instruction after this is **Add the numbers in the AC and SDR registers and store the result in the AC register**. You should note that this instruction does not have any data associated with it. This means it will take fewer ticks of the clock, so will fetch and execute quicker because it does not have to read the RAM a second time.

In general, instructions will take the form of 'what to do' followed by the 'data to do it with' – or, more formally, **Operation Code** followed by **Operand**. Other instructions will only have the Operation Code (often shortened to **Op Code**).

The actual program code and data are of course in binary, but we humans do not like to see lists of binary numbers or, for that matter, hex numbers. The consequence is that these programs are written down using **mnemonics** for Op Codes, so the instruction **Load the AC register with the contents of address 14** could be written as the mnemonic **LDA, 14** and the instruction **add 21 to the contents of the AC register** would be written as the mnemonic **ADD, #21**. The mnemonic **STA, 25** would mean **Store the contents of AC register at address 25**.

A program fragment containing these instructions is:

LDA, 14
ADD, #21
STA, 25

This means:

load whatever data is at address 14 into the AC register
add the value 21
store the result at address 25.

When a program is written in the form of

LDA, 14
ADD, #21
STA, 25

it is called assembly language.

Machine code

The program and data in RAM would in reality be just a set of numbers. If you write them down as numbers (in hex, decimal or binary, numbers are just numbers!), the resulting code is called **machine code**. This is what is actually run in the microprocessor using the fetch–execute sequence. Everything the CPU executes is machine code; when running Windows, the .EXE or .DLL files are machine code.

Assembly code

If you write down the same program using mnemonics, the resulting program code is called **assembly code**. The reason is that the mnemonics must be converted or 'assembled' into machine code with another program called an 'Assembler'. Writing a program using an assembler is much easier than writing directly in machine code. The sequence is to use a text editor to type the assembly code, then use the assembler to generate the machine code. This is then loaded into the RAM and the program run. With luck, it will do what you want it to!

If the assembly language

LDA, 14
ADD, #21
STA, 25

is converted to machine code with an assembler, it might give something like:

Address	Machine code
234	3A
235	14
236	8C
237	21
238	3E
239	25

What would be stored is just the machine code, i.e. 3A, 14, 8C, 21, 3E, 25. As you can see, machine code is not easy to read.

Actually writing commercial programs using assembly code (often just called assembler) is difficult, but one or two applications in computing are still written this way. Examples include very small but speed-critical parts of an **operating system**, or special high-speed animation sections of a game. Most programs are written using high-level languages such as C++ or Visual Basic, but eventually, after all the compiling and processing of these languages, everything the CPU executes is machine code. **Absolutely** everything!

2.6 Assembly language on real processors

The Intel 8086

It may seem odd to use a microprocessor first introduced in 1978 in a book written in 2002, but it has been done for simplicity. The 8086 has more registers than the simple microprocessor shown above. In place of the AC and SDR registers there are eight 16-bit registers, four of these being 'splitable' into two 8-bit registers as shown in Table 2.9. The register AH can be combined with the register AL to make AX, and so on for BX, CX and DX. AH can be taken as A High, and AL as A Low.

The layout or architecture of the 8086 is also more complex (Figure 2.25). It is not necessary to remember this layout, but the names and behaviour of the registers are important. The registers are connected via buses and the whole microprocessor is controlled via signals over the control bus, most of which has been left out for clarity. One important point to note is that the 8086 has an **instruction queue**, i.e. it can be executing an instruction whilst fetching another. This is one of the ways that microprocessors can yield an increase in execution speed. The 8086 is old enough not to have any floating point hardware. Modern microprocessors have integral floating point units that do floating point arithmetic such as 2.3×4.556

Table 2.9 *Intel 8086 general purpose registers*

AH	AL
BH	BL
CH	CL
DH	DL
SP	
BP	
DI	
SI	

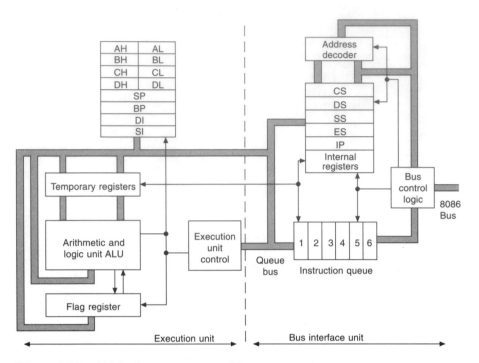

Figure 2.25   *8086 microprocessor architecture*

directly in one instruction; the 8086 would have to execute hundreds of instructions to achieve the same result. (An add-on chip was available, the 8057, that performed these operations.) The assembly code that follows will run on the modern microprocessors, as they are 'backwards compatible'.

An assembler

For the following exercises you will need an assembler. This is a piece of software that converts your program or **assembly code** to **machine code**.

There are several commercial assemblers available for the PC, but the shareware version called A86 is the cheapest and easiest to use. The author, Eric Isaacson, also claims it is the best! You can download A86 directly from his site at http://eji.com/a86/. Please read the legal notices that come with the package. From these you will see that to use the software for evaluation purposes is free, but that a small charge is made if you wish to keep and continue to use the software.

The 8086 instruction set

An **instruction set** is just a list of all the instructions that a microprocessor can execute.

If you have downloaded Eric Isaacson's A86 software (http://eji.com/a86/), you will find that it comes with the complete listing of the Intel microprocessor's instruction set. For the purposes of your course and this book this instruction set is rather too complex, so what is presented in Table 2.10 is an extract from that complete instruction set.

When writing assembly language programs, it is important to realize that almost no services are provided to the programmer. For

Table 2.10 *Subset of 8086 instruction set*

Op code	Example	Comment
ADD	ADD AX,12	Add 12 to what is in AX
AND	AND DH, 10011011b	Logical AND with DH and binary value 10011011
CALL	CALL 2000	Call routine at address 2000; it will end with a RET instruction
CMP	CMP SI,12	Compare SI register with value 12. Result sets flag in flag register
DEC	DEC AL	Subtract 1 from AL register
DIV	DIV DL	Divide AX by what is in DL. Answer, AL = Quotient, AH = Remainder
INC	INC SI	Add 1 to what is in SI register
INT	INT 021	Call DOS interrupt 21 (21 hex)
JA	JA 2000	Jump if above to address 2000
JAE	JAE 2100	Jump if above or equal to address 2100
JB	JB 3000	Jump if below to address 3000
JBE	JBE 1000	Jump if below or equal to address 1000
JC	JC 1000	Jump if carry flag set to address 1000
JMP	JMP 2300	Jump unconditionally to address 2300
JNZ	JNZ 2000	Jump is not zero to address 2000
MOV	MOV AX,23	Move 23 into AX register
MUL	MUL CL	Multiply AX register by what is in CL, answer in AX
OR	OR DI, 00110001b	Logical OR DI register with binary value 00110001
POP	POP AX	Take value from stack, put into AX, decrement stack pointer
PUSH	PUSH AX	Take value from AX, place on stack, increment stack pointer
RET	RET	Return from subroutine
SHL	SHL AX,3	Shift the value in AX 3 times to the left
SHR	SHR AX,3	Shift the value in AX 3 times to the right
SUB	SUB AX,8	Subtract 8 from value in AX register
XOR	XOR AL, AL	Logical eXclusive OR of AL with itself (sets AL to zero)

instance, if you wish to write a single character to the screen, you have several choices:

1. You could investigate the precise hardware details of your computer and get your assembly language programme to write directly to that hardware. This would involve knowledge of how the computer controls the screen hardware.
2. You could use somebody else's piece of code that outputs to the screen. Eric Issacson supplies such routines.
3. You could use the Basic Input Output System (BIOS) of your computer.
4. You could ask the operating system of your computer to output to the screen.

There is no instruction to print directly to the screen; this is a 'complex' task that involves many instructions. The instructions in assembly language are all very simple, such as ADD, STORE etc. Even an IF statement uses two lines of code.

Example program 1, P1.ASM

The programme below simply adds two numbers, and will not display the result.

```
MOV AX, [5210]
ADD AX,12
MOV [2007],AX
```

The first instruction, MOV AX, [5210], simply places the value stored at address 5210 into the AX 16-bit general purpose register. As AX is a 16 register, it will accept numbers up to one less than 2^{16}, or 65535, no larger. Eight-bit registers can accept up to one less than 2^8, or 255.

The second instruction adds 12 to the number in AX, and the result, 46, remains in the AX register.

The third instruction 'moves' the value in AX to the address 2007 in RAM. This is another example of a silly name in computing; the instruction **stores** the value, it does not **move** it.

In the instruction MOV AX,34, the MOV part is called the **Op Code**, short for Operation code (i.e. **what** to do). The AX,34 part is called the **Operand**, i.e. what the Op Code must **operate on**.

Comments

It is considered to be very bad programming practice to write code without some comments to tell you and others what pieces of code are supposed to do. It is tempting to get on with the interesting job of writing code and to leave the comments out, but in a short while it is easy to forget what you intended. If someone else has to work on your code, it is usually very difficult for them to find out your intentions. In the A86 assembler, comments are added after a ; character, so the code above may look like this:

```
MOV AX, [5210]    ;Get horizontal co-ordinate
ADD AX,12         ;Add offset
MOV [2007],AX     ;Store in frame buffer
```

Notice that comments are related to **why** the op codes are used and not to **what** they are doing. What follows is an example of silly comments!

```
MOV AX, [5210]    ;Get value at address 5210
ADD AX,12         ;Add 12
MOV [2007],AX     ;store in address 2007
```

They are silly because knowledge of the op codes themselves show what is happening; the comments should show **why**.

When a program is **assembled**, it produces an **executable file** that contains the **machine code** as shown in Table 2.11.

Table 2.11	*Assembly code and resulting machine code*
Assembly code	*The resulting machine code*

MOV AX, [5210]
ADD AX,12
MOV [2007],AX
	A1 54 14 05 0C 00 A3 D7 07

As you can see, even the rather obscure looking assembly code is easier to read than machine code! The processor uses machine code for everything, **absolutely everything** – Windows, Word, the whole thing is produced by the processor running machine code. You can see that the simple act of taking two numbers, adding them and storing the answer in RAM has generated three instructions that occupy 9 bytes of machine code. The Windows directory on the machine being used to prepare this book contains over 1 200 000 000 bytes; this is a very large collection of very simple operations and data that make up a complex operating system.

Table 2.12 illustrates how to use A86 to assemble a program.

Table 2.12	*How to use A86 to assemble a program*	
Step 1	Edit	Use any editor that will save simple ASCII files. These files are also known as text files. One of the very best is called UltraEdit, available from www.ultraedit.com, but you can use Microsoft Notepad etc. Save your file with the extension .ASM
Step 2	Assembly	Assuming you save your file as P1.ASM, at the DOS or Command prompt, type A86 P1.ASM and press enter. If everything has worked, this will result in the executable file called P1.COM and a symbol file called P1.SYM being in your directory. For the moment, ignore the symbol file
Step 3	Execute	At the DOS prompt, type P1 and press enter. With luck your program will work! If not, go back to step 1, edit the error and proceed to steps 2 and 3

What happens if it goes wrong

You will rapidly find out that there are almost no error messages! If you have some experience of high-level languages that produce executable code, this lack of error messages can be very frustrating. Often it looks as though it should work but simply refuses to do so. This is one of the reasons that high-level languages were designed! Reasons include the following.

1. The operating system hangs. Some errors will 'hang' the machine, i.e. stop it from running. This is because it is possible for your program to wander around in memory almost without restraint, overwriting important data. If this happens you will have to re-boot and start again at step 1.

2. You may have an error in a **symbolic address**, probably due to differences in spelling. In this case, A86 outputs the errors in a file with a .ERR extension. If your original file was p1.asm, the file will be called p1.err.

3. You may have some incorrect op-codes in your program, in which case A86 will output some error messages.

As an example, this program

```
MOV AX, [5210]
ADD AX,12
MOV [2007],AX
```

was modified to

```
MOVE AX, [5210]
ADD AX,12
MOV [2007],AX
```

and saved as **p1.asm**. The first MOV instruction has been changed to the incorrect spelling of MOVE. When assembled, A86 output the message

```
C:\>a86 p1.asm
A86 macro assembler, V4.05 Copyright 2000 Eric Isaacson
Source:
p1.asm
Error messages inserted into p1.asm
Original source renamed as p1.OLD
```

It is clear that your original file is now called p1.OLD and that p1.asm contains the error messages as shown below. If you correct the errors but leave the top two lines in place, A86 will remove the error messages next time you assemble the file.

```
  ~^
#ERROR messages will be removed if you leave these
first two lines in @@@@#
MOVE AX, [5210]
  ~   ^
#ERROR 01: Unknown Mnemonic
@@@@#
ADD AX,12
MOV [2007],AX
```

You can see that the incorrect spelling has been detected. To correct this, edit p1.asm, correct **only** the fault, then go back to step 2 – i.e. re-assemble the file.

Example program 2, P2.ASM

This program simply outputs the letter 'A' to the screen. Remember that ASCII 'A' is 65 in decimal, 41 in hex, or 01000001 in binary.

```
MOV DL, 65    ;ASCII A ready for DOS output routine
MOV AH, 2     ;DOS output routine number 2
INT 021       ;Call DOS routine number 2; it outputs whatever
                is in DL
INT 020       ;Call DOS to terminate program.
```

If you use the steps above to edit, assemble and test the program, you should get a single A character output at the DOS prompt when the program is executed.

Points to note about P2.ASM

The first line MOV DL, 65 could have been written in any of these ways:

MOV DL, 65
MOV DL, "A"
MOV DL, 'A'
MOV DL, 01000001b
MOV DL, 041

All the above lines are the same; the assembler simply converts the code to the correct value and inserts it into the executable file. It is easy to forget that all the code in a computer is binary, you may hear that it works on 'hex code' or the like, but in fact hex, decimal, ASCII etc. are only for humans, and the computer is pure binary. In this case, A86 uses the text format 65 as decimal, the quoted formats, "A" or 'A' as ASCII, and 041 (with a leading zero) as hex. Binary is taken as ending in b. **Whatever format you use, the output will be the same.**

As stated above, there is no single instruction in assembler to output to the screen. In this example, use has been made of a service provided by DOS. These DOS services or interrupts are called by number. The service used here is called DOS interrupt 21 (hex, so A86 uses 021), and, as this provides many simple functions, we have to use function number 2. For this to work, DOS expects the function number in the AH register and the letter to be output in the DL register. DOS interrupts are sometimes called system calls; although this is not completely accurate, is it useful to think of them this way – i.e. to ask the 'system' for a service. In effect, this calls a routine written by someone else to do what you need. A full list of these DOS interrupts is available on the Internet (search for DOS interrupt in Google), but is only of real value if you plan to write larger and more powerful assembly language programs.

Example program 3, P3.ASM

This program extends P2.ASM by including a 'loop' that will output the letter 'A' 10 times.

```
        MOV DL, 'A'    ;letter to be printed
        MOV AH, 2      ;DOS output routine number 2
        MOV CH, 10     ;start counter at 10
TOP:    INT 021        ;Call DOS routine number 2.
                       ;it outputs whatever is in DL
        DEC CH         ;count down by 1
        CMP CH, 0      ;see if counter has reached zero
        JNZ TOP        ;if counter has not reached zero,
                       ;jump to top of loop
        INT 020        ;if counter has reached zero, terminate
                       ;program
```

Points to note about P3.ASM

The first two lines are the same as for program P2.ASM.

The third line starts a register off at 10, ready to count down to 0.

The fourth line starts with TOP: This is called a **symbolic address** and the name TOP is called a **label**. When the program is assembled this address is converted into a real numerical address; in this case the address is 0106, but we would not have known that when the program was written, hence the use of a symbolic address. This is one of the services offered by an assembler and explains the appearance of the .SYM files in your directory; it is a file of the symbolic and numerical addresses to be used when reversing the assembly process – **un-assembly**.

The fifth line simply counts down by 1.

The sixth line checks to see if the counter has reached zero. When the DEC instruction is executed, the 8086 sets a **flag** in the **flag register** to record the result. A flag is simply a binary digit that is either 1 or 0 depending on the result.

Line seven is short for Jump if Not Zero to address TOP (remember the assembler converts the address TOP to the real numeric address at assembly time, in this case address 0106).

Lines five, six and seven form an 'if' statement.

Taking P3.COM apart with DEBUG

Supplied with DOS is a very odd but useful program called DEBUG. You can use DEBUG to look into your executable code. Assuming you have P3.COM in your directory, you just type DEBUG P3.COM and you will get a '-' character! You can then supply the command u for **u**nassemble. The result (all in hex) should look like this:

```
C:\>DEBUG P3.COM
-u
0E92:0100 B241      MOV    DL,41
0E92:0102 B402      MOV    AH,02
0E92:0104 B50A      MOV    CH,0A
0E92:0106 CD21      INT    21
0E92:0108 FECD      DEC    CH
0E92:010A 80FD00    CMP    CH,00
0E92:010D 75F7      JNZ    0106
0E92:010F CD20      INT    20
0E92:0111 06        PUSH   ES
0E92:0112 1000      ADC    [BX+SI],AL
0E92:0114 75E2      JNZ    00F8
0E92:0116 56        PUSH   SI
0E92:0117 BF0400    MOV    DI,0004
0E92:011A B5FF      MOV    CH,FF
0E92:011C B000      MOV    AL,00
0E92:011E 43        INC    BX
0E92:011F 3DF2AE    CMP    AX,AEF2
-q
C:\>
```

Points to note about the unassembly of P3.ASM

Ignore the first column that starts with 0E92, this is called a **segment address** and need not concern us here.

The next column tells us that the assembler has placed the program starting at address 0100 in RAM.

The third column is the **machine code**, the actual code that the processor uses to execute the program.

The last two columns contain almost the same code as you started with except that the symbolic address TOP has been converted to address 0106. DEBUG has unassembled the code, almost back to its original.

The value loaded into DL in the first line is still an 'A' because 41 hex = ASCII 'A'; DEBUG always outputs in hex.

All the bytes after the program, i.e. at address 0111 onwards are 'snow', i.e. meaningless data left over from whatever was in addresses 0111 to 011F when the machine used to prepare this book last used those addresses.

You quit from DEBUG with the command q.

Reverse engineering

The process of taking parts of an executable program and unassembling them is called **reverse engineering**. It is used to take code from other people or companies for use in new programs. Most of the time this is illegal as it contravenes the licence agreement. For example, Microsoft licence agreements refer specifically to 'Reverse Engineering, Decompilation, and Disassembly'. In the past, people have taken some useful parts of commercial programs, unassembled them, put this with their own code and re-assembled it for sale. There are ways to discover this has taken place and the programmers prosecuted.

Operating systems

This book is being prepared on a machine running Microsoft Windows 98. This operating system has as its core the older operating system called DOS, the Disc Operating System, with additions and modifications to suit Windows 98. Machines running Windows 2000 still offer a 'command prompt' but the underlying operating system is different. In this case calls to DOS services are emulated so should still work, but some things **may** not work correctly. For the exercises in this section it is preferable to use Windows 98 or older. Unfortunately, the more modern operating systems are not so easy to program using assembly language.

Example program 4, P4.ASM

This program extends P3.ASM by incrementing the letter to print ABCDEFGHIJ.

```
        MOV DL, 'A'    ;letter to be printed
        MOV AH, 2      ;DOS output routine number 2
        MOV CH, 10     ;start counter at 10
TOP:    INT 021        ;call DOS routine number 2.
```

```
                                   ;it outputs whatever is in DL
            INC DL                 ;represent next letter in alphabet
            DEC CH                 ;count down by 1
            CMP CH, 0              ;see if counter has reached zero
            JNZ TOP                ;if counter has not reached zero,
                                   ;jump to top of loop
            INT 020                ;if counter has reached zero,
                                   ;terminate program
```

Points to note about P4.ASM

The only difference from P3.ASM is the addition of INC DL. INC means increment, or 'add 1 to'. Since DL started by containing 65, or hex 41, it will become 66 then 67 etc., i.e. ASCII for ABC etc.

When DOS outputs the contents of DL, this is the first time that 65 means 'A'; before that it was simply a number. This is often hard to come to terms with; all the data in RAM are simply numbers, it is not until they are used that they have 'meaning'. An 'A' is for humans to read; to a computer it is no more than a pattern of dots on a screen produced by the DOS Interrupt 021.

Exercise 2.2

Modify program P4.ASM to print letters MNOPQRSTUVWXYZ, i.e. 14 letters starting at M. The answer is in Appendix A.

Exercise 2.3

Modify program P4.ASM to print numbers 0123456789. The answer is in Appendix A.

Example program P5.ASM

This program will output the string 'Mary had a little lamb', followed by a Carriage Return and Line Feed characters.

```
top:        jmp start
buffer:     db 'Mary had a little lamb',10,13,0
start:      mov si,buffer
L1:         mov dl,[si]    ;get first character
            cmp dl,0       ;see if end of string
            jz finprint    ;finish if end of string
            mov ah,2       ;initialize subroutine
                           ;int21 DOS call next
            int 021        ;write char using DOS
                           ;interrupt 021
            inc si         ;point to next char
            jmp L1         ;back for more chars
finprint:   int 020        ;back to DOS
```

Points to note about P5.ASM

Data and instructions all occupy the same address space, so the string 'Mary had a little lamb' is stored with the code used to process it. The code db in front of the line stands for **Define Byte** and tells the assembler to find some space in RAM and to keep the symbolic address as 'buffer'. There are four other symbolic addresses. Defining byte storage like this is done with an **assembler directive**, i.e. it **directs** the assembler how to behave, it does not generate machine code. Another assembler directive is DW, short for Define Word, in this case a 16-bit value. The Carriage Return is coded as 13 and the Line Feed is coded as 10. The 0 byte at the end is used to detect the end of the string. This kind if string, known as an ASCIIZ string, is common in programming languages such as C. It avoids the need to know the length of the string in order to control the loop that outputs it.

Terminology

As stated elsewhere in this book, some of the terms used in computing are confusing or downright silly. It is common to use the term 'word' to refer to a whole piece of storage. In the case of the 8086 microprocessor, this is a 16-bit value; in other processors it is 8 bits, 32 bits, 64 bits etc. The term 'word' has no bearing on the normal usage of the term – i.e. it is nothing to do with English **words**.

On the fourth line, use is made of the SI general purpose register. The op. code MOV DL, [SI] says 'put into DL the byte stored at the address that is in SI'. So if SI contains the address 0103, the instruction will have the same effect as MOV DL, [0103]. The reason this is used is so that SI can be incremented in order to **point** at the next address in memory. In this case, SI is being used as a **pointer**, an idea that is much used in high-level programs such as C or C++.

Addressing modes

In assembly language programming, much is made of **addressing modes**. This is to draw attention to such things as MOV DL, [SI] being different from MOV DL, 3 or MOV DL, [0103]. Each of these op. codes has a different effect, but a full discussion of addressing modes is best left until you wish to write larger and more complex assembler programs.

A different kind of loop from that used in program P3.ASM is in use here. In P3.ASM, the decision to terminate the loop was at the **bottom** of the loop, i.e. decrement the counter and see if it has finished; if not, jump back to the top of the loop. In P5.ASM, the **top** of the loop is marked with the symbolic address L1:. It contains the code that checks for the byte 0 at the end of the string; if it is found, the loop is terminated.

The line 'top: jmp start' is there because the processor cannot distinguish between data and machine instructions; they are all just numbers. If 'jmp start' was not there, the processor would attempt to execute the byte codes for 'Mary had a little lamb'. The hex dump of P5.COM is below to show this.

Hex dumps and binary files

A **hex dump** is when a file is presented as hex bytes. This is usually because the file is not made up of simple ASCII characters. Files that need to be shown this way are often called **binary files**. For example, if a program file contained the byte 08, 'printing' the file to the screen would result in a backspace (ASCII 8 is backspace) and not the character 8, a hex dump would show 08.

Hex dump of P5.COM

```
E9 19 00 4D 61 72 79 20 68 61 64 20 61 20 6C 69        ;e..Mary had a li
74 74 6C 65 20 6C 61 6D 62 0A 0D 00 BE 03 01 8A        ;ttle lamb.../.._
14 80 FA 00 74 07 B4 02 CD 21 46 EB F2 CD 20           ;._u.t.'.I!FeoI
```

As you can see, the machine code (written in hex bytes) does not seem to mean very much!

As assembly is a simple process of converting mnemonics directly to machine code; it can be reversed, the machine code can be 'turned back' to assembly code. Table 2.13 shows the result of this process, and provides a comment on what most of the bytes mean.

Unassembly of P5.ASM

Table 2.13   *Unassembly of P5.ASM*

Address	Contents	Mnemonic	Comments
0100	E91900	JMP 011C	;jump to the first instruction after the data
0103	4D	M	;data
0104	61	a	;data
0105	72	r	;data
0106	79	y	;data
0107	20	(space character)	;data
0108	68	h	;data
0109	61	a	;data
010A	64	d	;data
010B	20	(space character)	;data
010C	61	a	;data
010D	20	(space character)	;data
010E	6C	l	;data
010F	49	i	;data
0110	74	t	;data
0111	74	t	;data
0112	6C	l	;data
0113	65	e	;data
0114	20	(space character)	;data
0115	6C	l	;data
0116	61	a	;data
0117	6D	m	data
0118	62	b	;data
0119	0A	(line feed)	;data

(Contd)

Table 2.13 *(Contd)*

Address	Contents	Mnemonic	Comments
011A	13	(carriage return)	;data
011B	00	(0 used as end of string marker)	;data
011C	BE0301	MOV SI,103	;point to start of data at address 103
011F	8A14	MOV DL,[SI]	;get the data pointed to in DL ;processor register
0121	80FA00	CMP DL,00	;test to see if data is last in the string
0124	7407	JZ 012D	;if so, jump to last instruction in program
0126	B402	MOV AH,02	;put 2 into AH register, required for DOS ;function 2 call next
0128	CD21	INT 21	;call DOS int 21 function 2 to write ;character to screen
012A	46	INC SI	;point to next character in data string ;at next address
012B	EBF2	JMP 011F	;go back to address 11F to start again
012D	CD20	INT 20	;terminate program and return to DOS ;CLI (the DOS prompt)

Points to note about the unassembled program

There seem to be gaps in the addresses. This is not so, it is just that some instructions take up more than one address location. For instance, starting at address 011C there is the machine code instruction BE 03 01, which, when unassembled, gives the mnemonic MOV SI, 103. This instruction takes up the addresses 011C, 011D and 011E so the next instruction starts at address 011F. Some instructions only occupy 1 byte; for instance, at address 012A the instruction to add 1 to the SI register has the machine code 46 only.

Experiment with program P5.ASM

If you remove the top line (top: jmp start) and re-assemble the program, the first byte of the 'code' will be the ASCII code for 'M'. When you execute the program, most likely the machine will crash as the 4 bytes 'Mary' will be interpreted as op. codes DEC BP, DB 61, JB 017D.

Example program 6, P6.ASM

This program demonstrates that assembly language programmers must do everything for themselves! If a register holds a value such as 173, to print this to the screen will take a small program and not a single instruction as would be the case in a high-level language. The reason is that no op. code exists to convert the value 173 to the **three** ASCII characters required to print this to the screen.

Suppose at some point you wish to output the contents of the AX register as a multi-digit number. The code to do this is contained as a subroutine called OUTINT in the file LIB.ASM supplied in Appendix 1 and at www.anderh.com/repp. For the purposes of the National Certificate/Diploma in Computing, the detail of this subroutine takes assembly language too far; students would not be expected to write such code but would be expected to use it as a subroutine.

```
MOV AX, 173      ;the number to be printed by sub routine
CALL OUTINT      ;print the multi digit number
INT 020          ;terminate program
```

That's it!

To assemble the program with the file called LIB.ASM, just type at the DOS prompt

C:\>P6.ASM LIB.ASM P6.COM

This will assemble P6.ASM **with** LIB.ASM, and output the executable in P6.COM.

The only new op. code is CALL. This op. code causes the current address to be stored (on a **stack**) and a jump to be made to the address of the subroutine (remember the assembler will convert the symbolic address OUTINT to a real numerical address). When the RET instruction is reached, a jump is made back to the return address (held on the stack).

Stacks

A stack is simply a section of RAM that is handled in a particular way. A stack pointer (usually held in register SP) holds the address at the top of the stack. This is usually described as **pointing** to the top of the stack. If a value is to be stored on the stack, the op. code PUSH is used; this puts the value into the **address pointed to by the stack pointer** then **decrements** the stack pointer ready for the next use. In this way, the next value goes into the next location. To reverse the process, the instruction POP is used.

Example program P7.ASM

Now we know how to use a pre-written subroutine, we can practise with outputting a string:

```
        MOV SI, buffer
        CALL printstring
        INT 020
buffer: db 'I love Computing', 13,10,0
```

The string is terminated with a 0 byte as before, and SI is used to point to the string.

Assemble the program with:

C:\>A86 P7.ASM LIB.ASM P7.COM

Example program P8.ASM

This uses a DOS interrupt to get the current time and then the OUTINT subroutine to display it. It also demonstrates a common problem in assembly language, that of avoiding accidentally corrupting a register value. The OUTINT subroutine will not output a leading 0, so if the value to be output should be 02 instead of just 2, the program must check this first. To find the system time, a list of DOS interrupts is consulted to find out the 'rules' of the interrupt. This is what was found:

DOS interrupt 21 Function 2C, read system time.
Calling registers

AH = 2C

Return registers

CH = hours (0-23) in decimal
CL = minutes (0-59) in decimal
DH = seconds (0-59) in decimal
DL = hundredths of a second (0-99) in decimal

This means that 02C is put into AH before a call to the interrupt, then the values in registers CH, CL, DH and DL are used as hours, minutes and seconds.

```
        MOV AH, 02C   ;DOS interrupt 21 Function 2C,
                      ;read system time.
        INT 021       ;call DOS
                      ;now CH=hours, CL=Minutes
                      ;DH=seconds,DL=hundredths/sec

;..... now store to prevent overwriting by subroutine

        MOV hours, CH
        MOV mins, CL
        MOV secs, DH

        ;..... display the hours.................

        MOV AH,0      ;AX is AH and AL so clear top
        MOV AL, hours ;of AX (AH) ready for OUTINT
        CMP AX, 10    ;see if leading zero is needed
        JAE L20       ;jump if 10 or more without
                      ;outputting 0 first
        CALL leadingzero
L20: CALL OUTINT      ;output the time in hours

        ;..... now output a h:m:s separator...........

        MOV DL, ':'   ;hour:min:sec separator
        MOV AH, 2     ;DOS interrupt 21 function 2
        INT 021       ;call DOS to output ':'

        ;..... display the minutes.................
```

```
            MOV AH,0       ;AX is AH and AL so clear top
            MOV AL, mins   ;of AX (AH) ready for OUTINT
            CMP AX, 10     ;see if leading zero is needed
            JAE L21        ;jump if 10 or more without
                           ;outputting 0 first
            CALL leadingzero
     L21: CALL OUTINT      ;output the time in minutes

            ;..... now output a h:m:s separator............

            MOV DL, ':'    ;hour:min:sec separator
            MOV AH, 2      ;DOS interrupt 21 function 2
            INT 021        ;call DOS to output ':'

            ;..... display the seconds..................

            MOV AH,0       ;AX is AH and AL so clear top
            MOV AL, secs   ;of AX (AH) ready for OUTINT
            CMP AX, 10     ;see if leading zero is needed
            JAE L22        ;jump if 10 or more without
                           ;outputting 0 first
            CALL leadingzero
     L22: CALL OUTINT      ;output the time in seconds

            INT 020        ;terminate program

hours DB 0                 ;define some space
mins DB 0                  ;for variables
secs DB 0                  ;to store values
```

Exercise 2.4

Modify program P8.ASM to output the system date. The following information is required:

DOS interrupt 21 Function 2A, read system date Calling registers

AH = 2A in hex

Return registers

AL = day of the week (0=Sunday, 1=Monday etc.)
CX = year
DH = month
DL = day.

Hint, for storing the year you will need a DW directive to define a 16-bit word in place of the DB directive to define an 8-bit byte. The answer is in Appendix A.

Exercise 2.5

Modify program P8.ASM to output the DOS version number for your machine, preceded by the string 'DOS version number= '. The following information is required:

> **DOS interrupt 21 Function 30, return DOS version number**
> **Calling registers**
>
> AH = 30 in hex
>
> **Return registers**
>
> AL = Major version number (2,3 etc.)
> AH = Minor version number (2.1 returns 2 in AL and 10 in AH).
>
> The answer is in Appendix A.

> **Exercise 2.6**
>
> Modify programs P8.ASM and your answer to Exercise 2.4 to output both the system time and date on the same line with strings saying 'Time is now' and 'Date= '.
>
> The answer is in Appendix A.

2.7 Operating systems

An operating system has a number of functions:

- to provide an interface with the user
- to provide a range of services that are used by application software, such as disk management, printer control, time/date functions etc.
- to provide a development environment, i.e. compilers and run-time systems etc.

It is usual in operating systems (OS) to consider a layered architecture in a similar manner to layering in networks. The layers in a typical OS are:

- layer 4, applications
- layer 3, kernel
- layer 2, drivers
- layer 1, hardware.

Layer 1 is how the operating system communicates with the hardware, rather than the hardware itself. In PCs, this is generally the BIOS – the Basic Input Output System.

Layer 2, drivers, refers to pieces of software that 'talk' to specific device types such as disk drives. For example, in a PC, an ATAPI CD-ROM needs a device driver loaded because the operating system at layers 3 and 4 does not 'know about' CDs and how the data are organized in detail. The device driver provides this service.

Layer 3, the kernel, organizes the way that processes are controlled – i.e. if an application requests service from a printer, other application requests must not interfere.

Layer 4, applications, are the programs the user wishes to run in the machine. The OS must load them into memory and start them running.

Various operating systems have a layered architecture different in detail from that described here. No matter; the idea is that application software is supported or supplied with services by the OS. This means that an application programmer need not know how to control a printer or a disk drive; all that is needed is to ask the OS for these services. In the case of Microsoft Windows, this is done by the Windows API or **Application Programme Interface**. Application software calls for service from the Win API; the actual code for this is stored in .DLL files or **Dynamic Link Libraries**.

User interface

In the past, what the user saw was a screen prompt (or even a printer prompt!) like C:\>. This 'prompted' the user to type a command such as DIR to gain a service. (DIR requests a listing of the files on the current disk drive.) This style of user interface is called a CLI, or Command Line Interpreter, because the text typed at the prompt (the command line) is interpreted by the CLI and either a request is made to the kernel for service or an error message is issued. In Microsoft's DOS, the CLI is called COMMAND.COM. In the unix world there are many different command line interpreters; they are called 'shells' but do essentially the same thing – they provide a command line–user interface.

More modern PC operating Systems use a **Graphical User Interface**, or GUI. This is what you see when you use Windows, but it is **only** an interface; what underlies Windows 95 or 98 is mostly DOS. Windows NT or 2000 are very different although they look similar. Here the underlying kernel is not DOS but the GUI 'talks' to the kernel in a related fashion. If you run **Linux** on a PC, you use either a shell (the CLI) or a GUI that has a similar 'look and feel' to Microsoft Windows. There are several on the market.

Kinds of OS

Quite independently of the user interface, the OS must provide for ideas such as multi-tasking, and for multiple users.

Multi-tasking is not quite what it seems. To the user the machine is running multiple tasks all at once so, for instance, a download from the Internet is running at the same time as the user types into a wordprocessor. Of course the PC only has a single CPU, which can only do one thing at a time. The solution is to switch between tasks so quickly that the user is not aware of the switching. This is achieved using a number of system software techniques.

Multi-user operating systems must provide additional services to allow the identification of users; i.e. they must 'log in'. The OS must also provide security so that malicious or careless users cannot affect the work of others.

If more than one task or more than one user needs service from the OS, it must provide memory management. This means that the physical RAM must be organized so that users and applications are not able to infringe other areas. When using Windows, you may have seen the error message 'This program has performed an illegal operation'. A common cause of this is an application that attempts to access an address in memory that belongs to a different application or process. Windows cannot resolve the problem, so it shuts down the errant process.

2.8 ASCII and Unicode character sets

Before the days of computing, communication systems required each character to be sent as a code. Simple systems used 1s and 0s for transmission just like today, so binary numbers were used to encode characters. You could not send an 'A' character directly, but you could send binary 1000001 in its place. This eventually led to a 'standard' set of characters that were used to control printing devices before the widespread use of VDUs. ASCII stands for American Standard Code for Information Interchange, but there are other character encoding systems around like EBCDIC and LICS that work in a similar way. However, ASCII is the most widespread.

In ASCII, the codes from 0 to 31 are called 'Control Characters'. These were originally used to control the movement of the old mechanical printers, so we have terms like 'Carriage Return' (now known as Enter or just Return) that actually caused the carriage that held the paper to return to the left-hand side. Understanding this historical basis of the control characters helps you to understand the names they are given, which now seem a little odd. If a Control Character (written as CTRL A etc.) is sent to a printer or screen, it usually results in an action rather than a printable character. Because some of the codes only have real meaning for mechanical printers, the original names do not always make sense in modern usage.

Before the widespread use of Microsoft Windows, most machines responded directly to these control characters. As an experiment, try opening a DOS window and typing a command. Instead of pressing the Enter key, press CTRL M instead; you should find it does the same thing as pressing Enter. The Enter key is just a CTRL M key in DOS. (If you try this using Microsoft Word, CTRL M has a different effect.) If you are using Unix or Linux, try using CTRL H in place of the backspace key; it should work unless it has been re-mapped on your machine.

Table 2.14 lists the ASCII control characters.

Characters in ASCII are easy to remember; they run from A = 65 to Z = 90. This may look like an odd choice of numbers until you convert the 65 into binary and get 1000001, i.e. 64 + 1. This means that any letter is easy to calculate; it is 64 plus its position in the alphabet. M is the thirteenth letter in the alphabet, so in ASCII, M = 64 + 13 = 77. To make it lower case, just add 32. This is a good choice, as 32 encodes as a single binary digit. Lower case m is then 64 + 32 + 13 = 109. Of course it would be better to use hex, so A = 41, M = 4D, a = 61, m = 6D etc. Numerals are just as easy; '0' encodes as 48, '1' encodes as 48 + 1 = 49, etc.

The full set of 7-bit printable ASCII characters is shown in Table 2.15.

You will notice that the codes only extend to 127. This is because the original ASCII only used 7-binary digits and was referred to as a 7 bit code. Whilst there is some standardization of the codes 128 to 255; some machines will give different characters for codes 128

Table 2.14　*The ASCII control characters*

Dec	Hex	Keyboard	Binary		Description
0	0	CTRL @	00000	NUL	Null Character
1	1	CTRL A	00001	SOH	Start of Heading
2	2	CTRL B	00010	STX	Start of Text
3	3	CTRL C	00011	ETX	End of Text
4	4	CTRL D	00100	EOT	End of Transmission
5	5	CTRL E	00101	ENQ	Enquiry
6	6	CTRL F	00110	ACK	Acknowledge
7	7	CTRL G	00111	BEL	Bell or beep
8	8	CTRL H	01000	BS	Back Space
9	9	CTRL I	01001	HT	Horizontal Tab
10	A	CTRL J	01010	LF	Line Feed
11	B	CTRL K	01011	VT	Vertical Tab
12	C	CTRL L	01100	FF	Form Feed
13	D	CTRL M	01101	CR	Carriage Return
14	E	CTRL N	01110	SO	Shift Out
15	F	CTRL O	01111	SI	Shift In
16	10	CTRL P	10000	DLE	Date Link Escape
17	11	CTRL Q	10001	DC1	Device Control 1
18	12	CTRL R	10010	DC2	Device Control 2
19	13	CTRL S	10011	DC3	Device Control 3
20	14	CTRL T	10100	DC4	Device Control 4
21	15	CTRL U	10101	NAK	Negative Acknowledge
22	16	CTRL V	10110	SYN	Synchronous Idle
23	17	CTRL W	10111	ETB	End of Transmission Block
24	18	CTRL X	11000	CAN	Cancel
25	19	CTRL Y	11001	EM	End Medium
26	1A	CTRL Z	11010	SUB	Substitute or EOF End Of File
27	1B		11011	ESC	Escape
28	1C		11100	FS	File Separator
29	1D		11101	GS	Group Separator
30	1E		11110	RS	Record Separator
31	1F		11111	US	Unit Separator

to 255; for instance, older machines will give an é for code 130 whilst more modern machines will give an é for code 233.

It is not important to remember ASCII codes but it is often useful, especially when writing text- or string-handling parts of programs. If you remember that 'A' = 64 + alphabet position (40 in hex) and that 'a' = 'A' + 32 ('A' + 20 in hex), you can work out all of the alphabet. The '0' character is 48, and the digits are 48 + their value. If you also remember that a Carriage Return is 13 (0D hex) and that Line Feed is 10 (0A hex), you will be able to remember about half the codes and interpret some hex-dumped files.

Question 2.3

Write down the ASCII values in decimal and hex for the string 'I Love Computing'. Try to work it out without looking at the code table. Don't forget the spaces are ASCII characters as well.

	I		L	o	v	e		C	o	m	p	u	t	i	n	g
Dec																
Hex																

Table 2.15 *Seven-bit printable ASCII characters*

Char	Dec	Hex	Binary	Char	Dec	Hex	Binary	Char	Dec	Hex	Binary
Space	32	20	100000								
!	33	21	100001	A	65	41	1000001	a	97	61	1100001
"	34	22	100010	B	66	42	1000010	b	98	62	1100010
#	35	23	100011	C	67	43	1000011	c	99	63	1100011
$	36	24	100100	D	68	44	1000100	d	100	64	1100100
%	37	25	100101	E	69	45	1000101	e	101	65	1100101
&	38	26	100110	F	70	46	1000110	f	102	66	1100110
'	39	27	100111	G	71	47	1000111	g	103	67	1100111
(	40	28	101000	H	72	48	1001000	h	104	68	1101000
)	41	29	101001	I	73	49	1001001	i	105	69	1101001
*	42	2A	101010	J	74	4A	1001010	j	106	6A	1101010
+	43	2B	101011	K	75	4B	1001011	k	107	6B	1101011
,	44	2C	101100	L	76	4C	1001100	l	108	6C	1101100
–	45	2D	101101	M	77	4D	1001101	m	109	6D	1101101
.	46	2E	101110	N	78	4E	1001110	n	110	6E	1101110
/	47	2F	101111	O	79	4F	1001111	o	111	6F	1101111
0	48	30	110000	P	80	50	1010000	p	112	70	1110000
1	49	31	110001	Q	81	51	1010001	q	113	71	1110001
2	50	32	110010	R	82	52	1010010	r	114	72	1110010
3	51	33	110011	S	83	53	1010011	s	115	73	1110011
4	52	34	110100	T	84	54	1010100	t	116	74	1110100
5	53	35	110101	U	85	55	1010101	u	117	75	1110101
6	54	36	110110	V	86	56	1010110	v	118	76	1110110
7	55	37	110111	W	87	57	1010111	w	119	77	1110111
8	56	38	111000	X	88	58	1011000	x	120	78	1111000
9	57	39	111001	Y	89	59	1011001	y	121	79	1111001
:	58	3A	111010	Z	90	5A	1011010	z	122	7A	1111010
;	59	3B	111011	[	91	5B	1011011	{	123	7B	1111011
<	60	3C	111100	\	92	5C	1011100	|	124	7C	1111100
=	61	3D	111101	]	93	5D	1011101	}	125	7D	1111101
>	62	3E	111110	^	94	5E	1011110	~	126	7E	1111110
?	63	3F	111111	_	95	5F	1011111	del	127	7F	1111111
@	64	40	1000000	`	96	60	1100000				

Answer

	I		L	o	v	e		C	o	m	p	u	t	i	n	g
Dec	73	32	76	111	118	101	32	67	111	109	112	117	116	105	110	103
Hex	49	20	4C	6F	76	65	20	43	6F	6D	70	75	74	69	6E	67

Unicode

ASCII characters, although universally accepted, present one serious problem; there are not sufficient characters to cover all the symbols and characters from different languages. The solution adopted until the introduction of **Unicode** was to set up each computer with its own character set according to the country or language. This makes it harder to communicate files from computers set up for different countries; try finding the pound sign on an American keyboard! 'Normal' Unicode uses 16-bit characters, so there are $2^{16} = 65536$ possible characters, more than enough to cover all the world's main languages. The ASCII character set has been incorporated so character 65 is still an 'A', but the 65 is a 16-bit value. There is also a byte-oriented Unicode that allows for more than a million characters. The Unicode standard is developing all the time; the latest situation is presented on their web page at http://www.unicode.org/. This describes the current version, and the work in progress to add more.

Conversion of ASCII to Unicode is very easy as the codes are simply changed from 8 bit into 16 bit. Conversion from Unicode to ASCII may result in the loss of data as ASCII cannot support more than 256 different characters. Some operating systems will work with both character sets; the more modern ones will use Unicode as the native code.

2.9 Number bases

The Romans used a number system based on symbols, so I was 1 and V was 5. The number IV means 5 – 1, or 4, and VI means 5 + 1, or 6. This is a very difficult system to use if you want to do mathematics. In contrast, we use the Arabic system, which is based on **numbers by position**.

Consider the number 264. We all know this is two hundred and sixty-four because we have been brought up to be very familiar with numbers in this format. If you break it down, it means two hundreds, six tens and four units or 200 + 60 + 4. The digit 6 only means 60 because of its **position** in the number 264.

If you remember back to primary school days, you will recognize the sum

h	t	u
2	6	4
+1	2	2
3	8	6

The headings mean **h** for hundreds, **t** for tens and **u** for units.

A more mathematical approach would be to recognize that 100 is 10^2, 10 is 10^1, and units are 10^0 (any number to power 0 is 1). The sum then looks like this:

10^2	10^1	10^0
2	6	4
+1	2	2
3	8	6

This is the basis for numbers by position to a base, in this case, base 10. Each column is simply then number base raised to an integer power.

If you add 392 to 264 and set it out as below, the second column results in a **carry** operation.

10^2	10^1	10^0
2	6	4
3	9	2
carry 1		
6	5	6

This is how we are taught to 'carry 1' into the next column. What we are doing is simply using numbers by position; the sum of the second column, 6 + 9, is 15, the digit 1 in 15 refers to **10** rather than **1** so it belongs in the next column to the left.

> The only reason we use numbers to the base 10 is that humans are born with 10 fingers. If we were all born with, say, 12 fingers, we would use numbers to base 12 and think numbers to base 10 to be very odd indeed! The way we manipulate numbers, do addition, multiplication, division etc. is exactly the same in any number base.

Other number bases

The 6 in 264 means 60, or 6 tens, because we use numbers to the base 10. We could just as easily use numbers to any other base. If we used numbers to base 8 (called octal numbers), then the number 64 would mean 6 eights plus 4, not 6 tens plus 4.

If we were to use numbers to the base 8, the column headings would be $8^2\ 8^1\ 8^0$; if numbers to the base 5, the headings would be $5^2\ 5^1\ 5^0$.

The powers simply increase by 1 for each column to the left or decrease by 1 to the right.

The number of symbols required

To use any given number base, you need that number of symbols to write it down. As we use numbers to base 10, we use symbols 0–9. Binary numbers use base 2, so we need only two symbols, 0 and 1.

The common bases in computing are 2, 10 and 16. Binary is used because the electronic circuits operate in two states that can be modelled using 1 or 0; 1 for 'on' and 0 for 'off'.

Hex or hexadecimal numbers are often used in computing. This is because conversion to or from binary is very simple, and those people who need to work with 'bits and bytes' find hex convenient. Since hex numbers are to the base 16, we need 16 symbols, 0–9 and A–F. This makes numbers look a little odd, but 5D simply means 5 times 16^1 plus D, (or 13) times 1, so 5D hex is (5×16) + 13 = 93 in base 10 numbers.

Table 2.16 shows the same value in each row, but in various number bases.

Binary numbers

Knowing that binary uses the same **rule** as base 10 numbers, i.e. numbers by position, it is easy to understand a binary number.

The value shown in Table 2.17 in binary is 10110001010, or 2^{10} + 2^8 + 2^7 + 2^3 + 2^1 = 1024 + 256 + 8 + 1 = 1289 base 10. Ignore the leading zeros.

Table 2.16   *Various number bases showing the same value in each row*

Base 2 binary	Base 8 octal	Base 10 decimal	Base 16 hex
0	0	0	0
1	1	1	1
10	2	2	2
11	3	3	3
100	4	4	4
101	5	5	5
110	6	6	6
111	7	7	7
1000	10	8	8
1001	11	9	9
1010	12	10	A
1011	13	11	B
1100	14	12	C
1101	15	13	D
1110	16	14	E
1111	17	15	F
10000	20	16	10
10001	21	17	11
10010	22	18	12
10011	23	19	13

Table 2.17   *Decimal and binary numbers*

	2^{11}	2^{10}	2^9	2^8	2^7	2^6	2^5	2^4	2^3	2^2	2^1	2^0
Decimal value	2048	1024	512	256	128	64	32	16	8	4	2	1
Binary	0	1	0	1	1	0	0	0	1	0	1	0

Question 2.4

(a) Convert 110110011 to decimal.

Answer

2^{11}	2^{10}	2^9	2^8	2^7	2^6	2^5	2^4	2^3	2^2	2^1	2^0
0	0	0	1	1	0	1	1	0	0	1	1

$2^8 + 2^7 + 2^5 + 2^4 + 2^1 + 2^0 = 256 + 128 + 32 + 16 + 2 + 1 = 435$

(b) Convert 110001101 to decimal.

Answer

2^{11}	2^{10}	2^9	2^8	2^7	2^6	2^5	2^4	2^3	2^2	2^1	2^0
0	0	0	1	1	0	0	0	1	1	0	1

$2^8 + 2^7 + 2^3 + 2^2 + 2^0 = 256 + 128 + 8 + 4 + 1 = 397$

There are many way to convert backwards. One is to use knowledge of the values in each column, like this:

2^{11}	2^{10}	2^9	2^8	2^7	2^6	2^5	2^4	2^3	2^2	2^1	2^0
2048	1024	512	256	128	64	32	16	8	4	2	1

When converting 106 to binary, it is clear that all the columns 128 and higher have the value zero as 106 is lower than 128. A '1' is entered into the 2^6 column, and 64 subtracted from 106 to give 106 − 64 = 42. Because 42 is higher than the next number down, a '1' goes into the 2^5 column and 32 is subtracted from 42 to give 10; as 10 is 8 + 2, a '1' will go in each of the 8 and 1 columns as shown in Table 2.18. Therefore, 106 base 10 is 1101010.

Table 2.18 *Converting 106 to binary*

2^{11}	2^{10}	2^9	2^8	2^7	2^6	2^5	2^4	2^3	2^2	2^1	2^0
2048	1024	512	256	128	64	32	16	8	4	2	1
0	0	0	0	0	1	1	0	1	0	1	0

Checking backwards, 1101010 is 64 + 32 + 8 + 2 = 106.

Another way to convert a decimal number to binary is successive division by 2. In Table 2.19, the number 106 is divided by 2 using **integer arithmetic** – i.e. the fractional part of the answer is ignored. Also using integer arithmetic, the remainder after division is shown. This is known as MOD, so 106 MOD 2 = 0, i.e. there is no remainder after division by 2. Each quotient is then divided by 2 in the same way until a quotient of 0 is obtained. The binary value of the original number is now shown in the remainder column, **read from the bottom**. In this example, the value 106 is shown to be 1101010 as above.

Table 2.19 *Using integer arithmetic to convert a decimal number to binary*

	Quotient	Remainder
106 DIV 2 =	53	0
53 DIV 2 =	26	1
26 DIV 2 =	13	0
13 DIV 2 =	6	1
6 DIV 2 =	3	0
3 DIV 2 =	1	1
1 DIV 2 =	0	1

Hex and octal numbers

If we have an octal number, it is easy to convert it to base 10. Taking 523 as an octal number, this is:

5×8^2, or $5 \times 64 = 320$

plus

2×8^1, or $2 \times 8 = 16$

plus

3×8^0, or $3 \times 1 = 3$ (any number to power 0 is 1)

equals

$320 + 16 + 3 = 339$ (base 10).

As a further example, what is the octal number 1000 in decimal? The answer is easy to see if it is laid out as before:

8^3	8^2	8^1	8^0
1	0	0	0

so 1000 octal $= 1 \times 8^3 = 512$ base 10.

Converting numbers

You can convert numbers using Microsoft Excel spreadsheets. The functions OCT2BIN OCT2HEX, OCT2DEC, HEX2BIN, HEX2OCT, HEX2DEC, BIN2HEX, BIN2OCT, BIN2DEC, DEC2BIN, DEC2OCT, DEC2HEX can be used. If they do not work first time, see the help file about installing the Analysis Tool Pack 'add-in'.

The same rules apply if using hex or any other base. For example, the hex number 26A is:

2×16^2, or $2 \times 64 = 128$

plus

6×16^1, or $6 \times 16 = 96$

plus

A (or 10) $\times 16^0$, or $16 \times 1 = 16$

equals

$128 + 96 + 16 = 618$ base 10.

Converting Octal and hex to and from binary

As stated above, one reason that Hex or Octal numbers are used is that conversion to or from binary is simple.

Examples

1.   To convert the hex number 4A7 to binary:
     Take each digit and write it down in 4-bit binary.

     4 = 0100
     A = 1010
     7 = 0111

     so 4A7 = 0100 1010 0111, usually written with no spaces as 010010100111.

2.   To convert the hex number F0FF to binary:

     F = 1111

0 = 0000
F = 1111
F = 1111

so F0FF = 1111 0000 1111 1111.

3. To convert the other way, simply break the binary number into 4-bit sections **from the right** and write down the hex digit equivalent for each of the 4-bit groups. For examples to convert 10011000100111010100 to hex:

1001 1000 1001 1101 0100
9   8   9   D   4

so 10011000100111010100 = 989D4 in hex.

4. To convert 11110111001000001011 to hex:

1 1110 1110 0100 0001 1011
1 E   E   4   1   B

so 11110111001000001011 = 1EE41B in hex.

5. The only difference with octal numbers is that you use 3-bit groups instead of 4-bit groups. For example, to convert the octal number 216 to binary:

2 = 010
1 = 001
6 = 110

So 216 octal = 010001110 in binary.

6. To convert 110010011100001 to octal:

110 010 011 100 001
6   2   3   4   1

So 110010011100001 = 62341 octal.

7. One way to convert a hex number to an octal number is to convert to binary as an intermediary. For example, to convert 23FA to octal (notice that 23FA cannot be octal as octal only uses the digits 0–7):

23FA = 0010 0011 1111 1010, which when split into groups of three gives

0 010 001 111 111 010 = 21772 octal (ignore leading zeros).

If you have access to a PC running Windows and you do not have a scientific calculator that can handle numbers to different bases, you can check your answers with the Windows calculator. Go to start, programs, accessories, calculator. When started, click on the view menu and choose Scientific.

Question 2.5

Fill in table without using a calculator or any other aid.

Binary	Octal	Decimal	Hex
	233	155	9B
111110011		499	
		40	
			2E
101001010			
			BE
110111010			
	527		
	714		
		138	
		16	
		57	
			13E
		400	
			1FB
100011110			

Answer

Binary	Octal	Decimal	Hex
10011011	233	155	9B
111110011	763	499	1F3
101000	50	40	28
101110	56	46	2E
101001010	512	330	14A
10111110	276	190	BE
110111010	672	442	1BA
101010111	527	343	157
111001100	714	460	1CC
10001010	212	138	8A
10000	20	16	10
111001	71	57	39
100111110	476	318	13E
110010000	620	400	190
111111011	773	507	1FB
100011110	436	286	11E

Fixed point fractional numbers

In numbers to the base 10 using numbers by position, fractional numbers are represented in the same way, so

10^2	10^1	10^0	10^{-1}	10^{-2}	10^{-3}	10^{-4}
2	6	4	2	7	8	4

gives 264.2784 because

10^{-1} is $1/10^1$ or 0.1
10^{-2} is $1/10^2$ or 1/100 or 0.01
10^{-3} is $1/10^3$ or 1/1000 or 0.001 etc.

so $0.2784 = 2 \times 10^{-1}$ plus 7×10^{-2} plus 8×10^{-3} plus 4×10^{-4}.

In numbers by position, each power increases to the right and decreases to the left.

Question 2.6

Write down 452.0625 as a fixed point binary number.

Answer

$452 = 256 + 128 + 64 + 4 = 111000100$
$0.0625 = 2^{-4}$ or 0.0001

	2^8	2^7	2^6	2^5	2^4	2^3	2^2	2^1	2^0	2^{-1}	2^{-2}	2^{-3}	2^{-4}
Dec.	256	128	64	32	16	8	4	2	1	0.5	0.25	0.125	0.0625
	1	1	1	0	0	0	1	0	0	0	0	0	1

so 452.0625 = 111000100.0001.

Here the point is a bicemal point instead of a decimal point.

Just as one-third = 0.3333 recurring in decimal, i.e. 0.333 is not exactly one-third, it is possible to get inexact binary fractions. The decimal 1/100 or 0.01 gives an inexact binary fraction, which is unfortunate because £0.01, or one penny, cannot be represented exactly as a simple binary fraction. This can lead to errors, as will be shown in section 2.10. Decimal 0.01 is

0.00000010100011110101110000101000111101011100001010001111
to 56 binary places, **approximately**!

2.10 Floating point numbers

A floating point number (called a 'real' in Pascal) stores the number in several parts. For example, to change 382.070556640625 to a floating point number:

Step 1, convert to **fixed** point binary

382.070556640625 = 101111110.000100100001000000000000000

Step 2, move the binary point to the left until there is a leading '1'. This is called **normalizing**, and the number it produces is called the **mantissa**. Record the power of 2 required to achieve this; in this case it is 8. This value is called the **exponent**.

$$1.01111110000100100001000000000000000 \times 2^8$$

Step 3, to avoid the possibility of negative powers, add a fixed value to the exponent. This is called an **excess** value. A standard value to add is 127, and such a system would be called 'Excess 127'. Use the excess 127 rule on the exponent and convert to binary

$$8 + 127 = 135$$

$$135 = 10000111.$$

Step 4, store values, stripping the leading 1 of the mantissa. Since the mantissa will always have a leading '1' there is no point storing it.

Step 5, assign a 0 to a positive number or a 1 to negative number; this is called the **sign bit**.

Sign	Exponent	Fraction or mantissa
0	10000111	01111110000100100001000
bit 31	bits 30–23	bits 22–0

So as a floating point number,

382.070556640625 = 0100 0011 1011 1111 0000 1001 0000 1000

which viewed as hex would be:

0100	0011	1011	1111	0000	1001	0000	1000
4	3	B	F	0	9	0	0

or 43 BF 09 00.

IEEE floating point format

It is often said that the nice thing about standards in computing is that there are so many to choose from! Floating point numbers can and are represented in a wide variety of formats, which usually means the only program that can read them is the one that created them in the first place. Clearly it is desirable to have a common standard so all programs can read/write floating point numbers. The Institute of Electrical and Electronic Engineers (IEEE, home page http://standards.ieee.org/) has issued a floating point number standard, which is usually referred to as simply IEEE 754 (see http://grouper.ieee.org/groups/754/).

The IEEE standard defines several formats for floating point numbers, but for simplicity the most common is shown here. It is supported by many software providers.

Numbers are stored in the format N = 1.F* 2^(E-127), where

N = floating point number
F = fractional part in binary
E = exponent in excess 127 format, also known as bias 127 representation.

One bit represents the sign of the number and is known as the sign bit. 0 = positive. The next 8 bits contain the exponent field, and the last 23 bits contain the mantissa as a normalized number, leading zero not stored:

Sign	Exponent	Fraction
0	00000000	00000000000000000000000
bit 31	bits 30–23	bits 22–0

Floating point experiments

The following experiments with a spreadsheet, Visual Basic and Pascal demonstrate that floating point numbers are not always exact and that small errors can exist in their representation. These errors are small, but can be significant if appropriate steps are not taken to avoid them.

Use of a spreadsheet

This example is produced from Microsoft Excel 97.

In this experiment, the spreadsheet adds a value (called an increment) to a number and then adds itself again and again to the result. If the increment is itself not an exact floating point number, any errors get amplified to the point that they become visible. Once you have set up the spreadsheet, look at the first column in Table 2.20. You will see that the values increase at first as they should; each line is just 0.001 larger than the last, and any errors are not visible. If you look several hundred rows down, you will see that errors have appeared. Column 2 uses another simple floating point operation to make the errors appear larger. In this case an error is obvious in the very first row, as the answer should be 1, not 0.999999999999890.

Stage 1, set up the spreadsheet

1. Starting at cell A1, insert the values and formulas shown in Table 2.21. The cell that contains the string 'Starting value' is cell A1.
2. Format all rows from 4 onwards to 'Number' and 15 decimal places.
3. Copy down for more than 1000 rows.

Your results should be similar to those in Table 2.20.

(The $ characters in the formulas of Table 2.21 are to avoid indexing the cell reference during copying down; they have no effect on the calculation. The result will be that any reference with $ will not change; $B$2 remains a reference to B2, and will not become B3, B4 etc. as the formula is copied down. They are known as **absolute cell references**.)

Hiding rows

You may want to hide a large number of rows. To do this, select these rows by clicking on the first row number (shown on a grey background) and then moving to the last row and clicking again **whilst holding down the shift key**. Then use the menu sequence (in Excel) of Format-> Row->Hide.

Stage 2, experiment with different values

If you choose a starting value of 1, try different values for the increment. Increments that are exact binary fractions yield no error. For example, $2^{-3} = 0.125$, which in binary is 0.001. When normalized and converted to floating point, there is no error. Values that are not exact binary fractions, such as 1/100 or 1/1000, will cause a (small) error as shown in the Tables 2.20 and 2.21. Try these increments and decide if the resulting stored floating point numbers are exact:

0.0625
0.063
0.06
0.015625
0.05078125
0.0001.

Reduction of errors

Look at the last column in Table 2.20. It produces the values 1.001, 1.002, 1.003 etc. with no apparent errors. This is because there is no successive addition of inaccurate floating point numbers, so any error never gets any larger. Errors in floating point numbers are usually only significant when they are added, multiplied etc. many times. In the design of spreadsheets or when writing programs, effort should be made to avoid errors being amplified by unnecessary iteration. The same mathematical result can usually be achieved with smaller errors by avoiding successive operations.

Table 2.20 *Values*

Starting value	Amount to increment at each step		
1	0.001		
Results of successive additions	Results minus starting value multiplied by 1/increment	Number of additions	Alternative calculation avoiding floating point errors
1.001000000000000	0.999999999999890	1	1.001000000000000
1.002000000000000	1.999999999999780	2	1.002000000000000
1.003000000000000	2.999999999999670	3	1.003000000000000
1.004000000000000	3.999999999999560	4	1.004000000000000
1.005000000000000	4.999999999999450	5	1.005000000000000
1.006000000000000	5.999999999999340	6	1.006000000000000
1.007000000000000	6.999999999999230	7	1.007000000000000
1.008000000000000	7.999999999999120	8	1.008000000000000
1.009000000000000	8.999999999999010	9	1.009000000000000
1.010000000000000	9.999999999998900	10	1.010000000000000
1.011000000000000	10.999999999998800	11	1.011000000000000
1.012000000000000	11.999999999998700	12	1.012000000000000
1.013000000000000	12.999999999998600	13	1.013000000000000
1000 rows hidden to save space!			
2.013999999999890	1013.999999999890000	1014	2.014000000000000
2.014999999999890	1014.999999999890000	1015	2.015000000000000
2.015999999999890	1015.999999999890000	1016	2.016000000000000
2.016999999999890	1016.999999999890000	1017	2.017000000000000
2.017999999999890	1017.999999999890000	1018	2.018000000000000
2.018999999999890	1018.999999999890000	1019	2.019000000000000
2.019999999999890	1019.999999999890000	1020	2.020000000000000

Table 2.21 *Formulas*

Starting value	Amount to increment at each step		
1	0.001		
Results of successive additions	Results minus starting value multiplied by 1/increment	Number of additions	Alternative calculation avoiding floating point errors
=A2+$B$2	=(A4–$A$2)*(1/$B$2)	1	=1+$A$2*(C4*$B$2)
=A4+$B$2	=(A5–$A$2)*(1/$B$2)	=C4+1	=1+$A$2*(C5*$B$2)
=A5+$B$2	=(A6–$A$2)*(1/$B$2)	=C5+1	=1+$A$2*(C6*$B$2)
=A6+$B$2	=(A7–$A$2)*(1/$D$2)	=C6+1	=1+$A$2*(C7*$B$2)
=A7+$B$2	=(A8–$A$2)*(1/$B$2)	=C7+1	=1+$A$2*(C8*$B$2)
=A8+$B$2	=(A9–$A$2)*(1/$B$2)	=C8+1	=1+$A$2*(C9*$B$2)
=A9+$B$2	=(A10–$A$2)*(1/$B$2)	=C9+1	=1+$A$2*(C10*$B$2)
=A10+$B$2	=(A11–$A$2)*(1/$B$2)	=C10+1	=1+$A$2*(C11*$B$2)
=A11+$B$2	=(A12–$A$2)*(1/$B$2)	=C11+1	=1+$A$2*(C12*$B$2)
=A12+$B$2	=(A13–$A$2)*(1/$B$2)	=C12+1	=1+$A$2*(C13*$B$2)
=A13+$B$2	=(A14–$A$2)*(1/$B$2)	=C13+1	=1+$A$2*(C14*$B$2)
=A14+$B$2	=(A15–$A$2)*(1/$B$2)	=C14+1	=1+$A$2*(C15*$B$2)
=A15+$B$2	=(A16–$A$2)*(1/$B$2)	=C15+1	=1+$A$2*(C16*$B$2)
1000 rows hidden to save space!			
=A1016+$B$2	=(A1017–$A$2)*(1/$B$2)	=C1016+1	=1+$A$2*(C1017*$B$2)
=A1017+$B$2	=(A1018–$A$2)*(1/$B$2)	=C1017+1	=1+$A$2*(C1018*$B$2)
=A1018+$B$2	=(A1019–$A$2)*(1/$B$2)	=C1018+1	=1+$A$2*(C1019*$B$2)
=A1019+$B$2	=(A1020–$A$2)*(1/$B$2)	=C1019+1	=1+$A$2*(C1020*$B$2)
=A1020+$B$2	=(A1021–$A$2)*(1/$B$2)	=C1020+1	=1+$A$2*(C1021*$B$2)
=A1021+$B$2	=(A1022–$A$2)*(1/$B$2)	=C1021+1	=1+$A$2*(C1022*$B$2)
=A1022+$B$2	=(A1023–$A$2)*(1/$B$2)	=C1022+1	=1+$A$2*(C1023*$B$2)

Visual Basic

Start a new project and add the following controls:

- a text box called TxtIncrement with the initial value of the text property as 0.001
- a text box called TxtStartingvalue with the initial value of the text property as 1
- a list box called LstOutput
- a command button called cmdGo with a caption of Go
- a command button called cmdClear with a caption of Clear.

Add the code shown below:

```
Private Sub cmdClear_Click()
LstOutput.Clear
End Sub

Private Sub cmdGo_Click()
Dim i As Integer
Dim x As Double
Dim y As Double

x = Val(TxtIncrement.Text)
y = Val(txtStartingvalue.Text) + x
For i = 1 To 1050
  LstOutput.AddItem Str$(y)
  y = y + x
Next i

End Sub
```

When you run the resulting program, you should get something like Figure 2.26. Scroll though the list box to see the output. Errors due to successive additions of inexact floating point numbers are easily seen. Use the same increments as above to see if you get the same results:

0.0625
0.063
0.06
0.015625
0.05078125
0.0001.

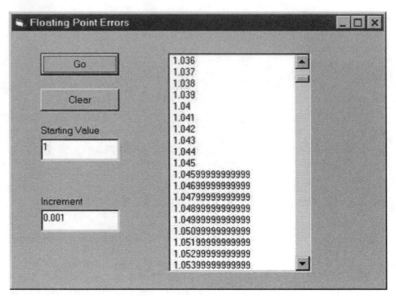

Figure 2.26   *Visual Basic experiment with floating point errors*

Pascal (Free Pascal or Borland Turbo Pascal version 6 or 7)

Start Turbo Pascal with a blank program editing screen, and enter the code below. Compile and run the code in a DOS screen. Errors in the output are easily seen; the program pauses every 100 rows until you press the Enter key (Carriage Return).

```
program fperror;

var i:integer;
  x,y,stvalue:real;

begin
  write('Starting value ');readln(stvalue);
  write('Increment ');readln(x);
  y:=stvalue+x;

  for i:=1 to 1050 do
    begin
      writeln(y:0:15);
      if (i mod 100)=0 then readln; {provides a
      pause every 100 lines}
      y:=y+x;
    end;
end.
```

Experiment with the same increments as before:

0.0625
0.063
0.06
0.015625
0.05078125
0.0001

You should get similar results.

2.11 User requirements

When considering the specification of PCs and associated equipment, there is more to consider than the machine itself. How do you know if you need the wonderful model on sale for £2000, or the lesser model selling for £500? A major reason for the ever-increasing power of computers being purchased is 'upgradeitus'. Some people will buy the latest computer/software simply because it is available. Operating systems like Windows are very hungry for disk space and RAM, and work very slowly unless run in a powerful machine. People often lose sight of the fact that Windows and many Windows applications offer features most do not even realize are present, let alone use or need. In a competitive commercial environment, a sound knowledge of why computers and software are specified is very important. There is no real point in upgrading a system just because it becomes available. As an example, if an application in one office is running perfectly well using an old 80286 PC running MSDOS and a dot-matrix printer, why change it? What **need** is there to change? Simply upgrading the computer is very easy, as is upgrading the software, but successfully running and paying for the change in work practice and staff training is often difficult and very expensive.

Cost of ownership

In order to own and run computers in a business for a period of time, the following items of value must be considered:

- hardware
- software licences
- staff training
- installation and maintenance
- business-specific data and documents
- staff experience and knowledge

Which of these are more significant? After working for some time, many data are generated in the normal course of the business and much knowledge and experience of the computer systems is built up in the staff. After a very short time, these data and the staff knowledge are much more valuable than the costs of the computers. Although the ongoing cost of IT support and maintenance is high, the value of the staff knowledge is probably greater. The cost of the hardware is often the lowest of these, and its value falls to zero in a very short time.

Therefore, **it is not sensible to upgrade unless there is a clear business need**.

Over the last few years, companies like Microsoft, Lotus, Corel etc. have put more and more features into their software. This has resulted in the perceived 'need' to upgrade the machines and staff training, often without any real thought. It is interesting to note that the 'cost of ownership' issue has become very prominent in recent times, and that these software companies have started to change their policies, making their software easier to use rather than having more features that require ever more powerful machines.

Figure 2.27 shows typical proportions of the cost of ownership found in many companies. The cost of the machines themselves is just one-fifth of the total. Simply upgrading machines and then upgrading the software often causes grief for no real benefit to the organization, because the extra training required and the cost of data conversion outweigh any benefits of newer machines. It makes sense to 'over specify' for a new installation so the machines will perform well for a reasonable period, but it does not always make sense to upgrade when new hardware or software become available.

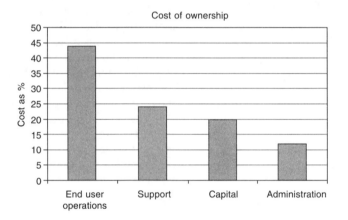

Figure 2.27   *An analysis of the cost of ownership*

General guidelines

Microprocessor

Do not be over-awed by CPU clock speeds. In practice, when running business software you are very unlikely to see the difference between a 1.2- and a 1.7-GHz machine; 1.7 is only $1.7/1.2 = 1.42$ (or 42 per cent) faster, and the overall speed of a machine is a result of much more than the CPU speed. A 1.1-GHz machine has only a 10 per cent faster clock speed then a 1-GHz machine – an even smaller difference. Machines fitted with faster CPUs are generally fitted with faster subsystems at the same time, so naïve users may be fooled into thinking it is all due to the heavily advertised processor 'inside'.

RAM

If running Microsoft Windows as a desktop operating system, performance improves up to about 128 Mb of RAM. Above this it is not likely to show a **marked** improvement unless the applications to be run all need simultaneous open windows or are themselves very demanding on memory. Running a PC as a server is very different, but is not in the scope of this part of the book. You will probably not **see** much difference between the latest RAM types unless you enjoy running benchmark software or timing long tasks with a stopwatch.

Video

The amount of RAM fitted to the video card depends on what you need the machine for. Running standard office applications does not usually require animated 3D, so you can calculate the RAM required from the resolution you intend to set. Many people do not like the highest resolution set for office applications as they cannot see the screen fonts, so if the target is the typical 800 × 600 you will see no benefit from an 8-Mbyte video card over a 4-Mb version. If you plan to use 3D applications and high-speed animated games, the more video RAM the better, but you will only see the benefit if the software designers make use of the hardware. More memory will have no effect on older software.

Monitor

Buy a good one! Overall, when using a PC it is better to have a good stable image with crisp resolution and well-saturated colours than something that is a few per cent faster. Spend the money you saved by not specifying the 'latest, fastest processor' on the monitor. Users will thank you for it. If you run a price comparison on machines with the latest CPU, you will see the price rises dramatically towards the faster end of the market. If one machine is 50 per cent more expensive but only 20 per cent faster, spend the difference on the monitor.

Disk Drive

A while ago it was thought that you could not buy a disk that was too large! This was mainly due to the ever-increasing size of the software and data files. Now that MP3, graphics and video are becoming more important, it looks as though the demand for disk space will now be dictated more by your data than the software. At one extreme, if you are only using the machine for typing plain text and you type at a good 'office' speed of 45 words a minute all day and all night, 7 days a week without a break for 40 years, apart from being tired and hungry, you will still only generate less than 5 Gb of data! At the other extreme, you are likely to fill a 60 Gb drive in a few months if you store MP3, graphics and video files. One hour of full broadcast quality video can be stored on a 10-Gb drive. The best option is to go for size, and only buy the more expensive fast drives if the applications really need it.

Floppy Disk Drive

Almost every PC has one, it is hardly ever used now but as soon as you specify a machine without a floppy drive, someone will arrive with an important file on a floppy disk.

CD-ROM

Almost all PCs are fitted with a CD-ROM or DVD drive. CD-R is now cheap and is an excellent system for backups of key data. Unless the budget is very tight, specify a CD-RW compatible drive wherever possible and use it for CD-R writing. DVD drives are gaining acceptance and offer much larger capacity, but most software is still distributed on CD. Speed is only an issue if you intend to use the drive as a continuous source of data; software installation speed is not seriously limited by CD-ROM drive speed. Do not get carried away with a '×40' drive; for most uses a '×20' is fine. Buy quality rather than speed.

Sound

Specify the cheapest possible sound if the system is for office use. Most users turn it off after a while, especially if the office is open plan. If you need good quality sound to support games or to edit music etc., it is better to output sound to a sound system than to spend on expensive PC speakers. In this case, buy a high quality sound card and leave the speakers in the shop.

Modem

Modems will soon be a thing of the past, at least if the promised ADSL connections become available for home use. Most offices use a direct LAN connection. Until this happens, 56 K modems are adequate. Buy quality, and avoid the 'plain wrapper' kind.

Modems

A modem is a 'MOdulator–DEModulator'. In English, to **modulate** means to **change** (like modify). The old telephone system (known to some as POTS, Plain Old Telephone System!) could carry only analogue sound signals. It was not possible to put a digital signal through such a system. Modern digital telephone systems are very different, but modems were designed for the POTS. A modem modulates a sound with digital information and demodulates this sound for received signals. The speed of a modem is given in bits/second; most are now 56 Kbits/sec. As each byte is encoded in either 9 or 10 bits, this means a 56 K modem will transmit about 5.6 Kb of data per second in an ideal world. Real world rates are nearly always slower. Having CPUs that are claimed to 'speed up the Internet' will make no difference at all!

Printer

For home or SOHO (Small Office Home Office) use, inkjets are fine; they are expensive to run if your output is high and are not as reliable as laser printers. For office use, the only real choice is a laser printer; they are fast, quiet, and reasonably cheap to run. Even for small offices, a printer with a large paper capacity will be appreciated by the users.

How to specify and buy a computer

First, clearly specify why you need a computer, what do you want to do with it, and who needs to be able to share your data. Next, decide on your budget.

The next step is to decide what software you will need to satisfy your business requirements, and only then should you specify what hardware is required to run that software. It is a great mistake to think 'I will need a 1.7 GHz Pentium IV' just because they are available and heavily advertised.

Due to the ever-increasing efficiency of hardware production and changes in Far Eastern economies, the actual costs of hardware are getting lower and lower. This means that the 'lowest' specification of some computer components now on sale is more than adequate for most people. For example, many machines now come with a disk drive with a 10 Gb capacity as standard. If you only need a wordprocessor this will meet your needs for a very long time. Some people seem to think that if they specify a 40 Gb drive the machine will be 'better' in some respect, but this is not true. Many machines are fast enough for normal business activities, and more speed is simply not required. A lot of people find that to run Windows 98 and Word 97 on a Pentium 266 with 32 Mb RAM fitted is quite adequate; why specify any more? In any case, what do you mean by 'more speed' in respect of a wordprocessor; always assuming that a Pentium IV is somehow 'faster', will it enable you to type faster?

Consider these typical applications:

- wordprocessing
- spreadsheets
- databases
- graphic arts
- technical design.

Now consider these things that would appear on a list of components when specifying a computer:

- disk speed
- disk capacity
- video resolution
- video RAM size
- monitor size
- monitor resolution
- monitor slot pitch
- monitor refresh rate
- main RAM size
- processor type
- processor clock speed
- internal bus speed
- internal bus type
- motherboard features, buses, expansion slots etc.

Now write down what is required (allowing for future expansion), rather than what you might 'like' to have. You will find that if you focus more on quality than on performance, the benefits will be higher. Clearly you need a machine that has sufficient performance, but you should next consider:

- cost/budget
- performance
- expandability
- ergonomics, i.e. how well the components 'fit' with the people who will use them
- needs of specific or specialist software, e.g. Autocad.

Some people are specifying notebook computers in place of desktop machines, but you should consider these points:

- they cost at least 50 per cent more for the same 'power', and often twice as much.
- sometimes, they will not run specialist software
- they are not as reliable as desktop machines, and are easy to damage
- they are not as expandable or configurable as desktops
- they are very portable
- they have an LCD screen (many people prefer this)
- newer versions of software make ever greater demands on the hardware, so notebooks go out of date quicker.

Now consider the questions shown in the sample assignment below and discuss your thoughts with your lecturer and fellow students. Keep your mind focused on what is **needed**, not on what is **desirable**, or what you may see advertised as 'The Computer Deal of the Century!'.

Sample assignment tasks

You are asked to specify computers for the six users below. For each of the users listed, choose a suitable machine and justify your choice. You should give a detailed explanation of your choices in terms of:

- cost
- capabilities
- performance
- upgrade path.

Very useful sources of information are the many computer magazines available at most newsagents. You should buy two or three of these and look at their buying advice; this is often very sound. Avoid the titles that are aimed at games players. The other useful source of information is the Internet; sites such as www.zdnet.com give excellent information.

The simplest way is to list the items fitted or specified in your chosen machine, and then explain the significance of each item and how it relates to the user's requirements. Write down the machine specification as a list of components in the same way as you would present it to a supplier.

User 1

This company supplies artwork, graphics etc. to the advertising industry, especially the glossy magazine trade. Their main expertise is in photo retouching, using very high resolution images. They only need machines for five graphic artists; the management function in the company is already computerized.

User 2

A small college runs 200 stand-alone PCs. A network company has offered a sponsorship deal and supplied a full network with cabling and servers to support the college, with the proviso that the college upgrades the user's machines. The current 200 machines are to be scrapped. The plan is to run the latest versions of Windows, MS Office and similar software on each user machine, but with the software stored on the servers; they have an **extremely tight budget** where every penny counts. You must achieve the **cheapest possible machine** that will run the software.

User 3

The PA to the Finance Director of a large shipping company requires a machine to do wordprocessing and e-mail. All the other computerized functions in the company are already running elsewhere.

User 4

A very experienced design engineer working on petrochemical plant designs has been on an Autocad course. The projects she works on involve 3D drawings of very complex pipework etc. During the course of the next year she will employ two assistants to computerize the existing paper drawings and to use Autocad themselves, so she needs three new networked PCs to run Autocad. The application requires that large amounts of data are stored and that the hidden line removal and other performance critical functions in Autocad are used to full effect.

User 5

A local private genealogy society has computer links to help in their research; they use an old PC with a 56-Kb/s modem. To reduce costs and speed up enquiries, they have decided to start a large database of family genealogy details. The eventual size of the database may be 200 Gb with the requirement of at least one level of back-up. Funds are very tight, but users will require a good service. To limit the expenditure, only one member will use the machine at a time, linked via a fixed modem on a pre-arranged time slot.

User 6

A financial accountant uses spreadsheets to model the financial behaviour of companies. The spreadsheets are very large and she is hoping to make them even larger, but is impatient with the recalculation time obtained with her current computer.

2.12 How to build a PC

There are so many options to consider when building a PC that it is difficult to provide specific instructions in a book of this nature. However, presented below are some of the main points.

A PC is generally fitted into a **system box** that contains several main components:

1. A **power supply**. This takes the AC mains voltage and converts it to 12 V DC for electric motors in the disk drives and 5 V DC for the logic circuits.

2. A **motherboard**. This is the main circuit board of a computer. When IBM first introduced a PC in the late 1980s, their design took no account of video graphics. For this reason a lot of PC motherboards do not contain any circuitry for video graphics, so a video card is added as an extra.

3. Peripheral items such as **hard disk drives**, **floppy disk drives** and similar accessories. Even the most basic PC now has one hard drive, one floppy drive and at least a **CD-ROM drive**.

Motherboards

On motherboards there is usually a set of parallel slots that are amongst the largest visible features. These slots house the bus that connects devices to the motherboard, and it is into these slots that accessories like a video cards, modems, television cards etc. are plugged. Over the history of the development of the PC motherboard there have been a number of types of these bus expansion slots. The first type, which is no longer made, had 8 data bits; later ones had 16 data bits, and this type became so common that it was called the industry standard architecture (or ISA) bus.

Several attempts were made by IBM and others to improve upon the speed of the ISA bus, and this has resulted in what is now called the PCI bus; it does the same job as the ISA bus but faster.

An expansion bus allows data to pass from the motherboard to the accessory cards and back again. As will as data, the bus also contains address information so that the data can be stored in particular places and has control wires to provide such things as the timing of events etc.

Electrostatic discharge

Installing the motherboard is very straightforward, but precise instructions must come from the manufacturer. It is very easy to damage the chips on the motherboard; this is done by accidentally applying very large voltages from your fingers when you touch the board. If you are wearing clothes made of nylon or similar synthetic materials and if the atmosphere is very dry it is extremely easy for you to build up a very large static voltage on your body. This can be of many thousands of volts. The problem with many silicon chips is that 30 or 40 volts will damage them. If you touch the board and have a static charge, it will discharge into the board and damage the electronics. One solution is to attach a copper wire from your wrist to a good earth; this will cause any static build-up from your body to be discharged, so you'll have zero volts on your body and cannot discharge into the electronics. If you are unable to take this precaution, simply touching a good earth like the screws in a light switch, or a heating radiator or some pipes, will at least reduce the static charge on your body and minimize the possibility of damage to electronics. If static electricity discharges from your body into the electronics, it is known as an **electrostatic discharge** (ESD).

To assemble the PC, the motherboard is fixed on some plastic pegs. The hard disk drive, CD-ROM drive and floppy disk drive are fixed into custom-made brackets and generally connected via a ribbon cable. This contains a large number of wires that are effectively an extension to the bus. Other wires coloured red, black, yellow etc. are to supply the 12 V or 5 V to motors in the disk drives or to the logic circuits.

Once these main components are in place, the accessory or expansion boards can be plugged in, again according to the manufacturer's instructions. You may have some components that plug into an ISA slot; these are the old-fashioned so-called **legacy devices**. The ISA bus is slower than the PCI bus, but if the device happens to be a modem the data rate is so slow that you will see no advantage from using a PCI version.

One application that requires very high-speed data transfer is video, and on many motherboards there is a special video slot called an **AGP slot**. This slot is dedicated to video data transfer from the processor to the video card and back again.

On the back of the PC there will be **legacy ports**. These are for connecting external devices to the PC; typically there is a **serial port** or possibly two serial ports, and a **printer port** (also known as a **parallel port**). Most modern PCs have more modern communication ports; the most common is called the **Universal Serial Bus** (USB), but you may find **FireWire** or SCSI ports. They are different in the way they work in detail, but in general are for communicating with external devices. SCSI stands for Small Computer Systems Interface, it is a standard that was designed not for the PC world but for larger computers. It has been adapted for PCs and is commonly used for such devices as disk drives and scanners. USB ports are used for connecting almost any peripheral devices such as scanners and even mice. FireWire is generally used to connect digital cameras. The older serial ports are used for connecting modems and mice, and the parallel port is used for connecting the printer. One reason for introducing USB was to reduce the number of different connections, but until USB is completely universal the old so-called legacy ports will be around.

Once the main PC box is assembled with the motherboard, drives, a power supply etc., the external devices are plugged in (the keyboard, monitor and printer). Once this is done the main electronic nature of the PC build is finished, but it is a long way from being a useful computer. At least three more things need to be done:

1. The BIOS of the computer needs to be configured. The **BIOS** is the **Basic Input Output System**. When you first turn on the PC, you will be instructed to press a particular key combination, e.g. ALT S or just the del key. This will present you with the BIOS control screen. The items on this screen must be configured according to the manufacturer's instructions for the components in your PC.

2. As part of the basic configuration of the PC, a hard disk must be **partitioned**. Partitioning involves taking a **physical disk** and creating one or more **logical disks**. In this way, the operating system is able to treat one physical disk as several logical disks. Disk partitioning is done with a program called **fdisk**. There are different versions of this supplied with different versions of Microsoft operating systems; you should use the

one that comes with the operating system that you intend to install. Unfortunately, the business of partitioning a disk is fraught with problems. A good source of information on using fdisk can be found from the Microsoft web site at http://support.microsoft.com/default.aspx?scid=kb;EN-US;q255867. Once the disk partitioning is complete, it must be **formatted** using the format program supplied with the operating system. Formatting means that details specific to the operating system are written to the disk. These things are **track and sector numbering**, the **file allocation table** and the **root directory** etc. The details of disk formatting are beyond the scope of this book; see http://support.microsoft.com/default.aspx?scid=kb;EN-US;q255867.

3. Once formatted, the operating system can be installed on the main disk. The operating system installation software is usually stored on CD-ROM. The operating system is sometimes supplied with a **bootable floppy disk**. This floppy disk is used to boot the machine, and contains **driver** software that will allow the CD-ROM to be visible to the installation program. There are many different operating systems available; the most common are the Microsoft Windows series (3.1, 95, 98, ME, 2000 and XP) the Microsoft NT series (NT Workstation and NT Server), and then there is **linux** from a whole range of suppliers. Linux is free and is based on the older **unix** operating system.

Switching the computer on

Simply turning on a computer and making the electronics come to life is not sufficient to get the computer working. Since everything in the computer is controlled by software, including the loading of software itself, simply turning on the computer with no software will cause a problem. The problem is that there is no software to control the loading process! In very old-fashioned computers there was a special program called a **loader**, which was set in the machine via switches. In other words, an operator set ones and zeros with the switches to load a very simple program into memory. The simple program, called a loader, simply loaded the rest of software into memory. In PCs this loader program is already placed in the BIOS chip. This loader will load whatever software it finds on the first sectors of the bootable or main disk. The software in these first few sectors is usually the operating system. Once this starts to load, it takes over and loads the rest of the operating system.

Booting

Why is starting a computer called **booting**?
There is an ancient philosophical problem that goes something like this:

'If I stand in front of you and I pull up very hard on your bootstraps, I notice that I can lift you off the floor. Now if you bend down and pull just as hard on your own bootstraps, you do not rise above the floor. Why is this?'

To the modern mind trained in engineering mechanics the problem is quite straightforward, but it puzzled the ancient philosophers. It is a problem that is related to computers because in one sense they have to 'pull themselves up with their own bootstraps', i.e. they need a program to load a program. The original loaders were called **bootstrap loaders** from this problem. There is more to starting the PC than simply turning it on!

The BTEC Unit 2 specifies that students undertake maintenance of software and hardware using appropriate disk tools, and locate and repair faults using appropriate faultfinding techniques. As there is a huge range of possible configurations of hardware and software, it is not possible to provide specific help on these topics.

2.13 Software licensing

It is very important to understand the legal position you are in when you install or use software on a computer. Software is generally supplied with a **licence**; it may come as a surprise that you generally cannot 'buy' software, it will only come with a licence to **use** the software. The software itself is called **intellectual property** and, except in a few rare circumstances, this intellectual property remains with the company that wrote or supplied the software.

There are various kinds of software licences. The first kind is called **freeware**. Here, a programmer has written a program and places it in the **public domain** for use according to the licence agreement that comes with it. There is no payment to be made, but the author usually asks that the software is not changed and that credit is given if the software is used in conjunction with a business. Some software is supplied under a licence written by the Free Software Foundation. This is known as the GNU General Public Licence. It generally means you can use the software free of charge unless you are using it for business (see http://www.gnu.org/copyleft/gpl.html).

The second kind is called **shareware**. This usually means you are free to load software on a machine and test it. If you like it, you pay some money to the software writer; if not, you delete it from the machine. Some shareware comes without any restriction and simply relies on your honesty to pay. Other kinds of shareware come with some kind of restriction, for instance, the inability to print or a restriction on the number of items you can use. Once you have paid the software writer the (usually small) sum of money to register the shareware, this restriction is lifted. Selling shareware is a very efficient way of supplying software. There are a large number of shareware download sites available on the net, including:

- http://www.shareware.com/
- http://www.jumbo.com/
- http://www.tucows.com/
- http://download.cnet.com/
- http://www.zdnet.com/

Alternatively, search for 'shareware download' on www.google.com.

Finally, there is the normal commercial software purchased online or from a software supplier, for instance Microsoft Office. This comes with a long and detailed licence agreement that sets out precisely how you can use the software and how you can't. Remember, all you have purchased is a licence to use the software, so in order to remain within the law you must use that software according to the licence agreement. Generally you are not free to let other people have a copy; this is in contrast to shareware, where most shareware authors encourage you to supply copies to your friends and colleagues.

Appendix A: answers

Exercise 2.1

(a)

A	B	C	D	E	F	G	R
0	0	0	0	0	0	1	1
0	0	0	1	0	0	0	0
0	0	1	0	0	1	0	1
0	0	1	1	0	1	0	1
0	1	0	0	0	1	1	1
0	1	0	1	0	1	0	1
0	1	1	0	0	1	0	1
0	1	1	1	0	1	0	1
1	0	0	0	0	0	1	1
1	0	0	1	0	0	0	0
1	0	1	0	0	1	0	1
1	0	1	1	0	1	0	1
1	1	0	0	1	1	1	1
1	1	0	1	1	1	0	1
1	1	1	0	1	1	0	1
1	1	1	1	1	1	0	1

Logic function = $(A \cdot B) + (B + C) + \overline{(C + D)}$

(b)

A	B	C	NOT A	D	E	R
0	0	0	1	0	1	1
0	0	1	1	0	0	0
0	1	0	1	1	0	1
0	1	1	1	1	0	1
1	0	0	0	0	1	1
1	0	1	0	0	0	0
1	1	0	0	0	0	0
1	1	1	0	0	0	0

Logic function = $(\overline{A} \cdot B) + \overline{(B + C)}$

(c)

A	B	C	D	E	R
0	0	0	1	0	0
0	0	1	1	1	1
0	1	0	0	1	0
0	1	1	0	0	0
1	0	0	0	0	0
1	0	1	0	1	0
1	1	0	0	1	0
1	1	1	0	0	0

Logic function = $\overline{(A \bullet B)} \bullet (B \oplus C)$

Exercise 2.2

Change the first line to MOV DL, "M" or MOV DL, 'M' or MOV DL, 77 or MOV DL, 04D ;(hex) or MOV DL, 01001101b ;(binary) as all these produce the same machine code output.
Change the third line to MOV CH, 14

Exercise 2.3

Change the first line to MOV DL, '0' (or 48 or 030 or 00110000b). Note, putting MOV DL, 0 is not correct; the result will be the first 10 control codes in the ASCII character set.

Exercise 2.4

```
        MOV AH, 02A     ;DOS interrupt 21 Function 2A,
                        ;read system date
        INT 021         ;call DOS
                        ;AL= day of the week (0=Sunday,
                        ;1=Monday etc.)
                        ;CX=year
                        ;DH=month
                        ;DL=day

; now store to prevent overwriting when subroutine
is used

        MOV year, CX
        MOV month, DH
        MOV day, DL

;..... display the day..................

        MOV AH,0        ;AX is AH and AL so clear top
```

```
        MOV AL, day      ;of AX (AH) ready for OUTINT
        CMP AX, 10       ;see if leading zero is needed
        JAE L20          ;jump if 10 or more without
                         ;outputting 0 first
        CALL leadingzero
L20:    CALL OUTINT      ;output the day

;..... now output  a  day/month/year  separator
............

        MOV DL, "/"      ;hour:min:sec separator
        MOV AH, 2        ;DOS interrupt 21 function 2
        INT 021          ;call DOS to output "/"

;..... display the month...................

        MOV AH,0         ;AX is AH and AL so clear top
        MOV AL, month    ;of AX (AH) ready for OUTINT
        CMP AX, 10       ;see if leading zero is needed
        JAE L21          ;jump if 10 or more without
                         ;outputting 0 first
        CALL leadingzero
L21:    CALL OUTINT      ;output the month

;..... now output a day/month/year separator ........

        MOV DL, "/"      ;hour:min:sec separator
        MOV AH, 2        ;DOS interrupt 21 function 2
        INT 021          ;call DOS to output "/"

;..... display the year...................

        MOV AX, year
        CALL OUTINT      ;output the year

        INT 020          ;terminate program

year  DW 0               ;define some space
month DB 0               ;for variables
day   DB 0               ;to store values
```

Exercise 2.5

```
        MOV AH,030       ;DOS interrupt 21 Function 30,
                         ;return DOS version number
        INT 021          ;call DOS

; now store values away to avoid overwriting by
subroutine

        MOV major, AL
        MOV minor, AH

; now output the string. Point SI to string for
subroutine

        MOV SI, string   ;copies ADDRESS of string to SI
```

```
        CALL
        printstring       ;printstring subroutine in
                          ; LIB.ASM

; now output major version . . . . . . . . . . . . . . . . . . . . . . .

        MOV AH,0          ;clear top of AX
        MOV AL, major     ;AX now contains
                          ;major version ready
                          ;for subroutine
        CALL outint       ;output to screen

; now output a separator . . . . . . . . . . . . . . . . . . . . . . .

        MOV AH,2          ;DOS interrupt 21 function 2
        MOV DL,"."        ;separator character
        INT 021           ;call DOS

; now output minor version. . . . . . . . . . . . . . . . . . . . . . .

        MOV AH,0          ;clear top of AX
        MOV AL, minor     ;AX now contains
                          ;minor version ready
                          ;for subroutine
        CMP AX, 10        ;see if leading zero is
                          ;needed
        JAE L20           ;jump if 10 or more without
                          ;outputting 0 first
        CALL leadingzero
L20:    CALL outint       ;output to screen

; . . . . . . . .terminate program. . . . . . . . . . . . . . . . . . . . .

        INT 020

major     db 0            ;variable to store major
                          ;version
minor     db 0            ;variable to store minor
                          ;version
string:   db "DOS version number= ",0
```

Exercise 2.6

```
;Assembly language program exercise 2.8. File ex5.asm
;Assemble with LIB.ASM for subroutines
;Modify programs P8.ASM and answer to exercise 2.6
;to output both the system time
;and date on the same line with strings saying 'Time
;is now'
;and 'Date= '.

; output string 1 "Time is now " . . . . . . . . . . . . . . . . . .

        MOV SI, string1
        CALL printstring

; now output the time
```

```
          MOV AH, 02C      ;DOS interrupt 21 Function 2C,
                           ;read system time.
          INT 021          ;call DOS
                           ;now CH=hours, CL=Minutes
                           ;DH=seconds, DL=hundredths/sec

;now store to prevent overwriting when subroutine
;is used

          MOV hours, CH
          MOV mins, CL
          MOV secs, DH

; display the hours.................

          MOV AH,0         ;AX is AH and AL so clear top
          MOV AL, hours    ;of AX (AH) ready for OUTINT
          CMP AX, 10       ;see if leading zero is needed
          JAE L20          ;jump if 10 or more without
                           ;outputting 0 first
          CALL leadingzero
L20:      CALL OUTINT      ;output the time in hours

; now output a h:m:s separator...........

          MOV DL, ":"      ;hour:min:sec separator
          MOV AH, 2        ;DOS interrupt 21 function 2
          INT 021          ;call DOS to output ":"

; display the minutes.................

          MOV AH,0         ;AX is AH and AL so clear top
          MOV AL, mins     ;of AX (AH) ready for OUTINT
          CMP AX, 10       ;see if leading zero is needed
          JAE L21          ;jump if 10 or more without
                           ;outputting 0 first
          CALL leadingzero
L21:      CALL OUTINT      ;output the time in minutes

; now output a h:m:s separator...........

          MOV DL, ":"      ;hour:min:sec separator
          MOV AH, 2        ;DOS interrupt 21 function 2
          INT 021          ;call DOS to output ":"

; display the seconds.................

          MOV AH,0         ;AX is AH and AL so clear top
          MOV AL, secs     ;of AX (AH) ready for OUTINT
          CMP AX, 10       ;see if leading zero is needed
          JAE L22          ;jump if 10 or more without
                           ;outputting 0 first
L22:      CALL leadingzero
          CALL OUTINT      ;output the time in seconds

; now output string 2 "Date= ".....................

          MOV SI, string2
          CALL printstring
```

```
; now output the date..............................

        MOV AH, 02A     ;DOS interrupt 21 Function 2A,
                        ;read system date
        INT 021         ;call DOS
                        ;AL= day of the week
                        ; (0=Sunday, 1=Monday etc.)
                        ;CX=year
                        ;DH=month
                        ;DL=day

; now store to prevent overwriting when subroutine
; is used

        MOV year, CX
        MOV month, DH
        MOV day, DL

; display the day..................

        MOV AH,0        ;AX is AH and AL so clear top
        MOV AL, day     ;of AX (AH) ready for OUTINT
        CMP AX, 10      ;see if leading zero is needed
        JAE L23         ;jump if 10 or more without
                        ;outputting 0 first
        CALL leadingzero
L23:    CALL OUTINT     ;output the day

; now output a day/month/year separator...........

        MOV DL, "/"     ;hour:min:sec separator
        MOV AH, 2       ;DOS interrupt 21 function 2
        INT 021         ;call DOS to output "/"

; display the month..................

        MOV AH,0        ;AX is AH and AL so clear top
        MOV AL, month   ;of AX (AH) ready for OUTINT
        CMP AX, 10      ;see if leading zero is needed
        JAE L24         ;jump if 10 or more without
                        ;outputting 0 first
        CALL leadingzero
L24:    CALL OUTINT     ;output the month

; now output a day/month/year separator...........

        MOV DL, "/"     ;hour:min:sec separator
        MOV AH, 2       ;DOS interrupt 21 function 2
        INT 021         ;call DOS to output "/"

; display the year..................

        MOV AX, year
        CALL OUTINT     ;output the year

        INT 020         ;terminate program

; variable declarations....................

year                    DW 0
month                   DB 0
```

```
day                 DB 0
hours               DB 0
mins                DB 0
secs                DB 0

; string declarations........................
string1:   db 'Time is now ',0   ;note trailing
                                  ;space
string2:   db ' Date= ',0        ;note leading space
```

This code can be downloaded from http://www.bh.com/companions/0750656840.

Appendix B: Assembly language subroutine library

```
;Library of subroutines in file LIB.ASM

;PRINTSTRING prints a string pointed to with SI
;register
;OUTINT writes a 16 bit number in AX to the screen
;as integer
;PRINTNUM writes a string as PRINTSTRING but with
;no spaces
;SHOWBITS writes a 16 bit number in AX to the screen
;as binary
;leadingzero writes a single 0 to the screen
;crlf writes an ASCII 13 Carriage Return
;then ASCII 10 Line Feed

rem       dw 0         ;16 bit variable for remainder
quo       dw 0         ;16 bit variable for quotient
space     equ " "      ;defines "space" as ASCII 32
numbuff: db 5 dup
          (space)      ;5 duplicates of "space"
          db 0         ;to give zero byte string
                       ;terminator
row       db 0         ;for MOVECURSOR
col       db 0         ;for MOVECURSOR

;.......... Subroutines ...................

printstring:           ;assume pointer to
                       ;string is in SI register
          mov ah,02
L1:       mov dl,[si]  ;get first character
          cmp dl,0     ;see if end of string
          jz finprint  ;finish if end of string
          int 021      ;write char
          inc si       ;point to next char
          jmp L1       ;back for more chars
finprint: ret          ;end of subroutine

;...... end of printstr .....................

; subroutine to show a 16 bit number in AX as binary

showbits:
          mov si,ax    ;copy of equipment config
                       ;number
          mov bl.16    ;counter for 16 bits
```

```
L1:        mov cx,si    ;cx is working register
           and cx,08000 ;mask off all but top bit
           cmp cx,0     ;if zero
           jz nought    ;then write a '0'

one:       mov dl,'1'
           mov ah,02    ;DOS write to screen function
           int 021
           jmp next

nought:    mov dl,'0'
           mov ah,02    ;DOS write to screen function
           int 021

next:      shl si,1     ;move all bits left one space
           dec bl       ;
           jnz L1       ;see if all 16 bits done
           ret          ;end of showbits subroutine

;.............end if showbits...................

;OUTINT subroutine
;this prints out a number in decimal held in AX
;register by storing it
;as ascii into a buffer and then pointing to this
;buffer with bx.
;Needs numbuff and space equ at top of file. A86
;seems to fall over if these are included within the
;code.

outint:
           mov cx,5     ;for each place in the buffer
           mov si,
           numbuff      ;
           mov dl,space ;
L21:       mov[si],dl   ;fill it with spaces
           inc si
           loop L21     ;the LOOP instruction
                        ;uses CX and does the
                        ;increment for you first
           mov si,
           numbuff +4   ;ready to start filling the
                        ;array

L22:
           mov dx,0     ;clear DX since DIV works on
                        ;DX:AX
           mov cx,10    ;divisor of 10
           div cx       ;divide by 10 and store
                        ;remainder
           mov quo,ax   ;store quotient for next time
           or dl,48     ;change remainder to ascii
           mov [si],dl  ;and store in buffer
           dec si       ;point to next location in
                        ;buffer
           mov ax,quo   ;ready for next div
           cmp ax,0     ;see if any numbers left
           jne L22      ;if there are, process them
```

```
                                     ;if not, write result to
                                     ;screen
                  mov si,
                  numbuff            ;point to the buffer
                  call
                  printnum           ;output the result
                  ret                ;return to whence you came
printnum:                            ;assume pointer to string
                                     ;is in SI register
                  mov ah,02
L51:              mov dl,[si]        ;get first character
                  cmp dl,0           ;see if end of string
                  jz
                  finprintnum        ;finish if end of string
                  cmp dl,32          ;see if space char
                  jz L52             ;do not print spaces
                  int 021            ;write char
L52:              inc si             ;point to next char
                  jmp L51            ;back for more chars


finprintnum:                 ret

;.............end if outint..................

;.............crlf subroutine.................

crlf:             pusha              ;save gen purpose registers
                  mov ah,2           ;DOS write char function
                  mov dl,13          ;Carriage Return (CR)
                  int 021            ;print it
                  mov dl,10          ;Line Feed (LF)
                  int 021            ;print it
                  popa               ;restore registers
                  ret                ;return from subroutine

leadingzero:
                  PUSH AX            ;keep AX to prevent
                                     ;overwriting
                  MOV AH, 2          ;DOS int 20 function 2
                  MOV DL, "0"        ;zero character to be output
                  INT 021            ;call DOS
                  POP AX             ;restore value to AX
                  RET                ;return to address after
                                     ;calling address
```

Unit 3 Business information systems

The aim of this chapter is to give students an insight into the way in which organizations function, by examining key resources such as people, hardware, software, data and information.

Throughout the chapter students will be directed to certain aspects of business information systems; each point will be clearly described and supported by an exercise or case study, which will provide clarity and understanding of certain issues.

The chapter is structured in such a way as to focus students' attention on the internal factors and impact of business information systems, the external implications, and, finally, a consolidation of the two through the use of cited models and case studies.

3.1 Data and information

What are data?

Data are random, unprocessed facts that have little or no value until they have undergone some sort of processing activity. The processing activity converts the data into information as shown in Figure 3.1.

Figure 3.1 *Conversion of data into information*

Data examples include:

- date (e.g. 15/01/2001)
- customer number (e.g. DY243/00PP)
- student registration number (e.g. NC899900000STG).

There are different levels of data within a given data set. Using the example of 'country', different levels of data can be as shown in Figure 3.2.

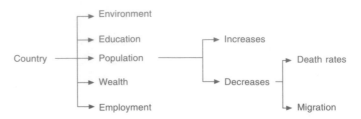

Figure 3.2　*Levels of data within a given data set*

Table 3.1　*Random data set*

CS10037900

PJ130336001

JH12779012

Without any knowledge of the data or the statistics, a string of numbers or characters is meaningless.

Table 3.1 identifies a given data set; however, it is unclear as to what the data set refers to. If further data were provided to complement the set, together the sets of data would transform into meaningful information as shown in Table 3.2.

Table 3.2　*Meaningful data set*

Student number	Student name
CS10037900	Jane Herring
PJ100379001	Mark James
JH100379002	Michael Hampshire

What is information?

Information is a set of meaningful data that is of use to somebody. Information is transmitted every second of every day, and it is the pillar and infrastructure to every organization and to life itself. If we could not transmit information, nothing in the world would be achieved; how would we know what people and systems want, when they want it, how they want, where they want it and in what quantity, for example? There are a number of ways in which information can be expressed, for example

1. verbal
2. physical
3. visual.

These can be identified as categories. Each category can further be divided into formats in which information is transmitted, for example through:

- speech
- sound
- graphics
- pictures
- body language
- writing
- sign language
- telepathy.

Exercise 3.1

Produce a table and match up each format of information to an appropriate category, providing an example of each format. For example, speech would be placed in the verbal category, with an example being 'giving directions'.

Format	Links		Category	Example
Speech	→	➤	Verbal	Giving directions
Sound				
Graphics				
Pictures				
Body language				
Writing				
Sign language				

Formats of information can in some cases be broken down further into actual contexts of information, i.e. what is used to project or represent that format, as shown in Figure 3.3.

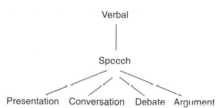

Figure 3.3 *Contexts of information*

Information

Category of information identifies the method of information
Format of information identifies the technique of information
Context of information identifies the tools of information.

Exercise 3.2

For each of the following scenarios, identify the format or formats of information that could be used.

1. Going to a library to find information about 'organizational structures'.
2. Guiding an aircraft to its correct position on the runway.
3. Getting information from one remote island to another that has no telecommunication sources.
4. Expressing happiness at seeing a friend.
5. Giving a presentation to a group of business colleagues.

Information in organizations

Information is pivotal to any organization; without information, a business cannot survive. In an organization information is used for many different purposes, such as negotiating contracts and terms, delegating day-to-day tasks, advising colleagues and peers, and instructing third parties on stock requirements or deliveries etc. Within an organization, information can be divided in terms of its generic or specialist qualities.

Generic information is common to any organization and the organizational need; this is illustrated in Figure 3.4.

Figure 3.4   *Generic information*

Specialist information is exclusive to the organization or the organization type. For example, information required by a bank would be different to that required by a retail organization that sells games consoles (Table 3.3).

Table 3.3   *Specialist information*

Organization type	Generic information	Specialist information
Bank	Marketing	New first-time buyers' mortgage rates
Games console shop	Marketing	Launch of new PS2 software
Bank	ICT	Upgrade of current cash machines
Games console shop	ICT	Installation of a new till

Exercise 3.3

1. Give three examples of specialist information for a school/college, a cinema and a restaurant using the following headings:
   - operations
   - financial
   - administrative.
2. Write a short summary stating why specialist information is important to an organization
3. Why might the specialist information required by an organization providing a service and by an organization that sells a product be dramatically different?

With too little information an organization cannot plan or forecast, or set targets or budgets. Therefore, both qualitative and quantitative information are needed.

Qualitative information

Qualitative information provides you with details, giving additionality to any existing information. For example, you might know that students have been studying at college for two years, but the qualitative aspect will identify the course, the mode, the subjects, and whether or not the students are enjoying the course etc. One of the best ways to extract qualitative information is through interviewing. Interviewing allows you to obtain controlled qualitative information that can serve as a balance to pure facts and figures.

Quantitative information

This type of information is based on facts and statistics – key information used for planning etc. Examples of this type of information include monthly expenditure, sales figures or employee performance status. Quantitative information is essential if you are working with large data sets because facts and figures are easier to map and model as opposed to descriptive qualitative information. To provide a good balance, any tool used for collecting information should incorporate both qualitative and quantitative information (see Figure 3.5).

Figure 3.5 *Balance of qualitative and quantitative information*

Table 3.4 is an extract from a questionnaire containing quantitative and qualitative information.

Table 3.4 *Consumer questionnaire*

Consumer questionnaire		
Name: Address:	Age (please tick the appropriate box 18 or below o 19–35 o 36–50 o 51–64 o 65 + o	
Which computer magazines do you buy?		
Why do you buy these magazines?		
How often do you buy computer magazines? (please tick the appropriate box) 2–3 times a week o Once a week o Fortnightly o Monthly o Ocassionally o		
What influences your decision to purchase a magazine? (please rate from 1–5, 1 = lowest, 5 = highest). Free cover disk Interesting articles and features Price Magazine format Loyalty		

Exercise 3.4

1. Design a questionnaire for one of the following:

   - to investigate shops used by students
   - to investigate the best film of the year
   - to identify the likes and dislikes of subjects on a course.

   For each questionnaire, include a mixture of 15 qualitative and quantitative questions. When the design is complete, print off or e-mail 10 copies to people within your group and get them to complete them.
2. From the information gathered, produce two charts and one graph based on the quantitative information, and provide a short summary detailing the findings of the qualitative information.
3. Identify which was the easier of the two sets of information to produce as graphical analysis and which as a written analysis. Why do you think this is?

3.2 Systems

What is a system?

A system can be described as a group or collection of resources that work in unison towards fulfilling a common goal. A system also implies a certain methodology that has been adopted to formalize the processing activity of the system. There is a variety of definitions that describe a 'system'; however, the most important aspect is that a system implies that an activity, task or series of events is taking place. Examples of systems include:

- a computer system
- a car system
- a booking system
- a reservations system
- a payroll systems.

The common element of all of these is that there are a number of components that contribute to the system.

Exercise 3.5

System	Component 1	Component 2	Component 3
Computer			
Car			
Booking			
Reservation			
Payroll			

1. For each of the systems identified in the table, identify three components that are needed to ensure that the system works effectively.

2. Are the components all unique to each system? If so, why?
3. Are there any common components that are shared across the systems? If so, which ones and why?
4. For each of the three components listed for each system, explain why they are essential to that system.

Systems do not work in isolation; they rely on information that feeds into the system so that a response or action can be generated. Using the example of a computer, which is a very complex multitasking system; without the use of an operator feeding in data and commands the system would not be able to process and output the data, thus becoming redundant (Figure 3.6).

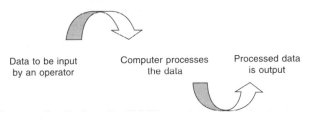

Data to be input   Computer processes   Processed data
by an operator   the data   is output

Figure 3.6   *Components required for data processing*

Systems objective

Every system has 'systems objective', which governs how the system works, who is involved with the system, the tasks that are carried out and the processing activities, and also quantifies when the system has reached its goal or objective.

System objectives can be very small and discrete or quite large and complex, depending on whether the system is working in isolation or as part of a bigger system. For example, taking a car and looking specifically at a single component, the brakes, the objective of the brakes is to stop the vehicle. You can quantify whether or not the system objective has been met if the vehicle stops (usually within a specific time range). Although the objective of the braking system might be straightforward, the braking system is part of a larger and more complex system.

Exercise 3.6

For the following systems, identify what their primary objective and any secondary objectives are. In some cases it might be difficult to distinguish, because a system can have multiple objectives all of equal importance.

System	Primary objective	Other objective
Attending college		
Getting a part-time job		
Doing assignments on time		
Socializing with friends		
Learning to drive		

Systems theory

Systems theory is based upon a model of feeding inputs into a system, a processing activity taking place, and a result or an output completing the process (Figure 3.7).

Figure 3.7 *Basic systems model*

The **processing activities** that occur will differ depending upon the type of system (for example, manual or computerized); examples of each can be see in Table 3.5.

Table 3.5 *Manual and computerized processing activities*

Manual	Processing activities	Computerized	Processing activities
Doing an assignment	• Read through task • Carry out research • Produce a draft copy • Submit final copy	Finding information about a customer	• Access a central resource such as a database • Search for information • Sort and select particular details

Certain activities go through the same sort of processing activity regardless of whether the process is manual or computerized. Examples of this include:

• performing a calculation, either by physically using a calculator or digitally by using a macro or program
• accessing information, physically from a resource or digitally from a file
• sorting information, physically by using files and alphabetical ordering or digitally by using a tool or wizard.

Systems should all have inputs, engage in processing, and produce outputs. However, the systems diagram is not complete because processing and information is only being channelled in one direction.

A true representation of a systems model is shown in Figure 3.8, where information is circulated in a continuous loop, offering both a control mechanism and feedback into the system.

Inputs are resources that trigger the system; they initiate the process and make things happen. These resources many include:

• people
• technology
• capital
• research and development
• a thought or idea
• raw materials or ingredients.

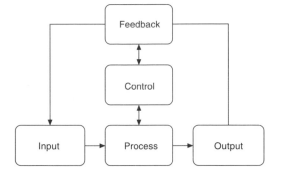

Figure 3.8 *Complete systems diagram*

Exercise 3.7

For the following systems, identify appropriate inputs, processing activity, output, and control and feedback mechanisms. For example, when producing wine to sell in a supermarket:

- Inputs: grapes
- Process: fermentation
- Output: bottled wine
- Control mechanism: quantity on sale, or price
- Feedback: consumer reviews or vintage rating.
  1. Completing an assignment
  2. Launching a new product onto the market
  3. Booking a holiday
  4. Making toast.

3.3 Organizations

Organization categories

An organization can be defined as 'a body of people' (Collins Shorter Dictionary, 1999). More specifically, an organization is a central body of resources working together for a common goal.

Organizations can be categorized by the nature of their business –for example, public sector, private sector, mutual or charity.

Public sector organizations

Public sector organizations are divided into government departments as shown in Figure 3.9, with each public sector function operating as an independent organization. Public sector functions are based upon the needs of the public, and assist in providing services such as health care and education. They are considered to be free provisions, although services are paid for indirectly through taxes and contributions.

Other areas that should also be considered within the public sector include environmental agencies, planning and building, and public functions such as emergency services.

Private sector organizations

The second category of organizations is private sector. The key

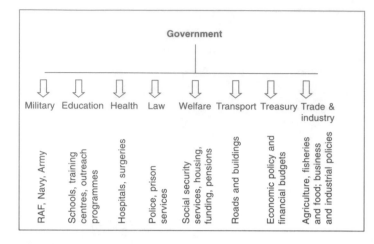

Figure 3.9 *Public sector departments*

objective for private sector organizations is to make a profit. These organizations are set up to provide a service or trade in a number of areas, including:

- finance
- insurance
- law
- retail
- manufacturing
- agriculture
- education and training
- technology
- logistics.

Mutual organizations

Mutual organizations are set up for the benefit of others in that they provide a co-operative function. Examples of mutual benefit organizations include trade unions, clubs and societies. Mutual organizations could be profit making or non-profit making. In some cases the members of the mutual organization will share the benefits and profits that are made.

Charity organizations

The final category of organization is classified as non-profit making, but does not fall under the umbrella of government public sector or private sector. Charities provide a social service similar to that of government utilities, but they rely on donations to support their infrastructure whereas the government relies on public contributions.

Organization functions

Within the above categories organizations can be classified further by their overall function. These functions can be grouped into one of four areas (Figure 3.10).

Primary organizations include farming and agriculture, for

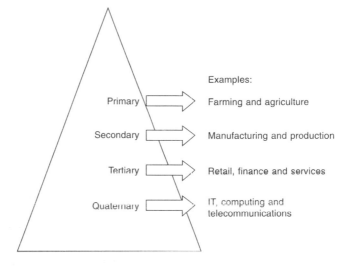

Figure 3.10 *Organization groupings*

example; i.e. those that are dependent upon natural land or sea resources. Secondary industries focus on manufacturing and production industries. Tertiary sector organizations are those that concentrate on retail and providing a service. Quaternary organizations have developed and grown over recent years to include such examples as computing, the Internet, and web-based and telecommunication businesses.

Clearly, organizations can differ in terms of their function and purpose – e.g. they can be profit or non-profit making. Organizations can also differ in terms of their size. The size of an organization will impact upon a number of areas, and on the information flows between these areas and other internal and external resources.

Organizational structures

Organizations can be modelled on two different types of structure: tall or flat.

Tall structures

Organizations that adopt a tall structure tend to be quite large in size. The name comes from the number of 'layers' within the organization, where each layer within the structure represents a level of management or user (Figure 3.11).

Flat structures

Flat-structured organizations tend to be smaller, with a narrower span of control and less management levels (Figure 3.12).

Over recent years some organizations have chosen to adopt a flatter structure because of the benefits that it can bring. This transition to a less rigorous structure is referred to as 'de-layering'. De-layering removes some of the more senior levels of management, as shown in Figure 3.13, making the lines of communication between lower and upper levels of users and management better.

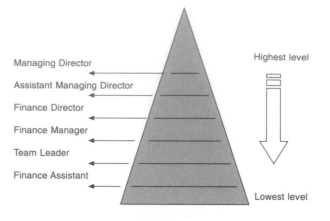

Figure 3.11   *Tall structure organization*

Benefits of a flat structure organization include:

- more direct communication between the lower and upper levels and vice versa
- reduced barriers to communication
- more open communication between the levels
- Examination of the information requirements of organizations – sales figures, staff information, profit/loss figures, competitor information etc. – is easier.

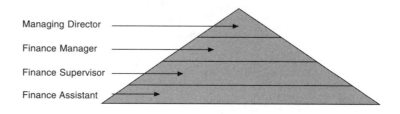

Figure 3.12   *Flat structure organization*

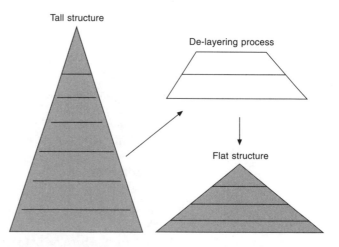

Figure 3.13   *De-layering process*

Flat and tall structure organizations both have their own benefits and drawbacks. The size of an organization can dictate its structure.

It would be impossible for a large multinational company to adopt a very streamlined flat structure because of the need for formality and rigour throughout the management levels. Smaller organizations can be flatter because the span of control is less rigorous. Decision making within an organization is also influenced by the structure. A tall structure organization might focus the emphasis of decision making on strategy planning and forecasting for the future, with less priority on day-to-day or routine tasks and decisions. A flat structure organization might be more orientated towards routine operational decisions and less towards visionary ideas and planning for the future.

Levels of decision making

The types of decisions that an organization makes are based on three levels, as shown in Figure 3.14. The strategic level represents the highest levels of management, i.e. managing director, chief executive and senior managers. Decisions at this level encompass planning for the future, strategy decisions such as mergers and take-overs, and forecasting markets and trends.

Question 3.1

1. What are the four types of organization groupings?
2. Provide four examples of government departments.
3. What is the primary difference between a charity and a retail outlet?
4. What is the process called that converts a tall structure to a flat structure organization?
5. What are the benefits of a flat structure organization?

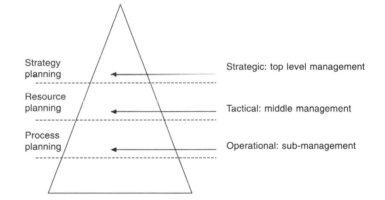

Figure 3.14   *Levels of decision making*

The tactical level represents middle management, to include heads of departments and assistant directors. The decisions focus on project plans, resource issues and financing.

The operational level focuses on day-to-day decision-making – the mechanics of the organization. This level, which is positioned at the base of the organizational structure, includes the majority of the workforce at sub-management levels.

Types of decisions

Decisions that are made within an organization are not only confined to different levels but also conform to various strata running through each level. These decisions can be identified in accordance to the nature of the decision to be made – for example, is the decision to do with routine processing and daily tasks, or is the decision more high level, focusing on issues of recruitment or company expansion? The three decision strata can be referred to as structured, semi-structured and unstructured (Figure 3.15).

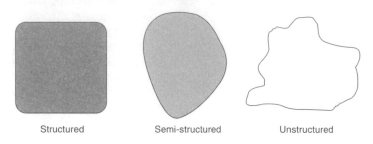

| Structured | Semi-structured | Unstructured |

Figure 3.15 *The three decision strata*

Structured decisions tend to be based on low level or repetitive decisions; for this type of decision there may be a limited number of outcomes.

Semi-structured decisions can be made at all levels of an organization. They strike the balance between everyday routine structured decisions, which require quite a limited thought process, and unstructured decisions, which are more thought provoking and less frequent.

Unstructured decisions tend to be based on higher level decisions, where there could be a wide range of outcomes based upon a complex problem. Unstructured decisions are usually made at management level, calling upon the expertise and knowledge of the decision maker. Decisions in this category are made more infrequently and on a much larger scale. An example of an unstructured decision could be whether or not to diversify and launch a new product line.

Each of the three decision types is not confined to a single organizational level; they will apportion themselves between each level. However, the bulk of a structured decision will fall within the operational level, and the bulk of an unstructured decision will appear within the strategic and tactical levels (Figure 3.16).

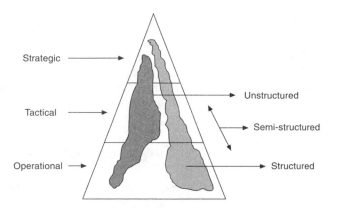

Figure 3.16 *Distribution of structured and unstructured decisions within an organization*

3.4 Functions of an organization

Organizations are built upon a collection of functions, the infrastructure of any organization being dependent upon the support provided by functional departments. Functional departments serve a specific purpose within the organization, and together the departments enable the organization to achieve its objectives.

Depending upon the size of an organization, is may have all the functional departments or it may have integrated departments. Smaller organizations may carry out the tasks and responsibilities of a functional department but without the dedicated resources to support it. A business such as a small kiosk selling refreshments would indeed need to sell, promote, get stock, distribute the stock and finance it, but all the roles may be performed by a single person.

The most common functional areas of an organization are illustrated in Figure 3.17.

Figure 3.17 *Common functional areas of an organization*

Sales

The sales department can serve a number of functions, and in some cases provides the supporting functions of other departments if there are no dedicated marketing or customer service departments. Primarily, the sales department deals with customers, its aim being to generate orders, which may extend from customer enquiries. The techniques used to generate sales vary between organizations, but some of the most common methods include:

- telephone canvassing
- door-to-door canvassing
- advertising (via marketing or promotional media).

The sales function is critical, because without it there would be no direct link between the customers and the organization.

Marketing

The marketing department is sometimes integrated with sales, its role being to advertise and promote the products or services of the organization. The marketing department is involved in the following activities:

- designing and developing promotional materials
- preparing marketing events such as launches and campaigns
- liaising with graphic design or PR (public relations) companies if advertising is not developed in-house

- website developments
- scrutinizing competitor developments.

Customer services

The customer services department focuses on serving the needs of the customer, acting as a focus for customer enquiries, complaints and appraisals. The customer services department is pivotal to the organization because the feedback that is received is channelled through to other departments so that they in turn can act upon and improve their provisions for customers.

IT

The IT department provides the technical hardware and software support for the organization. The IT department can provide a variety of services, including:

- maintaining the hardware and software systems
- upgrading systems
- user support and user training
- setting up and maintaining a website
- installations of new hardware and software
- Data back-ups
- Integrating and networking functional systems.

The IT department can be further divided into smaller functions each focusing on a specific area of IT, as shown in Figure 3.18.

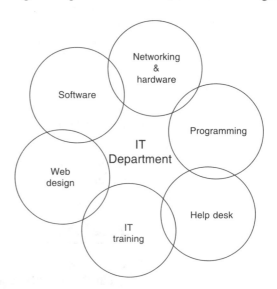

Figure 3.18 *Functional areas of an IT department*

Finance/accounts

This department serves a dual purpose within the organization. The primary function of the finance department is to ensure that there is financial stability within the organization and a steady cash flow to support day-to-day transactions. It is also responsible for:

- payments and transactions
- investments
- accounting procedures (profit and loss, balance sheets, end of year accounts)
- payroll
- budgets and forecasting.

Human resources

The human resources department provides support to the employees of an organization. Its primary function is the welfare of the staff, to ensure that they are advised, guided and motivated to enable them to work productively. Human resources personnel are also responsible for the 'hiring and firing' of staff. They are usually involved with the re-structuring of departments, and with any 'de-layering' activities that might take place.

Operations

Depending upon the organization type, one of the functional departments may be 'operations', where all the processing of products or services takes place.

An operations department would certainly be present in a large national or multinational organization offering a diverse range of products or services, and requiring one department to spearhead the developments.

Distribution

The distribution department is concerned with the delivery and logistics of physical stock items. Distribution may not be a discrete department in its own right; it may be linked to operations or sales functions.

Functional departments need to communicate with each other to ensure that information and good practice is shared throughout the organization. To ensure that this happens effectively and positively, a number of measures need to be taken. The first is to ensure that a good organizational structure is in place, with appropriate levels as mentioned previously. Secondly, steps need to be taken to ensure that the flow of information between the levels of the organization is open and fluent.

3.5 Information in organizations

Information is exchanged every second of every day, and the way in which information is communicated depends upon a number of factors. These include:

- format

- function
- sender and receiver
- transmission tool.

The format of information can be quite diverse, depending upon its function. What is the function of sending or receiving the information? Is it to inform, update, challenge? The information format can be quite generic. Examples include written formats of legally binding contracts, such as marriage certificates or contracts of employment, or verbal communication to greet and welcome a friend. The relationship between format and function is clearly very close.

Exercise 3.8

For the following information scenarios identify at least two information formats and justify why they are appropriate for that particular function:

1. Sending birthday greetings
2. Complaining about faulty goods
3. Catching up on the latest gossip with a friend
4. Sending invitations to a party
5. Expressing happiness.

The sender and receiver of the information play important roles in this transference process. There are a number of factors that can influence the success of the information flow, and these are shown in Figure 3.19.

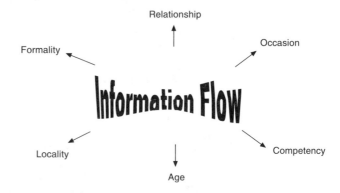

Figure 3.19 *Factors affecting information flow*

In an organization all of these factors are of vital importance. The relationship might be of a manager to a team member. The occasion might be a team briefing that could affect how information is transmitted. The competency or level of the sender and the receiver might be critical factors; what happens when a technical programmer tries to communicate at a very high specialist level to an end user who inputs data and has no technical knowledge? Age might need to be considered because people of different ages have different ideas and expectations.

The locality of the sender and the receiver might have an impact if the two are trying to communicate across different departments, offices, branches or companies that are situated miles apart.

Finally, the formality of the occasion might impact upon the flow of information. A manager relaying information to a member of the team at an appraisal may communicate the information in a completely different way to information shared over a working lunch.

In an organization the transmission tool depends upon all of the factors associated with the information format, function, sender and receiver. It might be electronic, verbal or written; in some cases combinations of tools are used. The types of transmission tools used in an organization are shown in Figure 3.20.

Computer (e-mail)	Talking	Memo
Fax	(through a resource	Letter
Telephone	such as a phone)	Report
Video conferencing	(without the use of a	Agenda
Bulletin board or	resource – just speech)	Minutes
newsgroup		

Figure 3.20   *Types of transmission tools used in organizations*

Flow of information in organizations

There are three ways that information can travel through an organization:

- upwards
- downwards
- laterally (across).

Upward communication signifies that the information is passed through each level with the source originating at the base level of the organization, possibly operational, and moving through the tactical and strategic levels (Figure 3.21).

An example of this information type might include a request from a data entry clerk for a supervisor to check the consistency of a piece of work. At a tactical level, the request might be from a manager to a head of department asking for more resources to support a project.

Downward communication is where the information is filtered through the organization from the top levels, or from higher levels (Figure 3.22). This type of communication might include a health and safety policy being implemented by the director of a company or, at a lower level, a manager setting up a staff appraisal with a member of the team.

Downward communication can be detrimental because it can be seen as a restrictive imposition, where the lower levels of the organization are being dictated to from above.

Lateral communication takes place across the organizational strata rather than up and down it (Figure 3.23). Lateral communication takes place between people of a similar position within

Strategic

Tactical

Operational

Figure 3.21   *Upward communication*

Strategic

Tactical

Operational

Figure 3.22   *Downward communication*

Team leader – Team leader OR Data entry clerk – Data entry clerk

Figure 3.23   *Lateral communication*

an organization. An example of this is two people within the same department sharing ideas, or working together on a project.

Uses of information in organizations

Information is required to maintain the everyday processing activities that occur in organizations, and provides the mechanics to keep organizational resources working. In an organization, information is used to:

- plan
- forecast
- make decisions
- structure
- model and control.

Information needs to be dynamic in order to keep processes up to date. Static information resources have little or no use apart from storing historical data for reference purposes.

Information that is used to plan, forecast and make decisions is based on a combination of quantitative and qualitative data. Planning might involve the collection of qualitative feedback from users or customers in order to improve a facility or service. Planning might also rely on a set of quantitative figures to see whether or not a project is financially viable.

Forecasting might depend upon qualitative historical data to establish what has been done in the past, analyse whether it was successful, and base forecasts on previous experiences. Forecasting can also be based purely on quantitative data such as profit and loss; for example, for this period we made this much money, if we increase production by x amount we should make y amount of profit in the future.

Decisions are also based on a combination of qualitative and quantitative data and information. For example, the decision to promote a member of staff could be based on his or her ability to meet all sales targets, or on personal recommendations from a peer.

Information is also used to structure, model and control. In these instances it could be argued that quantitative data are used more than qualitative data because in order to carry out each of these you need a measurable starting point, a specific tracking device and a mechanism that can accurately calculate or predict the distance travelled or progress made. This is quite difficult to do using qualitative information.

Planning and information

Everybody makes plans; these might involve writing a shopping list, or drawing up an action plan in order to prioritize tasks. Assignment schedules involve planning when a deadline needs to be met and you organize what you have to do in order to complete them (e.g. carry out research). In organizations, planning is crucial because it provides measurable progress steps for the future. Without planning you do not know where you are going – or recognize when you have got there!

There are a number of ways to plan in an organization, and the method chosen depends upon several factors. These factors evolve around a TROPIC cycle, as shown in Figure 3.24.

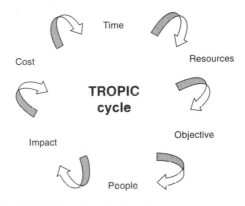

Figure 3.24 *TROPIC cycle of planning*

TROPIC requirements :

- **T**ime – how long is the plan?
- **R**esources – what is going to support the plan?
- **O**bjective – what is the purpose of the plan?
- **P**eople – who is involved with the plan?
- **I**mpact – who and what will the plan affect?
- **C**ost – how much is it going to cost to implement the plan?

If consideration is not given to all of these factors the plan may be incomplete and the chances of successful implementation greatly reduced. What is the point of generating a plan to network an entire department if you cannot afford the hardware or software, or if you cannot implement the network plan within a certain time period?

Within an organization, planning is carried out over certain periods of time (Table 3.6); these can be recognized as being:

- short term
- medium term
- long term.

Table 3.6 *Examples of planning*

Type of planning	Period	Example of plan
Short term	1–3 years	Introduce computers into a single department
Medium term	3–5 years	Ensure that all the departments within the organization are computerized and networked
Long term	5 years +	Expand and acquire new premises

Tools for planning

There are many tools available to assist with planning activities; some of these are very straightforward and involve setting out objectives and time scales in a simplistic plan such as:

- assignment schedule
- checklist
- personal development plan
- appraisal.

Other tools are more sophisticated and rely on specific timings of activities and task dependencies, for example:

- Gantt charts
- Critical path analysis.

Whichever planning tool is used, elements within the TROPIC cycle should always be referred to and used as guidance when setting specific planning goals and objectives.

Case study 3.1

Patricia and Richard Wright own Snooze Thatch Cottage (Figure 3.26), a guest house in rural Norfolk.

Figure 3.25 *Snooze Thatch Cottage*

The guest house is aimed at the more discerning guest, with a range of single, double and suite accommodation of the highest standard. The reputation of Snooze Thatch Cottage is such that no advertising is necessary; word of mouth has ensured that throughout the year rooms are always fully booked.

Although Patricia and Richard are actively involved with the management side and daily running of the business, they also employ six other staff members on a part- and full-time basis. Hazel is the housekeeper and ensures that all the day-to-day operations run smoothly; a chambermaid is also employed in the mornings to ensure that all the laundry and room preparation is complete. Mel is the general gardener and ensures that the half-acre grounds are kept in prime condition throughout the year. David is the handyman and his wife Pauline is the cook; another kitchen staff member also helps with daily food preparation and kitchen duties.

Owing to the success of the guest house Richard has been discussing the possibility of acquiring another property on the Norfolk coast and converting it to a second guest house. The initial outlay would be quite high because the fourteen-bedroom Victorian lodge needs complete renovation. It is estimated that, including the purchase price, £250 000 would be needed.

Tasks

1. Identify what sort of issues Richard and Patricia would need to consider in planning for this new venture.
2. Forecasting would be essential in this new venture; discuss why this is so, and identify what targets the owners would need to set for the short, medium and long term.
3. Identify six decisions that would need to be made if they went ahead with this venture.

3.6 Types of information systems

General information systems

Information systems are systems that have been set up to manage and support the day-to-day activities of an organization, and also the management. Almost every organization has an information system, ranging from quite a basic system that relies on simple application software to process, store and deliver the information required, through to quite complex, integrated systems that support the entire organization.

General systems that can provide information because of their ability to process, store and deliver information include:

- databases and database management systems (DBMS)
- spreadsheets.

Databases

Databases carry out a range of functions to support all types of users. Their primary function is to store volumes of data and specific formats to allow for easy processing and access. Data that is input into a database can be formatted into meaningful and useful information. Databases offer a range of features and tools to support an organization. Some of these are standard across a range of database software and some are more specific; examples include:

- menu systems
- security systems
- input screens – forms, tables (Table 3.7, Figure 3.26)
- output screens – reports (Figure 3.27), forms
- query and filter facilities
- validation functions
- analysis tools.

Note that forms can be a dual purpose, providing both input and output screens.

Table 3.7   *Example of a database table*

Field 1	Field 2	Field 3	Field 4	Field 5	Field 6	Field 7
Customer number	Surname	First name	Address 1	Address 2	Town	Postcode
J445/6	Jones	Anna	64 Kitts Road	Hampton	Norwich	NR13 1DD
P124/3	Martin	James	Oakley	6 High Street	Aylsham	NR45 6RD
R209/6	Robertson	David	31 Handy Close	Thorpe St Andrew	Norwich	NR7 8FT

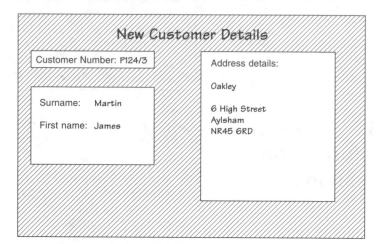

Figure 3.26   *Example of a database form*

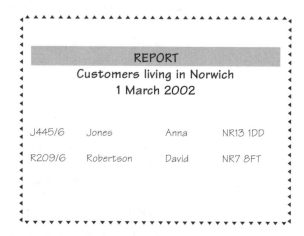

Figure 3.27   *Report form: report to identify all customers that live in Norwich, displaying the customer number, surname, first name and postcode only*

Spreadsheets

Spreadsheets meet the basic criteria of being information systems because they store, process and output data items in a variety of formats. Spreadsheets are commonly used to model numerical and financial data, and examples of their use include profit and loss accounts, monthly forecasting, expenditure and salary sheets (Table 3.8). Spreadsheets have a range of functions, including:

Table 3.8 *Monthly expenditure spreadsheet*

	Jan	*Feb*	*Mar*	*Apr*	*May*	*June*
Income	£	£	£	£	£	£
Wages	620	620	620	620	620	620
Expenses						
Entertainment	110	130	115	90	100	75
Car tax	20	20	20	20	20	20
Eating out	40	60	20	40	35	30
Clothes	150	220	100	120	135	170
Subtotal	320	430	255	270	290	295
Balance	300	190	365	350	330	325

- automatic calculations
- modelling and predictive facilities
- graphical outputs
- programming functions
- automatic updating.

Spreadsheets provide a clear and consistent worksheet format that helps you to understand and interpret data. Data can be typed in and stored as a skeleton template, and further additions and updates can then be added. Provided that formulas have been set up on the spreadsheet, new data can be incorporated and updated easily, providing the user with current facts and figures.

A spreadsheet that contains large volumes of data may not be easy to interpret. The graphical features offered by a spreadsheet can however be used to reflect certain data requirements. Some spreadsheet applications have built-in chart and graphic facilities to provide a more visual data interpretation; examples of these can be seen in Figure 3.28.

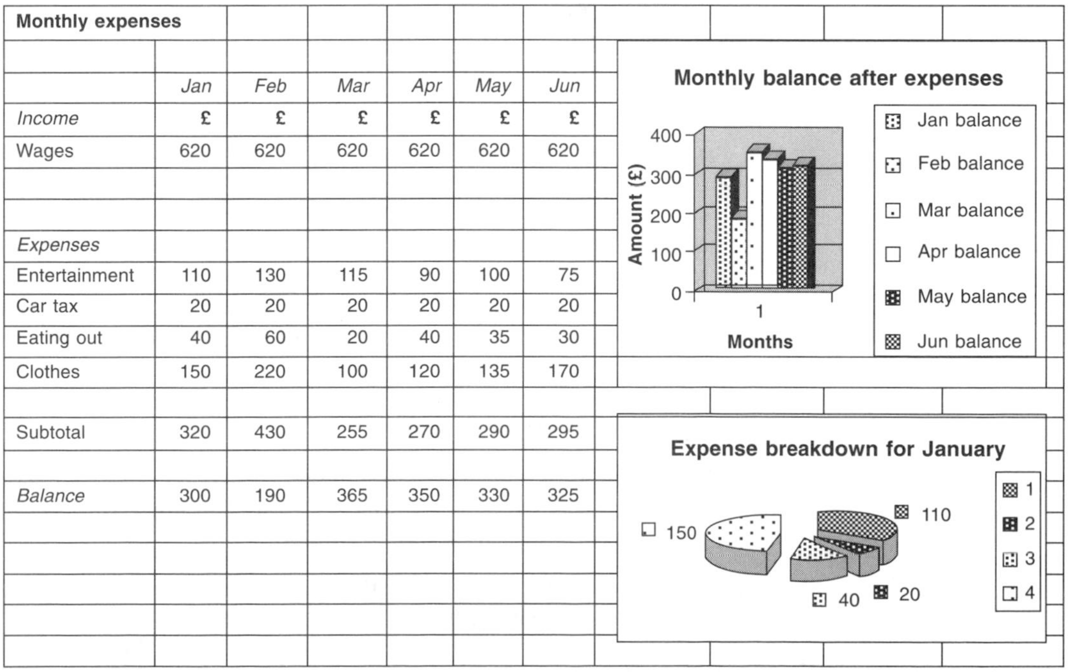

Monthly expenses						
	Jan	*Feb*	*Mar*	*Apr*	*May*	*Jun*
Income	£	£	£	£	£	£
Wages	620	620	620	620	620	620
Expenses						
Entertainment	110	130	115	90	100	75
Car tax	20	20	20	20	20	20
Eating out	40	60	20	40	35	30
Clothes	150	220	100	120	135	170
Subtotal	320	430	255	270	290	295
Balance	300	190	365	350	330	325

Figure 3.28 *Examples of the charts and graphs offered by spreadsheets*

Exercise 3.9

Using general information system software, design a small system to meet one of the following user requirements:

1. A library system that can store information about DVDs and videos for a hire shop, to include:

    *   customer details
    *   DVD/video details catalogue of titles
    *   rental status.

2. A stock control system template that will automatically calculate stock levels and re-order levels; information should show:

    *   Period extending from January to June
    *   Stock items (fan belts, spark plugs, adjustable wheel nuts, fuses and tyres).

Each stock item should have a stock level minimum requirement of 60 items, and when stock items reach below this level an indicator should show the need to re-order.

Template designs should be clear and fully functional (data are not required, but can be added to make the system more comprehensive).

Specific information systems

Databases and spreadsheets are two examples of general information systems that can assist organizations in the pursuit of manageable and supportive data systems. However, more specific information systems do exist, and examples of these include:

*   strategic level systems
*   management level systems
*   knowledge level systems
*   operational level systems.

Each of these information system types supports various aspects of an organization, from strategic and tactical levels down to operational levels. Specific information systems can also be set up and integrated into functional areas of an organization; for example, there may be a sales information system or a finance information system.

These four categories of information systems can also be broken down more specifically into actual information system types, as shown in Figure 3.29.

Strategic level systems

This level of information system supports senior executives in making unstructured decisions at a strategic level. The types of decisions that are made might include the following:

1. Should we consider diversifying into new markets?
2. Should we make a bid to acquire new businesses?
3. How could we embrace new challenges in the area of E-commerce?

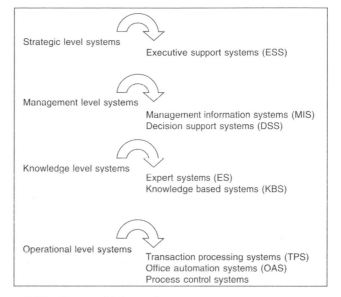

Figure 3.29 *Types of information system*

Strategic level information systems are set up to forecast, budget and plan for the future, extending over the long term of a period of five years and beyond. Within this category specific information systems can be set up, examples of this being Executive support systems (ESS).

Executive support systems

Executive support systems exist to support strategic personnel within an organization, their function being to provide the support and guidance needed to carry out long-term forecasting and planning. ESS use data and information collected from the current environment in order to establish trends or anomalies that can then be used for future planning. For example, an organization that may wish to transfer production to Europe over the next five years may look at a range of available data sources, including:

- cost of manufacturing (labour, transportation, premises)
- import and export issues (cost, initiatives, barriers to trade)
- existing businesses already trading in Europe and their profitability
- current financial status and whether there will be enough capital to finance such a venture in the future
- existing competition in Europe.

In order to identify specific trends, ESS may also rely on historical data to identify what has been done previously and whether it was successful.

A successful ESS has the characteristics shown in Figure 3.30.

Users who will be accessing ESS may have very limited IT knowledge or skills; senior executives will not necessarily be technically orientated, and therefore the ability to access the ESS easily and quickly is essential. Information required should be given by the ESS within a specified time period to enable further decisions to be made rapidly. An ESS must be able to interact easily and effectively with other systems in order to retrieve the data required. For example, decisions to be taken regarding whether

Figure 3.30 *Characteristics of a successful ESS*

or not to take over a new company may require the ESS to retrieve financial share price data from an external database source such as the London Stock Exchange. In order to make correct decisions the modelling and analytical tools should be first class, and the graphical user interface (GUI) must be easy to use, visual and instructive. Finally, an ESS has to be flexible and adaptable in order to support the ever-changing needs and requirements of an organization.

Management level systems

Management level systems are designed to support middle management in their role of making some unstructured and semi-structured decisions, but ones of a lower level than those offered by strategic level systems. These systems are put in place to offer support to management levels within an organization; they are not exclusive to managers only. Management level systems provide a category in which other information systems are embedded, including:

- management information systems
- decision support systems.

Management information systems

Management information systems (MIS) support management levels within an organization by providing them with data and information based on both current and historical records from which informed and detailed decisions can be made. MIS is typically based on internal data; examples include:

- financial status
- performance and productivity levels
- weekly, monthly and quarterly forecasts, and trend analysis
- sales targets and figures.

The term MIS has been used by some to include all information systems that support the functional areas of the organization. However, O'Brien (1993) makes reference to MIS as including operational and transaction processing systems that are only used indirectly by managers. The most important aspect of MIS is not the terminology but its role in supporting managers in their decisions, based on fact and figures taken internally from the organization.

Decision support systems

Decision support systems also support management levels within an organization, helping them to make dynamic decisions that are characterized as being semi-structured or unstructured. DSS have to be inherently dynamic in order to support the demand for up-to-date information, enabling a fast response to the changing conditions of an organization.

DSS are complex analytical systems that are designed explicitly with a variety of analysis and modelling tools to process, enquire and evaluate certain conditions.

Knowledge level systems

Knowledge level systems by definition provide support for knowledge users within an organization. This particular category of information system is not confined to a specific user (e.g. manager) or decision type (structured, semi-structured or unstructured).

The function of a knowledge information system is to assist an organization in the quest to:

* identify
* discover
* analyse
* integrate and
* collaborate

new ideas and information in order for the organization to be more efficient or profitable, or indeed to ensure high quality standards amongst the workforce, services offered and/or production lines.

Knowledge level system users in general are those who have achieved high academic degree or further degree status, or members of recognized professions, such as engineers, doctors, lawyers or scientists. Their role within the organization is to seek out technical facts, information and knowledge, which can then be analysed, processed and integrated into the organization. Examples of how knowledge level systems can be used in a hospital include:

* to discover new medicines to cure disease
* to identify certain patients who are more at risk of particular medical conditions
* to assess the impact of certain drugs upon particular categories of patients
* to assess the impact and monitoring of close relatives' medical history upon patients.

There are many ways that data can be extracted in order to provide the information required to carry out analysis or identify implications, impacts or trends. Some methods are quite straightforward and involve the sorting or filtering of information using conventional application software; however, there are specific tools and techniques available to serve this purpose. These knowledge tools include expert systems, and data mining.

Expert systems

Expert systems represent an advanced level of knowledge and decision support systems. Expert systems encapsulate the experience and specialized knowledge of experts in order to relay this information to a non-expert, so that they too can have access to the specialist knowledge.

Expert systems are based on a reasoning process that resembles human thought processes. The thought process is dependent upon rules and reasoning, which have been extracted by experts in the field. The primary function of an expert system is to provide a 'knowledge base' that can be accessed to provide information such as a diagnosis for a patient, to assist non-experts in their own decision-making process.

Data mining

Data mining is a generic term that covers a range of technologies. The actual process of 'mining' data refers to the extraction of information through tests, analyses, rules and heuristics. Information is sorted and processed from a data set in the hope of finding new information or data anomalies that may have remained undiscovered.

Data mining embraces a wide range of technologies, including rule induction, neural networks and data visualization, all working to provide an analyst with more informative and better understanding of the data.

Operational level systems

Operational level systems support operational managers and supervisors and assist them by tracking and monitoring activities that occur at this level. Such activities might include:

- sales figures for a set period
- production and productivity levels
- ratios examining daily work flow.

A system at this level will answer routine questions, such as:

- how much is being produced on a certain basis?
- how many items are in stock?
- when will production targets be met, based on current work flow levels?

Operational level systems will provide answers to structured questions and decisions where there may be a limited number of outcomes. Table 3.9 is a stock report which answers the question, how many items are in stock?

Table 3.9 *Stock report*

Stock report as at 1 March 2002			
Stock number	Stock item	Quantity	Location
RT1244000	Fan belts	136	Aisle 6B
Y45501	Spark plugs	26	Aisle 2A
FG2670911	Fuses	12	Aisle 1D
HI611098	Washers	180	Aisle 1B

Within the operational level category there are three different types of information systems:

- Transaction Processing Systems (TPS)
- Office Automation Systems (OAS)
- Process Control Systems.

Question 3.2

1. What are the four categories of information system?
2. For each category, identify the individual information systems that belong to it.
3. What are the main characteristics of the following systems?
   - management information system
   - transaction processing system
   - expert system.
4. Which of the following systems would be most appropriate to meet the following users' needs?
   - a non-expert requiring expert information
   - a senior executive
   - a manager requiring information in order to forecast future sales
   - an operational worker requiring repetitive task information.
5. Why do we need information systems in organizations?

Transaction processing systems

Transaction processing systems exist to support the operational level of organizations and assist in providing answers to structured routine decisions. The TPS is pivotal to any organization because it is the backbone of day-to-day activities and processing. Examples of TPS include holiday booking systems, customer ordering systems and payroll systems.

Office automation systems

Office automation systems are set up to identify and increase levels of efficiency and productivity amongst the workforce. To assist in this role, various tools and software are available to schedule, monitor and improve workforce activities. OAS will enable the workforce to:

- communicate more effectively
- promote collaborations and group synergy
- structure daily tasks and activities
- track and schedule appointments and activities
- increase productivity by reducing repetitive workload
- automate repetitive tasks.

Office automation systems can be quite simplistic, drawing upon the functions of application software such as wordprocessors, spreadsheets, databases, multimedia and communications software (e.g. e-mail).

More complex software tools can also be used to focus on a specific area of workflow or productivity, such as 'groupware', 'document imaging processing', 'workflow management systems' or 'electronic document management systems'.

Process control systems

Process control systems monitor, support and control certain process activities within a manufacturing environment. Applications that are used to support process control systems can help an organization by:

- improving quality control
- assisting with project planning of the product
- assisting with physical design
- identifying resource requirements
- identifying the development status or stage in the product life cycle.

There is a wide range of software available to support both general and specific activities that fall under the domain of process control systems, as identified in Table 3.10.

3.7 Information system development

Information systems need to be developed in order to meet business requirements. Development of an information system and its overall capabilities and applicability to an organization depend very heavily on whether it has been designed specifically or generically. Specific or 'bespoke' design ensures that the information system is tailored to an individual organization's needs. Generic information systems can be purchased 'off-the-shelf', and are used by a number of organizations. The benefits and limitations of the two types of systems are listed in Table 3.11.

Table 3.10 *Support available for process control systems*

Software type	Function
Spreadsheet	• Costs manufacturing items • Forecasts sales • Identifies break-even and profit margin points • Analyses work patterns and efficiency levels
Statistical packages	• Examines productivity levels to identify ratios of optimum working conditions • Identifies relationships between workforce and productivity
Project management	• Gantt charts identify timings of activities • Schedules of tasks and activities • Identifies task dependencies
Computer aided design (CAD)	• Interactive development of drawings and designs • Professional drafting tool
Computer aided manufacture (CAM)	• Controls production equipment more accurately • Integrates with other manufacturing systems • Ensures quality procedures

Table 3.11 *Benefits and limitations of bespoke and off-the-shelf systems*

Bespoke systems		Off-the-shelf systems	
Benefits	Limitations	Benefits	Limitations
Tailored to specific requirements	Can take a long time to develop	Can be cheaper than bespoke systems	May not satisfactorily meet the needs of the organization
Will incorporate user needs and requirements	Can be more expensive than 'off-the-shelf' systems	Can take less time to implement	Can be poor quality
Better quality system	Can be complex to use	Can be easier to use	May not be compatible with existing systems
Compatibility with existing systems		Standard formatting	

Exercise 3.10

A new company has decided to network two of its departments to improve day-to-day processing activities and efficiency. Each department affected will have brand new software installed onto the network. The departments involved are:

• finance (a highly specialized department requiring

software to assist in all aspects of budget control, payroll and daily accounting)
- sales and marketing (require general software to help with their decision making and advertising campaigns).

1. Provide software recommendations to meet the requirements of each department.
2. Fully justify all proposals, and state why you have rejected certain software options.

Systems life cycle

The systems life cycle is the oldest and most established method for building information systems. The methodology assumes that an information system has a life cycle similar to that of any other active organism, with a beginning, a middle and an end. Different information systems have different life cycles; however, the majority rotate around the generic stages of:

- project definition
- initial study
- design
- programming and specification
- installation
- review.

Project definition

Project definition sets out the requirements of the new system, identifying why a new system is needed, the objectives, constraints and costs, and the resources needed to support the new system. Within the project definition boundaries are also set to establish the scope of the project and the extent of its impact upon other functional areas or systems.

Initial study

The initial study phase starts to examine in more detail the problems of the existing system, and attempts, through investigation and fact-finding, to generate alternative system solutions and recommendations. During this stage a number of activities take place to ensure that the problems identified are a true reflection of the current system environment, and that proposals put forward meet the needs of the users and of the organization.

Fact-finding methods include:

- questionnaires
- interviews
- investigation of documentation
- observation.

Less formal methods of fact-finding can also incorporate:

- focus groups
- brainstorming.

As information is collected it is recorded using specific templates and documentation in preparation for the following stages of design, specification and implementation.

Design

The design stage can be broken down into two areas; logical and physical design.

Using set modelling and design tools and techniques, the system can be represented in paper format prior to the physical system design. The design stage identifies how the proposed system will work in key areas of functionality and practicality by examining the user interface, security issues and compatibility issues. The impact of the new system on existing resources is also examined.

Programming and specification

This stage translates the design specification into the required program or code. Customized programs may have to be written to support various levels in the system design. Suitable languages that may be used at this stage include Pascal, COBOL, C/C++, Java/J++, SQL, Visual or object-orientated languages.

Installation

This final stage involves the testing, training and conversion of the new or modified system, integrating it into the organization. Software is tested to ensure that there are no bugs or errors in the programs. Users may need to be trained to ensure that they understand and can operate the new system, and finally conversion of existing data and information from the old to the new system needs to take place.

Review

The review stage or post-implementation period provides the final checks and assurances once the system is up and running. A formal audit may take place to evaluate how well the system is performing against expected levels, and also to monitor user satisfaction and interaction with the new system.

Alternative system building strategies

The systems life cycle is very appropriate for large transaction processing systems and management information systems where requirements are highly structured and well defined. However, the prescriptive and rigorous framework of the life cycle makes it costly, time consuming and inflexible. For smaller, less complex systems a traditional life cycle pathway is too expensive and therefore alternative approaches to system builds have been explored.

The alternatives to life cycle development include:

- prototyping
- acquisition of application software
- development of bespoke software

- end user development
- outsourcing.

Prototyping

Prototyping provides the opportunity to design an experimental system or part of the actual system design to test whether or not it meets the specified user or system requirements. By building an actual working system refinements can be made, making it a flexible approach to system design.

Applications or bespoke software

If resources are limited, a viable alternative to a system build is to purchase appropriate software that can improve your existing system features. For example, a new finance system might be required; by purchasing either specific accounting software or general spreadsheet software the system is instantly updated and fulfils the requirements of the finance system expectations (providing the hardware is in place to support it).

The benefits and limitations of general application software and specific 'bespoke' software are listed Table 3.11.

End user development

This type of systems design has evolved from a culture of 'learning by doing', where end users are designing new systems with the help of modern day tools such as visual and graphical languages. Users are beginning to explore the capabilities of applications software, which enable them to create input and output screens, customize menus, introduce security measures and stipulate the functions of application software, modelling them into a specific information system.

Outsourcing

Outsourcing is an alternative to designing systems in-house either using traditional life cycle methodologies or drawing upon the skills and knowledge of end users.

The use of an external agency provides quality assurance and also reduces costs, as resources to be used are focused off site.

Methodologies and tools used for system design

There are a number of recognized tools and methodologies that can help in the process of designing an information system. Some of these can be categorized as:

- structured methodologies
- computer-aided software engineering (CASE)
- rapid application development (RAD).

Structured methodologies have been used since the 1970s, and have become increasingly popular since the development of SSADM in 1981 by Learmouth and Burchett Management systems (LBMS) for the Central and Telecommunication Agency (CCTA). The requirement for a standard information system that can be used generically across a range of government projects has ensured that SSADM remains one of the most popular information systems in current use.

Tools used in data flow diagrams

There are four tools that are used in the preparation of a data flow diagram, and these are shown in Figure 3.31.

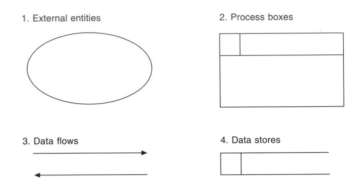

Figure 3.31 *Data flow diagram tools*

The four tools are used together to create a data flow diagram:

1. **External entities** identify people and organizations outside of the system under investigation.
2. **Processes** represent the activities that take place within the system.
3. **Data flows** provide the physical link between data sources that flow to, from and within the system.
4. **Data stores** detail the type of storage mechanism used to hold the data and information within the system.

External entities

External entities are used to represent people or organizations that have a role in the system but are not necessarily part of it.

External entities can appear in a system more than once; for example, a student would be part of a number of processes within a college system in terms of being enrolled on a course, having a personal tutor, being registered with the student union etc. To indicate that a student appears more than once in the system, we represent it as shown in Figure 3.32.

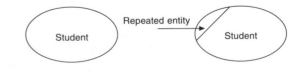

Figure 3.32 *Sample external entities*

Processes

Process boxes represent activities that take place within the system, and also activities that are linked to the system.

All activities have a process attached to them; something triggers the process and an action might become the output of that process. For example, Figure 3.33 illustrates the activity of producing an assignment.

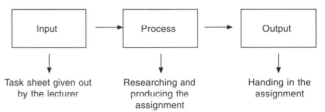

Figure 3.33 *Activity of producing an assignment*

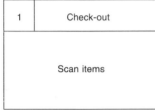

Figure 3.34 *Sample process box*

The process box has three distinct sections, each with its own identifier (Figure 3.34): (1) identifies the process box with a unique number; (Check-out) provides details of the location where the activity is taking place; and (Scan items) identifies the activity that is taking place.

Data flows

Data flows indicate the direction or flow of information within the system:

$\longrightarrow$ Feeding out to an output

$\longleftarrow$ Feeding in to an input.

Data flows provide the link to other data flow tools within a system; these links include connecting external entities to processes and processes to data stores, as identified in Table 3.12.

Table 3.12 *Data flow links*

Data flow links	Data store	External entity	Process
Data store	✗	✗	✓
External entity	✗	✗	✓
Process	✓	✓	✗

The matrix clearly defines that the flow of information within a system must always evolve around a process. The direct flow of information between processes indicates that two activities can take place without the intervention of an input such as a data entry clerk.

This is true in terms of automatic processing, where a program can receive a set of information and collate or process the information, which might then automatically trigger a second process – for example running off a report. Without the use of automated systems, direct links between processes would rarely exist and should therefore not be linked on a data flow diagram.

All data flows should be labelled clearly to identify the type of data or information that is being passed to and from sources and recipients, e.g.

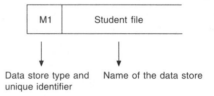

Data stores

Data stores represent different types of storage mechanisms, and there are four types:

1. D: a digitized or computerized storage mechanism such as a file on a database
2. M: a manual storage mechanism such as a filing cabinet
3. T (M): a manual transient data store, which is a temporary manual storage mechanism such as an in-tray on a desk
4. T: a computerized data store that is temporary – for example, e-mail, which may be read once and then moved to a permanent storage file or deleted.

There are two components to a data store, as identified in Figure 3.35.

M1	Student file

Data store type and unique identifier   Name of the data store

Figure 3.35 *Data store*

The information provided tells us that the data store type is manual and the identifier (1) is associated with the data store mechanism, which is a customer file. If the customer file is accessed again within the system, it will then become a repeated data store. All of the information remains the same, but we identify the repeated aspect by inserting a second line (Figure 3.36).

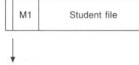

Figure 3.36 *Repeated data store*

Levels of data flow diagrams

There are three main levels involved with the preparation of a data flow diagram:

- **Level 0** (context diagram) provides a general overview of the system and how it relates to external entities outside of the system boundary.
- **Level 1** represents a detailed view of what and who is involved with the system. It examines what activities take place, who is involved with the data concerned, and appropriate storage mechanisms. A stepped outline for developing a level 1 DFD is outlined below.
- **Level 2** provides a specific breakdown of what is happening within a specific process. The process is expanded at level 2 so that more detail can be added, giving a clear and accurate picture of a specific activity.

Preparing a level 1 data flow diagram

The ten-step plan described here is a guide to preparing data flow diagrams; different people will use their own methods. However, the benefit of the plan is that you are constantly re-examining the information, and understanding the system is half the battle when preparing data flow diagrams.

Ten-step plan for preparing a level 1 data flow diagram

Step 1 Read through the information collected from:

- project brief
- fact-finding investigation
- user catalogues.

Step 2 Sort the information into clear sections identifying the following:

- the users external to the system (sources and recipients of information)
- the documents used in the system
- the activities that take place in the system.

Step 3 Produce a 'systems information table'.

Step 4 Convert external users to external entities.

Step 5 Convert documentation to data stores.

Step 6 Convert activities to processes, and identify where the activity takes place and who is involved.

Step 7 Start on a small scale by looking at the input(s) and output(s) to a single process, using data flows to represent the link(s) of data and information.

Step 8 Position the other processes in the diagram.

Step 9 Connect the remainder of the processes with their attributed input(s) and output(s).

Step 10 Check for consistency (examine the initial documentation to ensure that all information has been represented, and check back with the users or project sponsor that the diagram is correct).

The following is an example of the ten-step plan in use at a supermarket.

Step 1 Information is collected from the project brief and the fact-finding investigation carried out at Store-line Supermarkets. The systems boundary is fresh produce.

Steps 2 & 3 The information is sorted and a systems information table drawn up (Table 3.13).

Table 3.13 *Systems information table*

External entities	Data stores (documents)	Processes (activities)
Head office	Promotions file	Daily meeting
Supplier	Daily stock sheet	Put out and adjust stock
	Stock adjustment sheet	Check deliveries
	Stock cabinet	Order stock
	Stock order forms	
	Stock request forms	

Steps 4, 5 & 6 Convert the information into DFD tools (Figure 3.37).

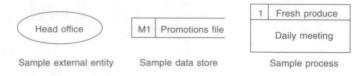

Sample external entity   Sample data store   Sample process

Figure 3.37 *Converting information into DFD tools*

Step 7 Single process DFD (Figure 3.38).

Figure 3.38 *Single process DFD*

Steps 8 & 9 Connection of the remainder of the processes (Figure 3.39).

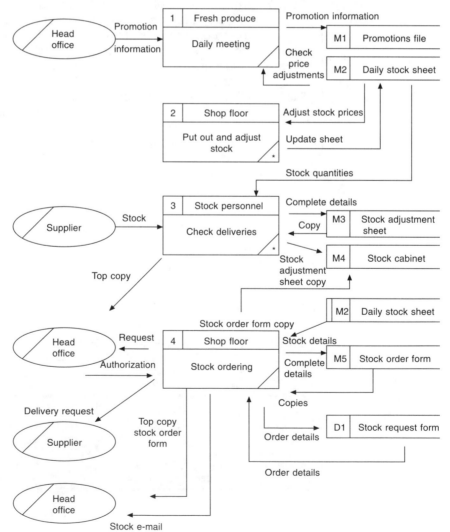

Figure 3.39 *Level 1 DFD for the fresh produce department at Store-Line Supermarket*

Step 10 Ensure that information is accurate and complete; check it against information provided by the personnel within the fresh produce department.

Exercise 3.11

Identify the system that you use for getting up in the morning and coming into college. Identify the activities that take place, who is involved with your system, and any documents that you might use to get you to college, ready for your first lesson.

Logical data modelling

Another tool that is used to identify and represent the activities of a system is logical data modelling (LDM). LDM provides a detailed graphical representation of the information used within the system and identifies the relationships that exist between data items.

Similarly to data flow modelling, logical data modelling uses a set of tools and associated textual descriptions.

The diagrammatic aspect of logical data modelling is referred to as 'logical data structures'. These structures have four main components (Figure 3.40):

1. Entities
2. Relationships
3. Degree
4. Optionality

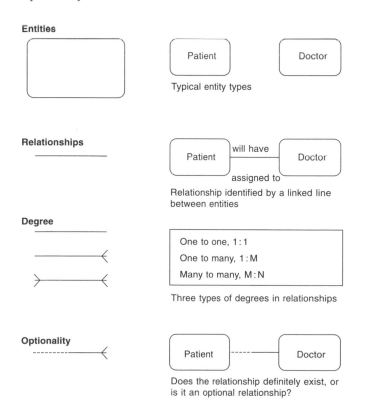

Figure 3.40 *Logical data structure notations*

Table 3.14 *Systems and entities*

System	Entities
Hospital	Patient
	Doctor
	Ward
	Treatment
	Diagnosis
College	Student
	Registration
	Course
	Tutor
	Enrolment
Ticket booking	Ticket
	Seat
	Booking
	Performance
	Reservation

Entities

Entities provide the source, recipient and storage mechanism for information that is held on the system. Examples of typical entities are illustrated in Table 3.14.

Each entity has a set of attributes that make up the information occurrences, for example:

Entity: Student
Attributes: Student number
                     Name
                     Address
                     Telephone number
                     Date of birth.

Each set of attributes within an entity should have a unique field that provides easy identification of the entity type. In the case of the entity type 'student', the unique key field is that of 'student number'. The unique field or 'primary key' will ensure that although two students may have the same name, no two students will have the same student number.

Relationships

To illustrate how information is used within the system, entities need to be linked together to form a relationship. The relationship between two entities could be misinterpreted, so labels are attached at the beginning and the end of the relationship link to inform parties exactly what the nature of the relationship is (Figure 3.41).

Figure 3.41   *Identifying entity relationships*

Degree

There are three possible degrees of any entity relationship:

1. One to one, 1:1, which denotes that only one occurrence of each entity is used by the adjoining entity (Figure 3.42).

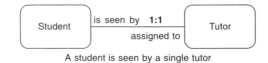

A student is seen by a single tutor

Figure 3.42   *Example of a 1:1 relationship*

2. One to many, 1 : M, which denotes that a single occurrence of one entity is linked to more than one occurrence of the adjoining entity (Figure 3.43).
3. Many to many, M : N, which denotes that many occurrences of one entity are linked to more than one occurrence of the adjoining entity (Figure 3.44).

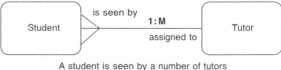

A student is seen by a number of tutors

Figure 3.43 *Example of a 1:M relationship*

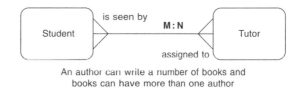

An author can write a number of books and
books can have more than one author

Figure 3.44 *Example of a M:N relationship*

Although M:N relationships are common, the notation of linking two entities directly is adjusted and a link entity is used to connect the two (Figure 3.45).

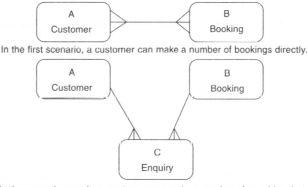

In the first scenario, a customer can make a number of bookings directly.

In the second scenario, a customer can make a number of enquiries that lead to a booking, while bookings result from a number of enquiries made by customers.

Figure 3.45 *Adding a link entity*

Optionality

There are two status types given to a relationship; first, those that definitely happen or exist, and secondly, those that may happen or exist. This second status is referred to as 'optional'.

A dashed rather than a solid link denotes optionality in a relationship (Figure 3.46).

In this scenario a customer may or may not decide to make a booking. If they do the booking will definitely belong to/be made by a customer.

Figure 3.46 *Optionality*

Logical data structures and data flow diagrams are examples of modelling tools that are used in SSADM to illustrate the analysis and design stages of a system build.

Flowcharts

Flowcharting is a traditional design tool that is still used today. System flowcharts detail the flow of information through an entire information system using specific symbols to characterize sequences and processes, as shown in Figure 3.47.

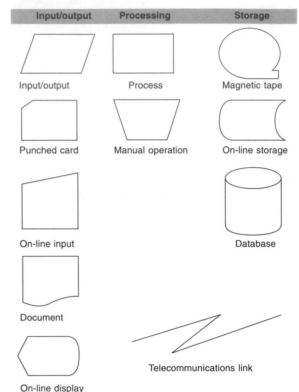

Figure 3.47   *Flowchart tools*

CASE

Computer-aided software engineering (CASE) tools reduce the amount of repetitive work by automating the steps involved with software and systems development. CASE tools can include project planning tools that assist in cost estimation and project scheduling, project management tools that assist in monitoring the progress of the development project, documentation tools, prototyping and simulation tools, and programming tools.

3.8 Security, health and safety

There are a number of health, safety and security issues to consider when working with computer and information systems. To protect organizations, users of information systems, and the general public (about whom information may be stored), a number of measures and guidelines have been introduced.

Data

There are a number of issues surrounding the use, storage and transfer of data on computer systems. These issues include data security and data protection. Although these two issues are closely related, data security examines the area of physical security issues and data protection looks at the measures that have been introduced to protect consumer data.

Keeping data secure can be quite difficult because of the environment in which users work and the levels of user access requirements. With the movement towards a totally networked environment, promoting a culture of 'sharing' the issue of data security is even more important and should be addressed at a number of levels (Figure 3.48).

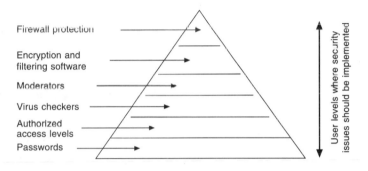

Figure 3.48 *Levels of security*

Security measures need to be integrated at each user level within an organization. The security measures should not be confined to a certain level; Figure 3.49 reflects on an organizational scale that should be implemented and the scale of implementation.

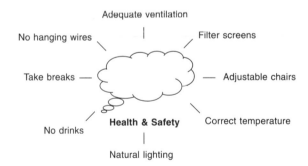

Figure 3.49 *Health and safety considerations*

The actual protection of data can be resolved quite easily by introducing good practice measures such as backing up all data to a secondary storage device. Data protection is also covered more widely under certain Acts, such as the Data Protection Act 1984.

Data Protection Act 1984 and 1988

The Data Protection Act applies to the processing of data and information by a computer source. The Act places obligations on people who collect, process and store personal records and data about consumers or customers, and is based upon a set of principles that bind a user or an organization to following a set of procedures offering assurances that data is kept secure. The main principles include:

- personal data should be processed fairly and lawfully
- personal data should be held only for one or more specified and lawful purposes
- personal data held should not be disclosed in any way incompatible to the specified and lawful purpose
- personal data held should be adequate and relevant, not excessive to the purpose or purposes
- personal data kept should be accurate and up-to-date
- personal data should not be retained for any longer than necessary
- individuals should be informed about personal data stored and should be entitled to have access to it, and if appropriate have such data corrected or erased
- security measures should ensure that no unauthorized access to, alteration to or disclosure or destruction of personal data is permitted, and protection against accidental loss or destruction of personal data is given.

Computer Misuse Act 1990

The Computer Misuse Act was enforced to address the increased threat of hackers trying to gain unauthorized access to a computer system. Prior to this Act there was minimal protection and difficulties in prosecuting, because theft of data by hacking was not considered to be deprivation to the owner. There are a number of offences and penalties under this Act, these include the following.

Offences

- Unauthorised access – an attempt by a hacker to gain unauthorized access to a computer system
- Unauthorized access with the intention of committing another offence – on gaining access a hacker will then continue with the intent of committing a further crime
- Unauthorized modification of data or programs – introducing viruses to a computer system is a criminal offence; guilt is assessed by the level of intent to cause disruption, or to impair the processes of a computer system.

Penalties

- Unauthorized access – imprisonment for up to six months and/ or a fine of up to £2000
- Unauthorized access with the intention of committing another offence – imprisonment for up to five years and/or an unlimited fine
- Unauthorized modification – imprisonment for up to five years and/or an unlimited fine.

Health and safety

General consideration should also be given to the working environment of users of computer and information systems. Issues covering environmental, social and practical aspects of working conditions are shown in Figure 3.49.

Users should work in an environment that has adequate ventilation and natural lighting; the temperature should also be suitable for a computing environment, bearing in mind that computers give out large quantities of heat.

Computers should have sufficient support peripherals (such as filter screens) to minimize glare, and height-adjustable chairs should be available to users.

When working at a computer, no food or drink should be consumed in case of spillages.

Wires should always be packed away in appropriate conduits and not left trailing across the floor.

The best measures for health and safety in the workplace are to use common sense and to adhere by standard ways of working. Organizations also offer guidelines and procedures for maintaining good working practice.

Unit 4 Introduction to software development

In general, software for computers is produced from a **high-level language**. Assembly language is a **low-level language** and, as described in Unit 2, each line in the code translates almost exactly to an op-code in the resulting **machine code**.

It is considered that machine code is a **first-generation language** as the original machines were programmed using straight machine code. As this is slow and very prone to errors, assemblers were produced to make life easier. Assemblers are considered to be **second-generation languages**. **Third-generation languages** use text that looks a little more like plain language; this is converted by a relatively complex system into machine code. Remember, whatever the language used to write software, the code executed by the processor is machine code. Always!

Well-known early third-generation languages are Fortran (FORmula TRANslation), COBOL (COmmon Business Oriented Language) and BASIC (Beginners All-purpose Symbolic Instruction Code). All predictions that these will be outclassed by more modern languages have so far proved to be inaccurate! The more modern third-generation languages are C, C++ and Java – very powerful languages, but not ideally suited to the beginner programmer. All these have been designed to suit given classes of problem; Fortran to solve more mathematical problems, COBOL for business applications etc. Pascal is a third-generation language that was specifically designed to teach the ideas of programming, and it has little or no commercial use. It does allow the development of programming ideas in a more formal way than BASIC, and this formal way is favoured in the development of larger projects. Whilst BASIC is a general-purpose language, it allows some sloppy programming practices that lead to bugs that are hard to find.

Some of the Pascal language files in this section can be downloaded from http://www.bh.com/companions/0750656840.

Bugs

Bugs are program errors. There is a nice story about why they are called 'bugs': it is said that Grace Murray Hopper, the designer of COBOL, first used the term to describe the removal of a moth (a 'bug') from a Mark II Aiken Relay Calculator, a primitive computer. There is a problem with this story: it is probably not true! At the very least, the story may have a *bug* in it! See http://www.jamesshuggins.com/ h/tek1/first_computer_bug.htm

---

Pascal

ALGOL is a programming language that was in use in the 1960s on large commercial machines, before the age of PCs. ALGOL was written by a team of people that included Professor Niklaus Wirth from the Swiss Federal Institute of Technology.

In order to achieve a better language that encouraged well-**structured** and well-organized programs, Wirth designed **Pascal** in about 1971. From the start, it was intended as a teaching language. Pascal added the capability to define new data types out of simpler existing types, and supported dynamic data structures – i.e. data structures that can change while a program is running.

4.1 How does a third-generation language work?

In Pascal, you can do a task (called **something** here; it does not matter what it is) ten times using the code:

```
for counter:=1 to 10 do {something};
```

Table 4.1 shows the same problem written in Pascal, assembler and machine code.

Table 4.1 *Simple program*

Pascal	for counter:=1 to 10 do {something};
Assembler	L1: mov al,1 {something} dec al cmp al,10 jne L1
Machine code as hex bytes	B0 01FE C8 3C 0A 75 F8
Machine code in binary	10110000 00000001 11111110 11001000 00111100 00001010 01110101 11111000

By reading the Pascal, even non-programmers can guess what is happening. The assembler code is not so easy to read and the machine code is nearly impossible unless you remember all the hex bytes. As for the binary . . .! It is all the same problem; count to 10.

Suppose the {something} was a task that had already been written, i.e. it was available in machine code. Assuming the typed code has been stored on disk, the business of converting a Pascal program is now split into the following steps:

1. Check that all the words and symbols in the Pascal code are correct, i.e. 'for' is not spelt 'four', the ':=' sign is not just a '=' on its own etc.

2. Make sure that all the words and symbols are in a meaningful order.
3. **Compile** the Pascal code into what looks like assembler code. This code is called **Object Code**.
4. **Link** this code with the pre-written code, in this case, the code that did {something}.
5. Write this linked code as a finished executable file. This is the finished **machine code**.

Notice that when the Pascal is converted to the assembler-like code, it does not 'know' how to do the task called {something}. If, for instance, the code for {something} needed to read a file of data, the Pascal code does not 'know' how to open and read a file. This ability is contained within prewritten **library files** that are supplied with the Pascal **Compiler**, i.e. the compiler converts the Pascal code and then a separate process **links** this code with the prewritten library code. In the past this **linker** software was supplied separately from the compiler; in the case of the Pascal system you are likely to use, the linking stage is largely hidden.

In this way, library files of object code can be written in (almost) any language, so providing a means of re-using software.

4.2 First steps in Pascal programming

You will need a compiler!

Pascal compilers

Turbo Pascal is a common Pascal compiler supplied by Borland that runs under DOS. Unfortunately, the version that runs under Windows has been discontinued. Borland Turbo Pascal version 7.0 is still available, but an **almost** identical version is available free of charge. It is called Free Pascal, and is available from http://www.freepascal.org/fpc.html to suit most operating systems. For the purposes of this book the Free Pascal version is preferred, as it comes with good quality disk-based help files and, unlike Turbo Pascal, is available for a range of operating systems. If you need Borland Turbo Pascal 7.0, see details on http://www.borland.com/pascal/

The stages in producing an executable program using Pascal are:

- edit the program text using a text editor
- compile the code
- link with library files
- load and execute the program for testing.

In both Free Pascal and Borland Turbo Pascal, all these stages are built into what they call an **Integrated Development Environment**, or **IDE**. Whilst this makes program development easier, you should not forget what is going on 'behind the scenes', i.e. the generation of machine code to suit the processor and operating system of your computer.

The Pascal IDE

Refer to your local centre to find out how to start the software. For a default installation of Pascal, under Windows, open a DOS window and type fp (or tp if using Borland). You should get the **IDE** as shown in Figure 4.1. This presents the main menu options.

Figure 4.1 *Free Pascal IDE, identical with Turbo Pascal*

To create a new program, press ALT then F for File, and choose N for New. You should get the screen shown in Figure 4.2.

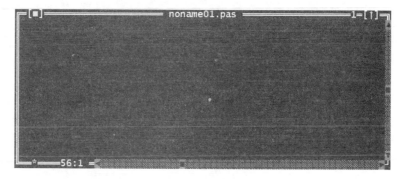

Figure 4.2 *A program window ready to enter Pascal text*

Now continue with the program codes given below.

Program 4.1

Type in the following program code, and remember to save it as 'prog4_1' by pressing the F2 key.

```
program prog4_1(input,output);
begin
  writeln('Hello World');
end.
```

Points to note
1. The first line finishes with a ';' character as does the third line.
2. The last line has a '.' after the word **end**.
3. The program is called prog4.1, but the top line shows it as prog4_1 because a '.' is not allowed in the program name.
4. The third line is indented using the TAB key.

So far, nothing has happened beyond editing and saving the code; the IDE has acted only as a **text editor**. The next stage is to compile and link your code to make it executable. Do this from the IDE by pressing ALT and C then choosing C for **Compile** (or just pressing the hot key ALT F9). You should get 'Compile successful, press any key'. Remember, the linking stage has been hidden by the IDE. If the compilation was successful, you now have an executable program. To run it, press ALT and R and choose **Run**. The screen will blink as the program runs then jumps right back to the IDE, so fast you cannot see your output! To actually see the output screen, press ALT F5. To get back to the IDE, press ALT F5 again. In the IDE, you can **toggle** the user output screen with ALT F5 at anytime.

The output screen should look something like:

```
Free Pascal IDE Version 0.9.1
Hello World
```

This is probably the most famous program in computing. Known as 'hello world', it is used to present almost every programming language available.

If things go wrong

Typical errors are forgetting the ';' or the '.', or spelling the words incorrectly

If you have made one of these errors, you will get a compiler error that says 'Compile failed' and then gives you a suggestion as to what has gone wrong. **Warning!** The compiler does its best to help, but sometimes gets it wrong! **Take compiler error messages as a guide only**. The error message will be in a new window.

Look at the top right-hand side of any window and you will see a number like 1 or 2 etc. You can always activate a window by pressing ALT and that number. Jump back to the window with your code in it, correct the error, and re-compile and run. You can close a window by clicking on the small square at the top left, as shown in Figure 4.3.

Figure 4.3 *'Compile failed' window*

Program 4.2

Now try a slightly longer program:

```
program prog4_2(input,output);
var counter:integer;
```

```
begin
for counter:=1 to 10 do
  writeln('I love computing');
end.
```

Start a new program with ALT F then New, and type in this new program. Press F2 to save it as prog4_2. Compile it, run it, then look at the output screen. You should have 'I love computing' ten times on the screen, together with the output of the last program.

To get rid of the previous output screen, first add the lines:

```
uses crt;
```

and

```
clrscr;
```

as in the listing for program 4_3 below.

Program 4.3

Now try:

```
program prog4_3(input,output);
uses crt; {adds a library file containing
  monitor control routines}
var counter:integer;

begin
clrscr; {clear the screen}
for counter:=1 to 10 do
  writeln('I love computing');
end.
```

Re-save it, re-compile and run it. Your output screen should now show just the output from this program; ten repeats of 'I love computing'.

The line **clrscr** is short for Clear Screen. The line **uses crt** adds a **unit**, in this case the crt unit. After compiling the code, the system links with a library file. This crt unit is an additional library file that contains the prewritten code that 'knows' how to clear the monitor screen.

> CRT is an old name that refers to a cathode ray tube, the device now called a monitor or VDU.

Points to note

1. Each Pascal **statement** ends with a ';' character (there are a few exceptions to this).
2. You can put a new line, tabs, spaces etc. in a Pascal statement to make it more readable. These are known as **white space** characters, and are ignored by the compiler.
3. Text inside { } brackets (often called braces) is also ignored by the compiler. They are used for comments in the program code. It is considered very good practice to put plenty of comments in your code. This makes it easier to understand your code, especially when looking at it some time after you

wrote it, on if someone else needs to understand it. If you work in a programming team, your colleagues will thank you for good comments.

4. The program uses TAB characters for indentation, again to make the program easy to read.

Consider the same program 4.3 presented below:

```
program prog4_3(input,output); uses crt; {adds a
library file containing monitor control routines} var
counter: integer; begin clrscr; {clear the screen}
for counter:=1 to 10 do writeln('I love
computing');end.
```

It will compile as before, but is much harder to read!

Having run these programs, look in the file system directory where you saved them. You should find files called prog4_1.exe, prog4_2.exe etc. These are the executable machine code programs, the files that are run by the system to produce your output.

Note on program layout style

You will see many references in this book to indentation, white space, and adding comments to make your program easier to read. You may find that longer programs get so indented that lines run off the right-hand side of the paper. If this is likely, use the options menu and choose environment, then editor. Change the tab size to 4 instead of the standard 8.

Another layout feature is the **case** of the reserved words and identifiers; upper case letters are CAPITALS, lower case are small letters. Pascal is not **case conscious**, i.e. it will react in the same way with WRITELN or writeln or Writeln. In some Pascal works you will see all the reserved words and identifiers in upper case. In this book all the code is presented in lower case in readiness for C/C++. These languages **are** case conscious, and (nearly) all the code is in lower case. For this reason, it is considered far better to become familiar with good layout to show **program structure**. If you are more comfortable using upper case for reserved words and identifiers, then you should do it consistently. Some examinations in programming require consistency rather than either upper or lower case code.

> In the old way of printing, when individual lead characters were set by hand into a frame, the capital letters were stored in a box (or case), that was above the case that stored the smaller letters. It has become standard language to refer to letters as upper or lower case according to where they were stored in the printing works!

4.3 Elements of Pascal 1

In this section are presented some elements of Pascal that will be used to develop the next set of programs. The point of the Software Development unit is to understand programs and how they are developed; not to master Pascal as a subject. For this reason, no attempt has been made to provide a comprehensive guide to Pascal, it is simply a means to an end.

It is strongly recommended that you obtain a copy of Free Pascal from http://www.freepascal.org/fpc.html, as the documentation that comes with it contains a great deal that is helpful. In particular, a file is supplied called **fpctoc.htm**, which is placed in the \doc directory inside wherever the software is installed (C:\pp by default). If you open this file in your web browser and follow the **reference** link, much useful information will be found.

Elements introduced here are:

- identifiers, reserved words
- variables of type: integer, real, string and char
- predefined functions and procedures. write, writeln, readln, val, trunc
- program structure: repeat..until
- data validation
- white space and indentation.

Identifiers and reserved words

Pascal uses **identifiers**. These identify something that has meaning. For instance, the identifier **writeln** used in the first program is the identifier to use when you wish to output to the screen followed by a **new line** character. When you write a Pascal program you can define your own identifiers; the first is usually the program name such as prog4_3. You must conform to the Pascal rules when naming identifiers, i.e.

- no spaces
- no punctuation marks, all characters must be letters, numbers or "_" (used to look like a space)
- the first character must be a letter
- you must not use one that is a Pascal **reserved word**; in Free Pascal, the complete list of these is: *absolute, and, array, asm, begin, break, case, const, constructor, continue, destructor, div, do, downto, else, end, file, for, function, goto, if, implementation, in, inherited, inline, interface, label, mod, nil, not, object, of, on, operator, or, packed, procedure, program, record, repeat, self, set, shl, shr, string, then, to, type, unit, until, uses, var, while, with, xor, dispose, exit, false, new, true*
- you can re-use identifiers such as **writeln** but it would be a little silly because you would not then be able to use the writeln feature of the language!

Therefore the following are allowed:

- tax
- income
- person_age
- counter
- list8

but the following will be thrown out by the compiler:

- 8list (the first character is not a letter)
- person_age?
- tax%

and you will get a compiler error such as the one shown in Figure 4.4.

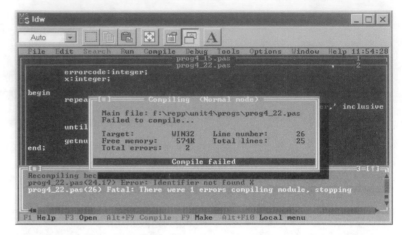

Figure 4.4   *Bad identifier*

Variables

Make sure you understand the section concerned with binary and floating point numbers (Unit 2) before you read this. Pascal uses both these methods for storing numbers. It can also store type **string**. Although not part of the original Pascal definition, this is now well understood to be part of every Pascal implementation. A string is simply a set of ASCII characters. Variables of type char are just single ASCII characters.

A variable is a named value that must be of a given **type**. Pascal supports a number of variable types, but three are introduced here, type **integer**, stored as a simple **binary number**, type **real**, stored as a **floating point number** and type **string** a set of ASCII characters. Tables 4.2 and 4.3 show the range of both numeric types.

It is not important for you to remember the exact limitations, but it is **very important** that you realize that every variable has limitations; integers are limited in range and have no fractions, real (floating point) types have a limited range and are not always accurate.

In situations where you cannot have superscripts to show powers, you can write 5E6 to mean 5×10^6, or 5 with 6 zeros = 5 000 000. Pascal uses this notation; the E stands for Exponent. For instance, variables of type real can store numbers from 5.0×10^{-324} to 1.7×10^{308} but only to 15 or 16 significant digits. Type integer can store numbers from −32768 to +32767, (-2^{15} to ($2^{15} - 1$)), a 16-bit number with the first bit used to denote + or −.

Different implementations of Pascal support variables differ in detail. The ones supported by Free Pascal are shown in Tables 4.2 and 4.3.

Table 4.2   *Free Pascal supported real types*

Type	Range	Significant digits	Size in bytes
Single	1.5E −45 to 3.4E38	7–8	4
Real	5.0E −324 to 1.7E308	15–16	8
Double	5.0E −324 to 1.7E308	15–16	8
Extended	1.9E −4951 to 1.1E4932	19–20	10
Comp	−2E64 + 1 to 2E63 − 1	19–20	8

Table 4.3 *Free Pascal supported integer types*

Type	Range	Size in bytes
Byte	0 to 255	1
Shortint	−128 to 127	1
Integer	−32768 to 32767	2
Word	0 to 65535	2
Longint	−2147483648 to 2147483647	4
Cardinal	0 to 4294967295	4
Int64	−9223372036854775808 to	
	9223372036854775807	8
QWord	0 to 18446744073709551615	8

To use a variable, you must first **declare** it with a **statement** like:

```
var counter:integer;
```

Points to note

1. The whole statement ends with a ';' character.
2. The reserved word var is used to denote that this statement declares a variable.
3. The identifier, called counter and chosen by the programmer, obeys the rules for identifiers above.

You can declare several variables in the same line as long as they are all of the same type and the identifiers are separated with commas. For example:

```
var totaltax, taxable_pay, salary:real;
```

Points to note in program 4.3

1. The first line is (nearly) always the same, <program> <your choice of name> <(input, output)>. Both Free Pascal and Turbo Pascal allow you leave out the whole line or just the '(input, output)' part.
2. The second part of the program contains all the **declarations**.
3. The last part of the program contains the **main program block**, with **begin** at the start and **end**. at the end. The word end. will only be found as the very last word in a Pascal program; the word end; (with a ; not a .) will be used many times.

So the structure for a simple Pascal program is:

```
Program yourname(input, output);
Declarations
Main program block
```

Pre-defined Pascal functions and procedures

Pascal comes supplied with a number of pre-defined functions and procedures. A **function** is some code that does a job, then gives you an answer in return that you can assign to something. For example, the **trunc** function converts a real type to an integer type; it does the conversion and gives you an answer. It could be used like this:

```
y=trunc(x);
```

where the answer is stored in variable y. A **procedure** is a code that does a job but does not give you an answer – for instance, the **writeln** procedure outputs data but does not return a value.

The Pascal functions and procedures **write, writeln, readln, val** and **trunc** presented here will be used to develop the next few programs.

The procedures **write** and **writeln** both output data, usually to the screen (unless you tell them to output elsewhere). The difference is that writeln outputs a new line at the finish, and write does not. You can put a whole line of **variables** or **constants** in a write or writeln statement; Table 4.4 provides some examples.

Table 4.4 *Examples of Pascal procedures*

write(x);	Outputs the variable x
write(x,y);	Outputs both the variables x and y with no space between
writeln('Total Tax= ', tax);	Outputs the **string constant** 'Total Tax= ' then the value of the variable *tax*. It will only output the space inside the ' ' marks
writeln('Total Tax= ', tax);	The same as above; the extra spaces before the variable *tax* are ignored. They are **white space** characters

The **readln** function reads or inputs data (usually from the keyboard unless you tell it otherwise), but waits for the **enter key** to be pressed at the end of the input. The enter key generates a new line.

The **val** procedure is used to convert a **string** to a numerical type, which can be of type real or type integer.

The **trunc** function is used to convert a real type to an integer type by cutting off the fractional part of the real and storing the returning number.

Program 4.4, using some of the above functions and procedures

```
program prog4_4(input,output);
var  x:integer;
     name:string;
begin
write('What is your name? ');
readln(name);
write('Hello ',name, ' now please give me a number with
no fractions ');
readln(x);
writeln('Thanks, you answered ',x);
end.
```

When you run this program, it simply asks your name with a readln procedure and then **echos** the numerical answer you give at the readln(x); line.

Run the program again, but this time type in a number with a decimal point. The program should crash, with an error message similar to the one in Figure 4.5.

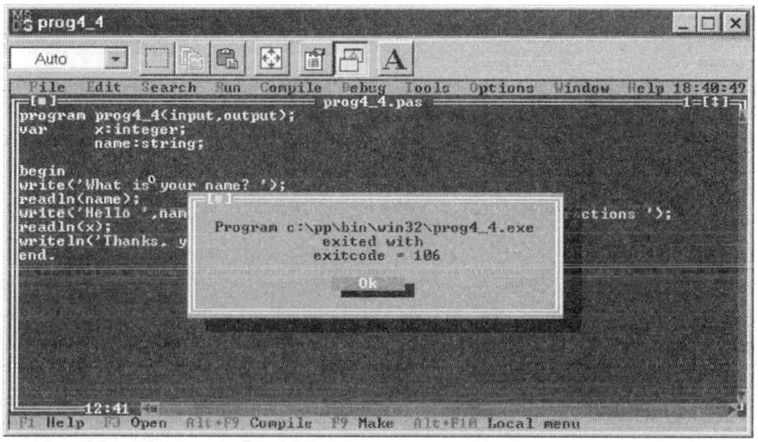

Figure 4.5 *Input error*

Points to note

1. The program crashes if you type a value with a decimal point, as Pascal interprets this as a **floating point** input. This is not the correct variable type for the variable x, which is an integer.
2. Pascal is said to be a **strongly typed** language, and this is one aspect of strong typing; it means the rules about variable types are enforced. Some programming languages, notably those based on BASIC, do not enforce data typing as strongly as does Pascal.
3. If you run program 4.4 and type 'two' instead of '2', it will crash again for similar reasons; 'two' is a **string**, a set of ASCII characters.

Program 4.5, a way around the program crashing

Type in:

```
program prog4_5(input,output);
var  errorcode:integer;
  y:real;
  name,numberstr:string;

begin
write('What is your name? ');
readln(name);
write('Hello ',name,' now please give me a number ');
readln(numberstr);
val(numberstr,y,errorcode);
writeln('Thanks, you answered ',y:0:3);
end.
```

Points to note

1. The programs are getting longer and harder to read, as there is little in the way of white space characters.

2. The required input, a number, is now achieved using a **string** type. This will prevent the program from crashing if the user types in an inappropriate value. Try running the program and entering different kinds of clearly wrong data, such as 'two' or 2.A. In these cases, the program outputs 0 as the value. This is not accurate, but is better than allowing the program to crash.
3. The code :0:3 in the last line specifies the output format of the real variable y. This is covered below.

Repeat of Program 4.5, clearer layout

The following program 4.5 has more white space, better indentation and comments and is therefore easier to read.

```
program prog4_5(input,output);
{start of declaration section}

var  errorcode:integer;
     y:real;
     name,numberstr:string;
{end of declaration section}

{start of main program block}

begin
     write('What is your name? ');
     readln(name);

     write('Hello ',name,' now please give me a number ');
     readln(numberstr);

     {now convert the input string with the val procedure}
     {errorcode will contain a non zero value}
     {if the conversion fails}
     val(numberstr,y,errorcode);

     writeln('Thanks, you answered ',y:0:3);
end.
```

Points to note

1. The text now has better comments.
2. The indentation clearly marks the start and end of the main program block. As your programs get longer and more complex, you will find that a small amount of effort taken in setting out the program will be of great benefit.
3. The val procedure requires three **parameters**; the first is the string to be converted to a number, the second is the variable that will hold that number, and the last is an error code. This will contain zero if all goes well, or a non-zero number indicating where in the string the conversion failed. The next program (below) will make use of this.

Program 4.5, an improvement on the last program

```
program prog4_5(input,output);
{start of declaration section}
```

```
var errorcode:integer;
    y:real;
    name,numberstr:string;
{end of declaration section}

{start of main program block}

begin
  write('What is your name? ');
  readln(name);

    repeat
      write('Hello ',name,' now please give me a number ');
      readln(numberstr);

      {now convert the input string with the val procedure}
      {errorcode will contain a non zero value if the }
      {conversion fails}
      val(numberstr,y,errorcode);
    until errorcode=0;

  writeln('Thanks, you answered ',y:0:3);
end.
```

The program now has a **repeat..until loop**. This will cause the program to go on and on executing all the code inside the words **repeat** and **until** until the **condition** specified after the word until is true. In this case, the variable **errorcode** will only be 0 when the conversion to a number has worked, i.e. the input of a number was valid. This is an example of **data validation**. Consider most (not all!) commercial programs. Will they crash if you make an invalid input, or give an error message? Program crashes are a Bad Thing, while error messages should be seen as useful.

Points to note

1. The indentation makes the position and meaning of the repeat..until loop much clearer and easier to see.
2. The input of the numerical value is now much more reliable, as it will accept as input any keyboard characters; errors are **trapped** by the code.

Program 4.6, an addition to the last program using the trunc procedure

```
program prog4_6(input,output);
{start of declaration section}

var errorcode:integer;
    y:real;
    name,numberstr:string;
{end of declaration section}

{start of main program block}

begin
  write('What is your name? ');
  readln(name);
```

```
repeat
    write('Hello ',name,' now please give me a number ');
  readln(numberstr);

  {now convert the input string with the val procedure}
  {errorcode will contain a non zero value if the }
    {conversion fails}
  val(numberstr,y,errorcode);
until errorcode=0;

writeln('Thanks, you answered ',y:0:3);

  writeln('The integer part of you number was ',trunc(y));
end.
```

Points to note

1. The final program in this section, program 4.6, introduces two more ideas. First, it uses the trunc function to convert a real type into an integer type. Second, use is made of Pascal's ability to have a function or expression as a parameter for a procedure. The example here is the last writeln:

    ```
    writeln('The integer part of you number was ',trunc(y));
    ```

    The conversion using **trunc** is itself a parameter for the **writeln** procedure.
2. It could have been done in two lines like this

    ```
    x:=trunc(y)
    writeln('The integer part of you number was ',x);
    ```

    providing x was an integer type.

Formatting numbers in write or writeln statements

When Pascal executes a statement like

```
writeln('Your tax= ',tax);
```

it uses the exponential format for variables of type real unless you tell it otherwise.

In this example, if the variable tax had the value 13.34, Pascal would output 1.33400000000000E+001, which means 1.334×10^1. If the value was 1344, the output would be 1.33400000000000E+003, or 1.334×10^3.

If you want a normal decimal output, use the **format specifier** for type real immediately after the variable name, as in

```
writeln('Your tax= ',tax:0:2);
```

The :0 means 'use any number of screen columns', the :2 means 'use two decimal places'.

If you had used the format specifier :8:4, it would have meant use eight screen columns and four decimal places.

You can use a **format specifier** with type integer as well but with only one part, as in

```
writeln('Your service in whole years= ',service:5);
```

This will output the integer service using five screen columns.

Elements of Pascal 1: Practice

The following programs use only the elements introduced in the first part of this section, **Elements of Pascal 1**.
The elements introduced were:

- identifiers, reserved words
- variables of type: integer, real, string and char
- predefined functions and procedures: write, writeln, readln, val, trunc
- program structure: repeat..until
- data validation
- white space and indentation.

Now write programs to suit the tasks below.

Program 4.7

Calculate the area of a rectangle. Ask the user for the length of each side and output the result to two decimal places. Do not put any data validation in place.

Possible answer

```
program prog4_7(input, output);
var side1,side2,area:real;

begin
  {get the size of the rectangle }
  write('Please type the length of side 1 ');
  readln(side1);
  write('and now the length of side 2 ');
  readln(side2);

  {now calculate the answer}
  area:=side1*side2;

  {now output the answer }
  writeln('The area = ',area:0:2);

end.
```

Points to note

1. Format specifier :0:2 to give any number of screen columns and two decimal places.
2. Sensible variable names.

Program 4.8

Calculate the foreign currency equivalent to UK pounds. Ask the user for the exchange rate and the amount to be converted. Do not put any data validation in place.

Possible answer

```
program prog4_8(input, output);
var amount,exchangerate:real;

begin
  write('What is the exchange rate? ');
  readln(exchangerate);
  write('What amount of currency to convert? ');
  readln(amount);

  {now ouput the result}
  write(amount:0:2, ' equals ',amount* exchangerate:0:2
                              ,' pounds');

end.
```

Points to note

1. Statements can be split across lines with any number of white space characters.
2. Use of write instead of writeln when getting user input.
3. The final writeln can contain the calculation.

Program 4.9

Calculate the area of a circle given the formula Area = 3.14159 × diameter × diameter. Do not put any data validation in place.

Possible answer

```
program prog4_9(input, output);
var diameter,area:real;

begin
  write('What is the diameter? ');
  readln(diameter);

  {calculate the result}
  area:=3.14159*diameter*diameter;

  {now output the result}
  writeln('When diameter= ',diameter:0:2, ', area= ',
  area:0:2);
end.
```

Points to note

1. Inside the statement `writeln('When diameter= ', diameter:0:2, ', area= ',area:0:2);` there is a comma **inside** the ' ' marks to be output.
2. Format specifier :0:2.

Program 4.10

Calculate the temperature in degrees F given the formula degrees C = F − 32 × 5/9. Be careful about precedence levels when using subtraction and multiplication. Do not put any data validation in place.

Possible answer

```
program prog4_10;
var degreesF, degreesC:real;

begin
  write('What is the temperature in degrees F ');
  readln(degreesF);

  {calculate the answer}
  degreesC:=(degreesF-32)*5/9;

  writeln(degreesF:0:2, 'F = ',degreesC:0:2, 'C ');

end.
```

Points to note

1. The (input, output) has been left off in the first line. Although not standard Pascal, it is normal practice in both Free Pascal and Turbo Pascal.
2. Use of brackets to ensure the subtraction occurs before the multiplication.

Programs 4.11 to 4.14

Add some data validation to all four programs 4.7 to 4.10 to prevent the programs crashing if the user types inappropriate data.

Possible answers: Program 4.11, modified program 4.7

```
program prog4_11(input, output);
var side1,side2,area:real;
  errorcode:integer;
  inputstr:string;

begin
  {get the size of the rectangle }
  repeat
    write('Please type the length of side 1 ');
    readln(inputstr);
    val(inputstr,side1,errorcode);
  until errorcode=0;

  repeat
    write('and now the length of side 2 ');
    readln(inputstr);
    val(inputstr,side2,errorcode);
  until errorcode=0;

  { now calculate the answer}

  area:=side1*side2;

  {now output the answer }
  writeln('The area = ',area:0:2);
end.
```

Possible answers: Program 4.12, modified program 4.8

```
program prog4_12(input, output);
var amount,exchangerate:real;
  inputstr:string;
  errorcode:integer;

begin
  repeat
    write('What is the exchange rate? ');
    readln(inputstr);
    val(inputstr,exchangerate,errorcode);
  until errorcode=0;

  repeat
    write('What amount of currency to convert? ');
    readln(inputstr);
    val(inputstr,amount,errorcode);
  until errorcode=0;

  {now output the result}
  write(amount:0:2, ' equals ', amount*exchangerate:0:2,
  'pounds');

end.
```

Possible answers: Program 4.13, modified program 4.9

```
program prog4_9(input, output);
var  diameter,area:real;
  inputstr:string;
  errorcode:integer;

begin
  repeat
    write('What is the diameter? ');
    readln(inputstr);
    val(inputstr,diameter,errorcode);
  until errorcode=0;

  {calculate the result}
  area:=3.14159*diameter*diameter;

  {now output the result}
  writeln('When diameter= ',diameter:0:2, ', area= ',
  area:0:2);
end.
```

Possible answers: Program 4.14, modified program 4.10

```
program prog4_14;
var degreesF, degreesC:real;
  inputstr:string;
  errorcode:integer;

begin
  repeat
    write('What is the temperature in degrees F ');
    readln(inputstr);
```

```
        val(inputstr,degreesF,errorcode);
     until errorcode=0;

     {calculate the answer}
     degreesC:=(degreesF-32)*5/9;

     writeln(degreesF:0:2, 'F = ',degreesC:0:2, 'C ');

end.
```

Points to note, programs 4.11 to 4.14

1. The data validation is basically the same in all cases; each write/readln pair of statements is enclosed inside a repeat..until loop, the data is read as a string and converted.
2. You could add uses crt; and clrscr; as found in program 4.3 to clear the screen for each program.

4.4 Elements of Pascal 2

Below are some more elements of Pascal that will be used to develop the next set of programs.

- assignment
- expressions and operators
- constants
- if..then..else statement and boolean variables
- compound statements
- case statement
- for..to/downto statement
- while..do statement
- repeat..until statement.

Variable assignment

In **Elements of Pascal 1,** assignment was used to give a variable a name without explanation. Assignment effectively means 'store a value in a variable'. Unfortunately, the symbols used in many programming languages cause some confusion.

In Pascal, if you want the variable x to take on the value 12, you would write:

```
x:=12;
```

This **assignment statement** ends with a ';' in the usual way, and the assignment **operator** ':=' is used to tell the compiler to generate code to store the value 12 **in memory** at a **location** (or **address**) that Pascal remembers as 'x'.

The confusion comes in some languages (e.g. BASIC) where the same assignment task is written as x = 12, i.e. the '=' on its own is used. It would be better to write x⟸12, i.e. x with an arrow pointing to the left. It would then read easily as 'x is assigned the value 12' and there would not be confusion with the 'equals' sign. The problem is that standard keyboards do not generate a left pointing arrow; it is not an ASCII character. Although it works on some machines it is not standard (the S in ASCII stands for Standard).

The problem gets worse when you consider a very common operation, adding 1 to a variable. In Pascal, this can be written as x:=x+1; clearly x cannot equal x + 1. When you read Pascal programs and see an assignment, it is best to say 'x is assigned', not 'x equals'.

Assigning a value to a variable

When Pascal assigns a value to a variable, it must do two things.

1. It must 'know' where to store it in memory. During compilation, when Pascal comes across a declaration statement like

   ```
   var x:integer;
   ```

   it finds 2 bytes of space in memory (2 bytes for a 16-bit integer), then 'remembers' where that place is.
2. When an assignment is required, the value is store in the correct location.

It would generate code something like

```
MOV [SI], AX
```

assuming the value 12 is in the AX register and the SI register already **points** to the address of the variable x.

The main point to understand is that the value 12 gets **stored in memory** at a **location** (or **address**) that Pascal remembers as 'x'.

A variable can be assigned values from more than simple constants (see Table 4.5).

Table 4.5 *Assigning values*

x:=12;	Simple assignment of a constant 12
x:=y;	Simple assignment of another variable. Because Pascal is **strongly typed**, the assigned variable must be compatible with x within the Pascal rules, i.e. integer types, real types etc. but not mixed
x:=y+12;	x is assigned the value of an **expression**, i.e. a piece of code that must be evaluated before assignment takes place
x:=(salary-tax)*taxrate;	x is assigned the value of a more complex **expression**
x:=trunc(y);	x is assigned the value of a **function**
x:=trunc(tax)+ trunc(taxallowance)/12;	x is assigned the value of an **expression** that contains a **function**

The value to the right of the assignment operator ':=' must evaluate to be type compatible with the variable. If x was of type integer, the following code would not compile:

```
x:=25.4*size_in_mm;
```

because the code will generate a type real result. If x were type real, there would be no problem.

Expressions and operators

An **expression** is a piece of code that must be evaluated before assignment takes place. You can use functions in expressions but not procedures; functions return a value that can be used in the expression, whereas procedures do not.

Expressions are evaluated according to normal rules of arithmetic, i.e. BoDMAS, which means Brackets of Divide Multiply Add Subtract. Ignoring the old word for multiply (of, because 7 **of** 6 = 42 the same as 7 × 6), the expression evaluator will:

- work out the values inside brackets first
- perform divisions and multiplications next
- then perform the additions and subtractions.

In fact it is a little more involved that that, but just remembering BoDMAS will help. The actual precedence (importance) of the operators is shown in Table 4.6, where the highest precedence comes first.

Table 4.6 *Precedence of operators*

Operator	Precedence	Category
Not, @	Highest (first)	Unary operators
* / div mod and shl shr	Second	Multiplying operators
+ − or xor	Third	Adding operators
< <> < > <= >=	Lowest (last)	Relational operators

The **operators** here are:

*	= multiply
/	= divide
div	= integer divide (no fractions or remainder)
mod	= remainder after integer divide
and	= logical or bitwise **and** operation
shl	= logical or bitwise shift left (effectively divides by two)
shr	= logical or bitwise shift right (effectively multiplies by two)
+	= add
−	= subtract
or	= logical or bitwise **or** operation
xor	= logical or bitwise **xor** operation
<	= less than
<>	= not equal to
>	= greater than
<=	= less than or equal to
>=	= greater than or equal to.

Constants

A very important aim is to make the program code easier to read. Pascal supports **constants** to help in this respect. A typical use for a constant is:

```
program demo(input, output);
const daysinyear=365;
var monthlysalary,annualsalary:real;

begin
  { some code left out for clarity }
  monthlysalary:=annualsalary / daysinyear;

  { the rest of the program left out for clarity }
end.
```

Points to note

1. The declaration of constants is usually before the declaration of variables.
2. If used throughout a long program, any change need only be made once, in the declaration.
3. If the use of constants makes the code easier to read and understand then you should use them; if not, leave them out.

If .. then ..else statement and boolean variables

The **if** statement is used to control what code is executed, e.g.

```
if (name='Fred') then writeln('Hello Fred');
```

The part between the **if** and the **then** must evaluate to **true** or **false**. It may be an expression or a **boolean** variable. A **boolean variable** is one that can be just true or false, nothing else.
   Typical code is:

```
if (salary>taxfreepay) then tax:=salary*taxrate;
```

where (salary>taxfreepay) has only the value **true** or **false**; the expression does not evaluate to a number. Either salary is greater than the taxfreepay or it is not. If the expression evaluates to false, the code on the right of the **then** reserved word is not executed.
   It is often useful to add the else clause to the if statement, for example:

```
if (age<16)
  then
    childsfare:=true
  else
    childsfare:=false;
```

Points to note

1. There is no ';' after the line `childsfare:=true` because the ';' character means **end of statement**.
2. The indentation and white space makes the code much easier to read.
3. The assignments are to a **boolean** variable but can be any valid Pascal statement.
4. The code after the *else* clause is only executed if the expression evaluates to false.

George Boole

George Boole was born on 2 November 1815 in Lincoln, Lincolnshire, England. He went to school in Lincoln, and by the age of 12 he had become very skilled at Latin – so much so that it provoked an argument. He translated an ode by the Latin poet Horace, and this was published by his proud father. His schoolmaster disputed that any 12-year-old could have written with such depth. The schoolmaster was wrong.

From the age of 16 Boole was an assistant teacher. He maintained his interest in languages and intended to enter the Church, but from 1835 he began to study mathematics on his own. He began publishing in the *Cambridge Mathematical Journal* and was awarded the Royal Medal from the Royal Society for his work on the solution of differential equations.

In 1849, Boole was appointed to the Chair of Mathematics at Queens College, Cork. He taught there for the rest of his life, gaining a reputation as an outstanding and dedicated teacher.

In 1854 he published *An investigation into the Laws of Thought, on Which are founded the Mathematical Theories of Logic and Probabilities*. Boole had reduced logic to simple algebra, and it began the algebra of logic called **Boolean algebra**.

He died on 8 December 1864 in Ballintemple, County Cork, Ireland, aged just 49.

Compound statements

A statement is one piece of code that ends with a ';' character. It is often required to 'join' several statements together to make them act as one. This is done with **begin** and **end**, as in the example below.

```
if (salary>taxfreepay) then
  begin
    writeln('Salary will be taxed');
    tax:=salary*taxrate;
  end;
```

If the expression after the **if** evaluates to true, both the statements here will be executed; they have become a **compound statement**. You can make many statements into a compound statement, but if you have too many it is probable that re-writing the code with a better structure will make it clearer and easier to read and understand.

If you had written:

```
if (salary>taxfreepay) then
    writeln('Salary will be taxed');
    tax:=salary*taxrate;
```

The line `writeln('Salary will be taxed');` will only be executed **if** `(salary>taxfreepay)` evaluates as true, **but** the line `tax:=salary*taxrate;` will **always** be executed because it does not 'belong' to the **if** statement. This is a very common mistake in Pascal programs. If you want more than one statement to be executed as a result of a decision, they must be made into a single compound statement with a **begin end**; pair.

Points to note

1. At the risk of being too emphatic, the white space and indentation make the code easier to read and understand. This is especially true if you forget to type **begin** and **end**; to make it into a compound statement. When you become more practised, the indentation will reflect the program logic and you will be able to see such errors very quickly. People who think they can add the indentation later to finish off a program are making a fundamental mistake; the indentation, comments and white space are used to help you write the program in the first place, to aid understanding.
2. There is a ';' character after the line `tax:=salary*taxrate;`, i.e. the line before **end**;. It is possible to leave this off, as **end**; marks the end of the compound statement. It does no harm to leave one there!

Case statement

The case statement acts like many **if** statements in the line. For example:

```
case choice of
  'a' :writeln('You pressed the a key');
  'b' :writeln('You pressed the b key');
  'c' :writeln('You pressed the c key');
  'd' :writeln('You pressed the d key');
else
  writeln('Invalid key pressed');
end;
```

In this statement, the variable **choice** is expected to have the value 'a' or 'b' or 'c' or 'd'. The appropriate writeln is executed depending on this value, or a suitable error message is displayed.

Points to note

1. In place of a variable you can have an **expression**.
2. The statement ends with **end;**.
3. You could have written the same logic with a set of **if** statements. There is not a clear choice whether you choose **case** or a set of **if** statements; it is a matter of style. Some languages do not support **case**.

More complex case statements are possible, for example

```
Case choice of
  'a','e','i','o','u': writeln ('vowel pressed');
else
  writeln ('key was not a vowel');
end;
```

where choice can have any value from 'a','e','i','o' or 'u'. If any other value is entered, the statement in the **else** clause is executed. The variable choice would be of type char.

You could also write a case statement with the case constants in a range like this:

```
case choice of
'a'..'m':writeln('Thank you');
else
writeln('That was not correct');
end;
```

The clause 'a'..'m' is evaluated as any ASCII character between a and m. The variable choice would be of type char.

For..to/downto statement

If you need to execute a statement a known number of times, you can use the construction below, the **for loop**.

```
for count:=1 to 10 do {something};
```

which takes the variable count (an integer type, not a real type) from the value 1 to the value 10 and executes the code, in this case, ten times.

You could use variables, as in

```
for i:=start to finish do {something};
```

or expressions, as in

```
for y:=(x-1) to (x+20) do{something};
```

You can also count down just by changing **to** to **downto** as in

```
for count:=100 downto 20 do {something};
```

As an example of a **for loop**, here is a program that will write the 13 times table.

```
program timestable(input,output);
var count,table:integer;

begin
  table:=13;

  for count:=1 to 12 do
    writeln(count, ' times ', table, ' = ',count*table);

end.
```

Points to note

1. The writeln statement uses several parameters separated with commas.
2. Only the spaces inside the ' ' marks are significant in the writeln statement.
3. If you wish several statements to be executed by the for loop, they must be made into a compound statement.

While..do statement

This is another loop, but one that is more flexible than the **for loop**. Its construction is

```
while <condition> do {something}
```

It is more flexible because the condition can be anything that evaluates to a **boolean**, i.e. true or false; it need not be based on numbers. While the loop is running, the condition that determines when it is finished must have the chance to change, otherwise the loop will go on forever. The usual rule applies about compound statements.
    For example

```
x:=1;
while x<=100 do
  begin
    writeln(x);
    x:=x+23;
  end;
```

This will write the sequence 1, 24, 47, 70, 93.

Points to note

1. Indentation!
2. If you missed the statement x:=x+23; the loop would go on forever.
3. You could have achieved the same output with a for loop, but this is easier to understand.

Repeat..until loop

This is another loop. The main difference from a **while loop** is that the condition that terminates the loop is at the end and not the beginning. The only important difference, therefore, is that a **repeat loop** will always execute at least once; a **while loop** has the possibility that it will not execute at all, depending on the condition.

For instance, the code

```
x:=1;
repeat
   writeln(x);
   x:=x+23;
until x>=100;
```

will generate the same number sequence as in the **while loop** example. Some programming languages do not support **repeat loops**, as the same effect can be achieved by using the right conditions and a **while loop**.

Points to note

1. The repeat loop does not need the begin end; pair to make a compound statement. Some people see this as an inconsistency in Pascal.
2. Unless you indent the code, it is even harder to see where the repeat..until loop is in a long program.

Elements of Pascal 2: Practice

The following programs use the elements introduced in the first part of this section, **Elements of Pascal 2**.

The elements introduced were:

- assignment
- expressions and operators
- if..then..else statement and boolean variables
- compound statements
- case statement
- for..to/downto statement
- while..do statement
- repeat..until statement
- constants

Now write programs to suit the tasks below.

Program 4.15

Modify program 4.14 to:

- output an error message if non-numeric input is typed
- prevent temperatures below −459°F being entered.

Possible answer (modifications shown in **bold**)

```
program prog4_15;
var  degreesF, degreesC:real;
   inputstr:string;
     errorcode:integer;
     temp_in_range:boolean;
```

```
begin
  repeat
    write('What is the temperature in degrees F ');
    readln(inputstr);
      val(inputstr,degreesF,errorcode);

      {new lines for program 4.15}
      if errorcode<>0 then writeln('Error in input');

      if (degreesF< -459) then
          temp_in_range:=false
          else
          temp_in_range:=true;

  until (errorcode=0) and (temp_in_range);

  {calculate the answer}
  degreesC:=(degreesF-32)*5/9;

  writeln(degreesF:0:2, 'F = ',degreesC:0:2, 'C ');

end.
```

Points to note

1. The error message is produced by an **if** statement testing the value of the variable **errorcode**.
2. The program uses a boolean variable; the value is set to **true** or **false** depending on the temperature entered. If below −459°F, the boolean temp_in_range is set to false; any temperature above that, temp_in_range is set to true.
3. The line

   ```
   until (errorcode=0) and (temp_in_range);
   ```

   could have been written as

   ```
   until (errorcode=0) and (temp_in_range=true);
   ```

   i.e. the last expression tested explicitly against the value **true**. In general with programming languages this is not required as the expression evaluator only comes back with true or false, so a simple boolean variable is all that is required.
4. Try removing the brackets from the line `until (errorcode=0) and (temp_in_range);` and then try to re-compile the program. The missing brackets may be wrong, but the error message is less than helpful (see Figure 4.6)! Do not always believe compiler error messages!

Program 4.16

Write a program that outputs the area of either a circle or a rectangle. The program should:

- take an input of a single keyboard character, R for rectangle and C for circle (allow r for R and c for C).
- have data validation for all inputs.

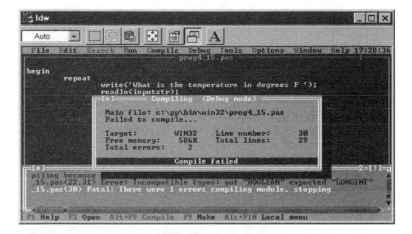

Figure 4.6 *Program 4_15 compilation failure*

Possible answer

```pascal
program prog4_16(input, output);
var  diameter,side1,side2,area:real;
     errorcode:integer;
     inputstr:string;
     choice:char;

begin
  writeln('Press C for circle or R for rectangle');
  writeln('Then press ENTER');
  repeat
    writeln('Choice? ');
    readln(choice);
  until (choice='c') or (choice='C') or (choice='r')
      or (choice='R');

  case choice of

  'c','C':
    begin
      repeat
        write('What is the diameter? ');
        readln(inputstr);
        val(inputstr,diameter,errorcode);
      until errorcode=0;

      {calculate the result}
      area:=3.14159*diameter*diameter;

      {now output the result}
      writeln('When diameter= ',diameter:0:2,
        ', area= ',area:0:2);
    end;

  'r','R':
    begin
      {get the size of the rectangle }
      repeat
        write('Please type the length of side 1 ');
        readln(inputstr);
```

```
        val(inputstr,side1,errorcode);
      until errorcode=0;

      repeat
        write('and now the length of side 2 ');
        readln(inputstr);
        val(inputstr,side2,errorcode);
      until errorcode=0;

      { now calculate the answer}

      area:=side1*side2;

      {now output the answer }
        writeln('The area = ',area:0:2);
    end;
  end;
end.
```

Points to note

1. The **end**; reserved word is underneath the beginning of the statement it belongs to.
2. The variable choice is of type **char**.
3. The validation of the key press could be done in a more elegant way; more of that later.
4. The choice between rectangle and circle is done via a **case** statement.
5. The case statement uses compound statements delimited with **begin** and **end**;.
6. The same program is presented below without white space, indentation or comments. Which is easier to read? Program code layout is done to help **you**.

```
program prog4_16(input, output);
var diameter,side1,side2,area:real;
errorcode:integer;
inputstr:string;
choice:char;
begin
writeln('Press C for circle or R for rectangle');
writeln('Then press ENTER');
repeat
writeln('Choice? ');
readln(choice);
until (choice='c') or (choice='C') or (choice='r') or
(choice='R');
case choice of
'c','C':
begin
repeat
write('What is the diameter? ');
readln(inputstr);
val(inputstr,diameter,errorcode);
until errorcode=0;
area:=3.14159*diameter*diameter;
writeln('When diameter= ', diameter:0:2, ', area= ',
area:0:2);
```

```
end;
'r','R':
begin
repeat
write('Please type the length of side 1 ');
readln(inputstr);
val(inputstr,side1,errorcode);
until errorcode=0;
repeat
write('and now the length of side 2 ');
readln(inputstr);
val(inputstr,side2,errorcode);
until errorcode=0;
area:=side1*side2;
writeln('The area = ',area:0:2);
end;
end;
end.
```

Program 4.17

Write a program to input the ages of six people and output the average age. Use data validation to cope with bad inputs. Clear the screen as the first instruction.

Possible answer

```
program prog4_17;
uses crt;

var total,age,average:real;
    counter,errorcode:integer;
    inputstr:string;

begin
  clrscr;
  total:=0; {initialize the variable to ensure it contains
  0}

  for counter:=1 to 6 do
    begin
      {validate the input}
      repeat
        write('What is the age of person ', counter, ' ');
        readln(inputstr);
        val(inputstr,age,errorcode);
      until errorcode=0;
      total:=total+age;
    end;
  average:=total/6;

  writeln('The average age= ',average:0:2,' years');
end.
```

Points to note

1. The line write('What is the age of person ',
    counter, ' '); has a quoted space at the end to provide
    space between the value of variable counter and the user input.

2.   The **for loop** uses a compound statement.
3.   Each input is added in turn with the line `total:=total+age;`
4.   The variable **total** has been initialized to zero with the line `total:=0;`.

Initializing variables

Since the act of declaring a variable simply asks the compiler to find space in memory for the value, if there is already some (unknown) value at that address the variable may appear to take on that value. It is therefore good practice to set all variables to known values. This will help you to be ready for languages that do not initialize them for you, e.g. C/C++. In some languages (e.g. BASIC) this step is not required, because each variable is always set to zero at compilation time.

As an experiment, try this program.

```
var x:real;
begin
   writeln(x:0:3);
end.
```

As the variable x has not been initialized, it may output any number, depending on two things:

1.   Whether your Pascal compiler initializes variables.
2.   What is currently in your computer's memory – a freshly booted system may output 0.000 because there is the value 0 at the address used to store the value of variable x. A machine that has been used for a few different programs without a reboot may output whatever value happens to be at the location where x is stored.

Program 4.18

Write a program that calculates the average age of an unknown number of people. Use data validation to cope with bad inputs. Clear the screen as the first instruction.

Possible answer

```
program prog4_18;
uses crt;
var total,age,average:real;
    counter,errorcode:integer;
    inputstr:string;
begin
    clrscr;
    total:=0; {initialize the variable to ensure it
    contains 0}

    age:=0;
    counter:=1;

    while age<>-1 do {use -1 as a sentinel value to end
    the loop}
        begin
```

```
                    {validate the input}
                    repeat
                      write('What is the age of person ', counter,
                      ' ');

                      readln(inputstr);
                      val(inputstr,age,errorcode);
                    until errorcode=0;

                    if (age<>-1) then
                      begin
                        total:=total+age;
                        counter:=counter+1;
                      end;
                end;
              average:=total/(counter-1);

              writeln('The average age of ',counter-1,
              ' people was ',average:0:2,' years');
end.
```

Points to note

1. Use is made of a **while loop** because the number of ages to average was unknown at **compile time**. A **repeat..until loop** could have been used.
2. The counter was initialized to 1 not 0.
3. A sentinel value has been used to terminate the loop, in this case −1. The assumption is made that −1 is not a valid age!

4.5 Elements of Pascal 3

Below are some further elements of Pascal that will be used to develop the next set of programs:

- more pre-defined functions and procedures
- user-defined procedures
- parameter passing by value and by reference
- user-defined functions
- scope of variables.

More pre-defined functions and procedures

The documentation that comes with Turbo Pascal or Free Pascal lists a large number of pre-defined functions and procedures. Some of these are standard Pascal, such as writeln or readln, and some are not. No distinction is made here between the two.

Some useful string functions are shown in Table 4.7. Table 4.8 shows some useful numerical functions.

Making programs modular

As you can see from program 4.16 onwards, when programs get longer they get harder to understand. One way to make programs easier to write, read and understand, and to make them more reliable,

Table 4.7   *Some useful string functions*

Name	Example	What it does
chr	y:=chr(65);	Returns ASCII character, in this case, 'A'
lowercase	name:=lowercase(name);	Returns a string in lower case
upcase	name:=upcase(name);	Returns a string in upper case
copy	s:=copy('ABCDEFGH', x,count);	Returns a substring starting at position x, count bytes long
str	str(x,outputstr);	Converts number x into a string
length	y:=length(name);	Gives the length of a string

Table 4.8   *Some useful numerical functions*

Name	Example	What it does
abs	y:=abs(value);	Gives absolute value of argument, i.e. removes the minus sign.
int	y:=int(x);	Returns the integer part of a type real
odd	x:=odd(y);	Returns true if y is odd, false if y=true
pi	area:=pi*d*d;	Returns the value of Pi = 3.1415926535897932385
power	y:=power(10,2)	Returns base to power x, in this case, $10^2 = 100$
random	y:=random(x);	Returns a random number $\geqslant 0$ and $< x$. Always generates the same random numbers unless randomize is used first
randomize	randomize;	Generates a new seed value for the random number generator
round	y:=round(x);	Rounds x to nearest integer
frac	y:=frac(x);	Returns the fractional part of x
sqr	y:=sqr(counter);	Returns square of its argument. Warning, this means square root in other languages!
sqrt	y:=sqrt(x);	Returns square root of x

is to split them into smaller pieces and write/test each piece on its own.

The two main methods of splitting standard Pascal programs into pieces are to write **procedures** and **functions**. You will recall that a **function** is some code that does a job then gives you an answer in return, while a **procedure** is code that does a job but does not give you such an answer.

You have already used procedures like writeln and val, and functions like trunc. They are used like this:

```
writeln(x);
```

or

```
val(inputstr,age,errocode);
```

You also often use **functions** by **assignment** or as part of an **expression**, like this:

```
y:=trunc(x);
```

or

```
if trunc(tax) > maxvalue then taxfree:=4000;
```

Pascal provides the means to write your own functions and procedures.

User-defined procedures

A procedure that displays a welcome message is **declared** like this:

```
procedure welcome;
var name:string;

begin
  write('Hello, what is your name? ');
  readln(name);
  writeln('Welcome ',name, '. Please press the ENTER
  key to continue');
  readln; { a readln on its own simply waits for enter,
  any input is "thrown away" }
end;
```

The structure is similar to that of a program; the first line starts with the reserved word **procedure**, and this is followed by a **user-defined identifier** that follows the standard Pascal rules already described. This is followed by an optional **parameter list**. This parameter list is missing from the welcome example, but will appear shortly.

To **use** the declaration above is very easy; you simply type welcome – i.e. the procedure name. That way it can be used as often as you like.

Program 4.19

This is program 4.9, but with the addition of the **procedure declaration** and its **procedure call** (when it is used) shown in **bold**.

```
program prog4_19(input, output);
var diameter,area:real;

procedure welcome;
var name:string;

begin
  write('Hello, what is your name? ');
  readln(name);
  writeln('Welcome ',name,
  '. Please press the ENTER key to continue');
  readln; { a readln on its own simply waits for enter,
  any input is "thrown away" }
end;

begin { start of main program block }
```

```
welcome; {call the procedure defined above }
write('What is the diameter? ');
readln(diameter);

{calculate the result}
area:=pi*diameter*diameter;

{now output the result}
writeln('When diameter= ',diameter:0:2, ', area= ',
area:0:2);
end.
```

Points to note

1. The procedure declaration belongs in the declaration section of the main program. The structure for a Pascal program with procedures or functions is:

```
Program yourname(input, output);
Declarations {including declarations of procedures
and functions}
Main program block
```

2. The procedure declaration has the same structure as a simple program declaration.
3. The procedure is **called** by name with the line **welcome**;
4. You can have many statements in a procedure, but remember, the point of a procedure (or a function) is to split the code into easily managed pieces – therefore long procedures are probably a sign of a badly designed program.
5. You can have variables (or indeed other procedures) declared inside a procedure. The variable **name** is defined inside the **welcome** procedure.
6. The first code statement to be executed is the first statement in the **main program block**, even if there are declarations of executable code 'above it' in the declaration section.
7. The statement `area:=pi*diameter*diameter;` uses the function **pi** in place of 3.1415926535897932385.

Decimal places

Some people seem to think that a large number of decimal places must be a Good Thing. Taking pi as 3.1415926535897932385 implies that the calculation you are performing has an accuracy to 19 decimal places. Suppose the calculation was for the area of a circular piece of concrete to be laid for the erection of a flag pole. The concrete is to be 10 metres in diameter. The area is **approximately** pi $\times$ 5 $\times$ 5 = 78.5398163397448309616, because the value of pi can never be set down with perfect precision; it is an **irrational number**. Now consider the answer against another problem. An atom is roughly 10^{-10} metres in diameter, so a square 1 atom by 1 atom is $10^{-10} \times 10^{-10} = 1 \times 10^{-18}$ so the calculation of the concrete area is ten times more 'accurate' than a square 1 atom by 1 atom!

Parameter passing by value and by reference

Passing by value

If you split a program into pieces, there must be a mechanism for the pieces to share data. One of the best ways it to 'send' that data to the procedure (or function) when you call it. You have already used this form with `writeln('Hello ', name);` the data is sent, or more correctly **passed**, to the procedure in the constant 'Hello' and the variable **name**. Pascal supports two ways to pass variables to procedures; **by value** or **by reference**. They are used in different ways, as will be shown here.

```
program prog4_20;
var i,j:integer;

procedure doit(x:integer);
var y:integer;
begin
   writeln('You passed the value ',x,' to this procedure');
   x:=x*2; { multiply the local value by 2 }
   writeln('Twice the value is ',x);
   y:=51;
   writeln('The local variable y = ', y);
   writeln('But you cannot see it outside of this
   procedure!');
end;

begin {start of main program block}

   writeln('This is the first piece of code to be executed');
   i:=12;
   doit(i);
   j:=34;
   doit(j);
end.
```

This program outputs:

```
This is the first piece of code to be executed
You passed the value 12 to this procedure
Twice the value is 24
The local variable y = 51
But you cannot see it outside of this procedure!
You passed the value 34 to this procedure
Twice the value is 68
The local variable y = 51
But you cannot see it outside of this procedure!
```

Points to note

1. The variable x is **passed by value** to the procedure. This means that it is 'called' x **inside** the procedure but you can pass any type-compatible variable to it. In the main program block, the variables i and j are passed to the procedure **doit** and Pascal places a **copy** of the value into variable x for its own internal use.

2. The value x is changed inside the procedure with the line x:=x*2; but it has no effect on the variable that was passed. So when the procedure was called with doit(j); the value in variable j was copied to variable x inside the procedure but variable j was not affected.

3. The variable x is not visible outside the procedure. The variable y, declared inside procedure doit, is also not visible outside the procedure **doit**. These are called **local variables**.

Passing by reference

```
program prog4_21;
var i,j:integer;

procedure changeit(var z:integer);
var y:integer;
begin
   writeln('You passed the value ',z,' to this procedure');
   z:=z*2; { multiply the local value by 2 }
   writeln('Twice the value is ',z, ' inside the procedure');
end;

begin {start of main program block}

   writeln('This is the first piece of code to be executed');
   i:=12;
   writeln('Variable i = ',i);
   changeit(i);
   writeln('Variable i = ',i);

   j:=34;
   writeln('Variable j = ',j);
   changeit(j);
   writeln('Variable j = ',j);
end.
```

This program outputs:

```
This is the first piece of code to be executed
Variable i = 12
You passed the value 12 to this procedure
Twice the value is 24 inside the procedure
Variable i = 24
Variable j = 34
You passed the value 34 to this procedure
Twice the value is 68 inside the procedure
Variable j = 68
```

Points to note

1. The syntax of the procedure declaration changes just a little; there is the reserved word **var** in the **parameter list**. The parameter list is the part inside the brackets of the declaration. Apart from that, the declaration is the same.

2. When passing by reference, the variable passed to the procedure **can** be changed.

3. In the main program block, the variable i starts with a value of 12. This is passed by reference to the procedure but it is 'called'

z inside the procedure. When z is changed by the line `z:=z*2;`, the variable i is also changed. You have already used a procedure in this form. In the programs that used `val(inputstr, age, errorcode)`, the variables **age** and **errorcode** are **passed by reference** as they are changed inside the procedure.

4. Look at the program output, you will see that both variable i and variable j have been changed by the procedure.
5. The variable types to be passed are declared in the parameter list, and other local variables are declared in the procedure's declaration block, in this case the variable y.

Passing by reference

The mechanism used when passing by reference is to send the **address** of the variable. When a variable is declared, Pascal finds free space in memory (RAM) and keeps a 'note' of where it is, i.e. it **points** to the address in memory. When passing by reference, this address is passed to the procedure, not a copy of the data, so the variable inside the procedure **points to the same place**. The reason that variables passed by reference can be changed is that there is only one address where the value is stored.

User-defined functions

Functions are declared in the same place as are procedures, in the declaration block, using a similar syntax. The difference is that a function needs to **return a value**, and that value will have a **type**. Remember, Pascal is a **strongly typed** language. You can also pass variables to functions in a parameter list just like procedures. You can pass by **value** or pass by **reference**, but normal practice would be to pass by value as the function itself returns a value.

A simple user-defined function is:

```
function twice(x:integer):integer;

begin
  twice:=x *2;
end;
```

In this simple function, a variable is passed by value to the function twice, and the function will return a value of type integer.

It is used in assignments or expressions like this:

```
y:=twice(x); { used in an assignment }

if z=twice(score) then writeln('Good!'); { used as an
expression }
```

Points to note

1. The return value of this function is of type integer, and is made to return by assigning a value to the function name in the line `twice:=x *2;` inside the function declaration.

2.   The variable type passed to the function does not need to be the same as the return type.

Program 4.22

A second example function outputs the times table of your choice.

```
program prog4_22;
var i,counter:integer;

function getnumber(lower,upper:integer):integer;
var inputstr:string;
  errorcode:integer;
  x:integer;

begin
  repeat
    write('Type a value between ',lower,' and ',upper,
    ' inclusive');
    readln(inputstr);
    val(inputstr,x,errorcode);
  until ((errorcode=0) and (x>=lower) and (x<=upper));
  getnumber:=x;
end;

begin {start of main program block }

  counter:=getnumber(2,12);
  for i:=1 to 12 do
    writeln(i,' times ',counter,' = ',i*counter);

end.
```

Points to note

1.   The function getnumber is declared with two variables of type integer in the parameter list.
2.   The function validates the input for non-numeric input, and an upper and lower value.

Scope of variables

So far, variables declared in procedures have been referred to as **local**. This means that the variable has no meaning outside of the procedure. Variables declared in the main program are said to be **global**, and can be used anywhere. The term applied to this is **scope**; the scope of a variable is local or global.

In program 4.22, the variable x is declared inside the procedure **getnumber**. As an experiment, try adding the line `writeln(x);` in the main program block. You will find that the program will not compile; the compiler will give the error message 'Identifier not found x', because x is **out of scope** (Figure 4.7).

How to confuse a programmer with variable scope

You could define a global variable x in the main program block and another local variable also called x inside a procedure. If you

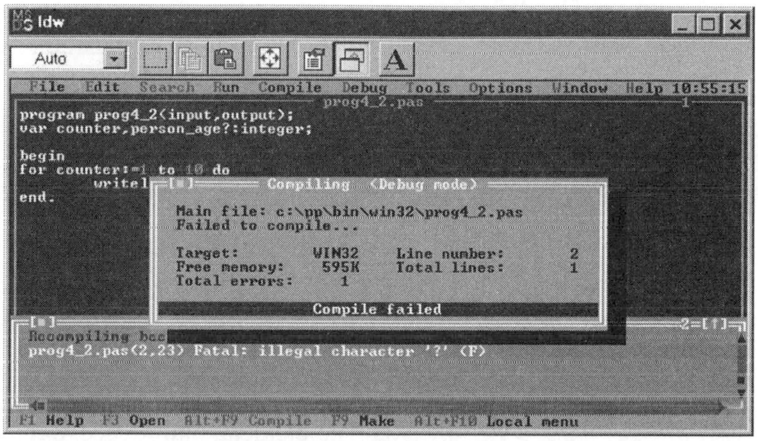

Figure 4.7 *Compiler error message*

then had a statement like `writeln(x);`, which x is being referred to? In fact the local one has precedence, as the following experiment will confirm. The global x has a value of 90, the local x has a value of 34. Inside the procedure dummy, both variables are **visible**, i.e. they are both in scope, but the local one has precedence; the writeln statement outputs 34.

Small program experiment

```
var x:integer, { a global variable }
procedure dummy;
var x:integer; { a local variable }

begin
  x:=34;
  writeln('X= ',x);
end;
begin
  x:=90;
  dummy;
end.
```

You can confuse many programmers with this problem! The solution is to have the lowest possible number of global variables (none at all is best!). Another solution is to use a naming convention. One such convention is to use L as the first letter in every local variable name, and G in front of every global name. Many programmers find this leads to ugly variable names, so we will not do it.

It is an excellent idea to write small experiments like the one above to ensure you understand particular points. They only take a few moments to put together and are a powerful way to improve your understanding.

Why have local and global variables?

In larger programming projects, the overall task of writing the code is spilt between more than one person. If only global variables were used, there would have to be a system that avoided variable names clashing in different parts of the program. For instance, if you used 'counter' as a variable in your code and someone else used 'counter' inside a procedure that was used by your code, the value of the variable would at the very least be confusing. In reality, the value would not be as either programmer had planned. It is much better to have a piece of code, a procedure or function, that stands on its own without relying on the value of a global variable. Values that must be supplied for the procedure or function to work with are passed by value or by reference as described above.

Elements of Pascal 3: Practice

The following programs use the elements introduced in the first part of this section, **Elements of Pascal 3**.
The elements introduced were:

- more pre-defined functions and procedures
- user-defined procedures
- parameter passing by value and by reference
- user-defined functions
- scope of variables.

Now write programs, procedures and functions to suit the tasks below. To test a function or procedure, write the simplest possible main program block.

Program 4.23

Use a function that returns a string in Title Case, i.e. all lower case but first letters in upper case. It should convert 'this is a test string' to 'This Is A Test String'.

Possible answer (does not run in Turbo Pascal, no **lower case** function)

```
program prog4_23;

function titlecase(name:string):string;
  { returns string with first letter=capitals }

var  p,i:integer;
     ch:string;
     done:boolean;
     convert_to_caps:boolean;
     outputstr:string;

begin

  name:=lowercase(name); { first ensure everything is
  lowercase }

  done:=false;
  repeat {a loop to ensure that any leading spaces are
  removed }

    if copy(name,1,1)=' ' { if first char is a space }
      then
        { get rest of string only }
```

```
              name:=copy(name,2,length(name)-1)
          else
            { assign boolean to end the loop }
            done:=true;
    until done;

    convert_to_caps:=true; { initialize boolean for use
    in for loop }
    outputstr:=''; { initialize string to null ready to
    build output string}

    for i:=1 to length(name) do {look at each character in
    string }
      begin
        ch:=copy(name,i,1); { get one char at a time }
        if convert_to_caps=true
          then
          begin
            { add upper case char to output string }
            outputstr:=concat(outputstr, upcase(ch));
            { set boolean ready for next time}
            convert_to_caps:=false;
          end
          else
          begin
            { add lower case char to output string }
            outputstr:=concat(outputstr,ch);
          end;

        { see if next char must be capital }
        if ch=' ' then convert_to_caps:=true;
      end;
    titlecase:=outputstr; { assign finished string to
    the function }
end;

begin {start of main program block }
  {simply to test function output}

  writeln(titlecase('this is a test string'));
end.
```

This program outputs:
```
This Is A Test String
```

Program 4.24

Use a procedure to ask a simple question to be used to build an arithmetic test program. The question is 'What is x + y', where x + y = a maximum number you specify. You should pass a boolean variable by reference, and specify the maximum answer.

Possible answer

```
program prog4_24;
var rightanswer:boolean;

procedure showquestion(maxanswer:integer;var correct:
boolean);
```

```
var answer,errorcode,num1,num2:integer;
    inputstr:string;

begin
  randomize; { so that the random numbers are always
  different. }
    { Leave this line out for program testing then}
    { all the random numbers will be the same each }
    { time the program runs }
  num1:=random(maxanswer);
  num2:=random(maxanswer-num1);
  repeat
    writeln('What is ',num1,' + ',num2,' ?');
    readln(inputstr);
    val(inputstr,answer,errorcode);
  until errorcode=0;

  if answer=(num1+num2) then correct:=true else
  correct:=false;
end;

begin { start of main program block }

{ very simple program to test procedure }
showquestion(1200,rightanswer);
if rightanswer then writeln('Well done') else
writeln('Wrong');

end.
```

Points to note

1. The procedure generates the possible numbers to be added, num1 and num2 based on a random number.
2. The element in the parameter list `var correct:boolean` declares the variable **correct** by reference, i.e. it can be changed inside the procedure and the changed value is available once the procedure is finished.

4.6 Design of larger programs

The programs presented so far have been small enough to cope with without thinking too hard about the design. This is normal for small programs, but most commercial applications require programs of significant size and complexity.

How to design a product for a customer

Stage 1 The first requirement is to find out exactly what the customer wants. It is hard to believe, but it is at this stage that most design projects fail. People who do not find out what the customer wants usually end up designing something based on a false idea. The writing of the **customer's** or **user's specification** involves writing down the customer's needs in non-technical terms.

Stage 2 Once the customer specification is done, you can write out the **technical specification**. The technical specification defines performance and other technical details.

Stage 3 Once the technical specification is complete you can write out a list of possible solutions. At this stage of the design process you should **not** attempt to **evaluate** any the solutions. If you are using the design team to arrive at a possible solution, meetings should disallow any adverse comments about other people's suggested design solution. The idea here is to encourage the entire team to be imaginative. This allows new ideas to be considered. If a climate of derision exists, people tend to be wary of suggesting new and possibly better ways of doing things.

Stage 4 Having decided on the whole range of solutions, one solution is selected for further work.

Stage 5 In the case of programming, there are often at least two aspects to design, often more. These two are:

- what the computer user sees on the computer output, known as the **Human Computer Interface** or **HCI**
- the internal processes of the software.

These two aspects are often designed and written by separate teams. For instance, if the program is a database application, the manipulation of the data is best left to a database specialist and the design of the user screens to someone with greater experience in designing user interfaces. The screen designer needs to know little about databases and database design, and needs only be concerned with screen design. One useful benefit from this technique is that the screen designer can produce a prototype before the rest of the software is finished, and this can then be approved by the customer before any more work is done. Most people would call this **prototyping**, although, as is usual with computing, this word can have other meanings.

Stage 6 Once the prototypes and the final program are complete, the software is tested. If it is found not to perform to the technical specification, go back to stage 4 or even stage 3, depending on what has failed.

This process can be summarized as:

1. Define customer needs
2. Define technical needs
3. List possible solutions
4. Select detailed design
5. Make prototype
6. Evaluate and test prototype.

These ideas do not apply to software design alone; this design scheme can be used to design almost anything.

You should notice that detailed design does not start until Stage 4.

> There is a problem with learning design strategies at the same time as learning programming, and this is that you will be unfamiliar with the programming language and methods whilst at the same time being unfamiliar with using a structured design technique. For this reason, the following sections will take everyday objects as examples for considering design.

The scheme outlined above does not take account of the use of **top-down design** or **bottom-up design**.

Top-down design is where you start with the whole problem in mind; you consider all the larger aspects first. Once these are clear, you concentrate on the next level of detail and so on until you have designed all the elements.

As an example of top-down design, consider the design of a car (Table 4.9). (A real design would of course be more detailed, but the purpose here is to describe the process, not the car!)

Table 4.9   *Designing a car – top-down design*

Determine the needs of the customer	Four adult seats, space for their luggage, have maximum safety features, be able to cope with rough country roads, and be able to run on fuel available anywhere
Write technical specification	Size and shape of seating and internal space, determination of possible weight and hence the power output of the engine, determination of the ground clearance to cope with rough roads, definition of fuel type based on survey of what kinds are available world-wide (i.e. do not assume it is a petrol engine!)
List possible solutions	Four-wheel drive, two-wheel drive either front or back, tracked vehicle (remember, at this stage no one is allowed to make adverse comments about a possible solution!). Normal piston engine, rotary engine, turbine, steam engine. Fuel diesel, petrol or LPG
The actual design	A Landrover!
Prototyping	Make a four-wheel drive for testing on a test track
Testing	Ensure that the car meets the customer's needs

The point about top-down design is that details such as the engine and layout of the wheels etc. are not decided first; rather, the whole problem is considered and then progressively refined.

Bottom-up design is the opposite of this. In this method, important details are decided first, then more and more is added until the whole product is finished. This is a very poor technique for something like a car; the result is often a lovely engine mounted in an ugly car without space for all the passengers. You may well have travelled in one!

However, bottom-up design is useful for some programming problems. Consider a program that takes a scanned image of some text and converts it to editable text. This is known as **Optical Character Recognition**, or **OCR**. The finished product must be easy to use and able to take input from all sorts of graphics devices/files etc. – just the kind of complex product that should result from top-down design. There is, however, a key problem here, which is to be able to recognize the characters reliably with an acceptable error rate. Until this problem is cracked, the rest of the project is not required. Early attempts at OCR failed at the recognition stage. A product of this nature is designed by concentrating first on the key problem, the recognition. Once this has been achieved, the rest of the program code can be built around it. This process, starting with a detailed part of the product, is called bottom-up design. It suits small design tasks that may have difficult technical features, but it does not suit larger and more complex products.

Most professional designers actually use both techniques. Although top-down design is usually preferred because it concentrates on customers' needs first and then produces a solution, some problems need detailed treatment first.

More formal techniques used to develop business software are described elsewhere in the book.

4.7 Translating a design into code

For smaller projects or the components of larger projects, use can be made of **stepwise refinement** and **pseudo code**.

Stepwise refinement

In order to design an efficient solution to a given problem, it is best to break the task down into manageable parts. As an example, consider the task below. Assume that both the customer specification (i.e. what the customer wants) and the technical specification have been completed. (This problem is only to illustrate the idea of stepwise refinement; it is not intended to be a guide to income tax!)

You are asked to write a program that calculates income tax, national insurance etc., not for a company, just for individuals.

Define customer needs

This is done by agreement with the customer. She needs a small program that will act as a handy tax calculator to give away with her main product, an employment advice package. She would like users to type in their annual salary and their tax allowance as issued by the Inland Revenue; the program will then **estimate** their annual tax. It has been accepted that actual tax calculations can be complex, and the program will act as a tax estimator only.

Define technical needs

This is done in consultation with a tax specialist, with all the complex aspects of tax to be left out and only a simple PAYE calculation to be completed. The specification is to include details such as the data to be validated, age range only 16–100 years, marital status (married, single, divorced, widowed, separated etc.).

List possible solutions

Your first task is to find out the relevant taxation rules and rates for income tax and national insurance etc. before you proceed. These are available from the Inland Revenue webpage at www.inlandrevenue.gov.uk. There are few possible solutions, as the rules have been laid down elsewhere.

Detailed design

You discover that you need at least these details: age, gender, marital status, salary and tax allowance from the user, and the 'tax bands' (currently 10%, 22% and 40%) charged at various levels of salary. You also discover that the tax bands and the salary levels are often changed, so cannot be fixed in your program.

You could write the program such that when a value is calculated, the result is output straight away. This is a style of coding that will eventually lead to an over-complex program, so should be avoided. It is better to break the program into three pieces:

1. Get user details
2. Do the calculations
3. Output the result.

These can be represented on a diagram as in Figure 4.8.

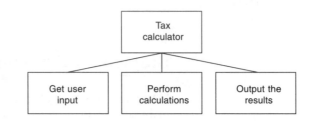

Figure 4.8 *Main parts of tax program*

There is not yet sufficient detail to write a code, so each of the three parts is broken down further. The **Get user input** section can be broken down or **refined** into more pieces, i.e. the get and validate user input. The validation is done to conform to the validation rules set out in the **technical specification** (Figure 4.9).

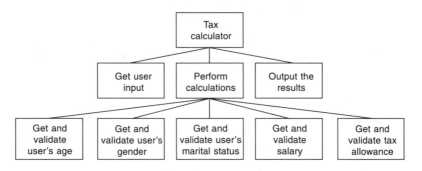

Figure 4.9 *First stage of stepwise refinement*

Likewise, the **Perform Calculations** section can be broken down into more pieces (Figure 4.10).

In this program, the **Output results** section is already simple enough and does not need further refinement.

When finished, the process of stepwise refinement should leave you with tasks that can be written as program code.

Pseudo code

You could now take each task from your stepwise refinement and write **pseudo code**. Pseudo code is not a real programming language but is an 'English-like' representation of a real language. It will

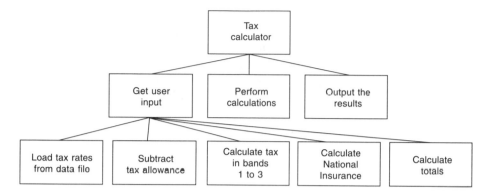

Figure 4.10 *Second stage of stepwise refinement*

translate **approximately** line by line to a real language. For instance, the pseudo code:

Repeat
   Obtain users age from keyboard
until age is in range 16 to 100

would be used as the pseudo code for the Get and validate user's age section. This may translate into the Pascal:

```
repeat
   write('Please give your age in years ');
   readln(inputstr);
   val(inputstr,age,errorcode);
until (errorcode=0) and (age>=16) and (age<=100);
```

Each task is written in this way until the whole program is coded.

Evaluation and testing

The finished program is then tested to see if it conforms to both the customer and technical specifications.

A typical technique used for this testing is to prepare **test data** and set them out as shown in Table 4.10. In this case, the test data would be constructed with the aid of a tax specialist to ensure they are correct.

Table 4.10 *Tax calculator test data*

Inputs	Age	Gender	Marital status	Salary	Tax allowance
	34	M	S	23000	4535
Expected outputs	Tax band 1 188	Tax band 2 3648.70	Tax band 3 0	Total tax 3836.70	NI 1380
Actual outputs	Tax band 1 188	Tax band 2 3648.70	Tax band 3 0	Total tax 3836.70	NI 1231
Output valid?	Yes	Yes	Yes	Yes	No

The test data have previously calculated values. You can see that the table has space for **inputs** and the **expected outputs** when these input values are used, together with a space to show if the outputs are correct. In this example, the value for NI (National Insurance) is not correct, indicating a problem with the coding.

Well-designed test data are invaluable for program testing, and should include:

- normal input values, i.e. ages, salaries etc. in the usual range
- invalid inputs to check on the validation routines
- values at the extremes of the validation ranges, which will discover such errors as

```
until (age>16) and (age<100)
```

when you meant to put

```
until (age>=16) and (age<=100).
```

In the former case, an input of age 16 would have been thrown out as invalid.

A number of these tests should be performed to show that your program is performing to specification.

4.8 Debugging inside the IDE

Both Free Pascal and Borland Turbo Pascal offer a debugger. This is a tool that 'stops' the execution of the program at a **breakpoint**, then displays the value of a **watch** (Figure 4.11). Figure 4.11 shows program 4.17 with the debugger turned on and a watch set for the variable **total**. The program is running but has stopped at the **breakpoint**, which is set on the line `readln(inputstr;)`. This allows inspection of the watch set on the variable total. Breakpoints and watches are set in the Debug menu.

Figure 4.11   *Debug and watch screen*

In this example the variable total is showing the expected result, but 'bugs' can be found using this technique.

Trace tables

The expected value of a variable can be set out in a **trace table**, then use made of the **debugger** to see if the variable actually has the right values. For instance, if a program had the code

```
repeat
  {do something}
  x:=x+0.001;
until x=10;
```

it may well fail. You will remember from the section on floating point numbers that repeatedly adding a value like 0.001 to a floating point number may well give inaccurate results. The loop here will only finish when x = 10 **exactly**. It may well be that because of the floating point error, x will never be exactly 10, only very near. Unfortunately computers do not 'think', so when it would be obvious to a human that the calculation should finish, the computer will go on and on round the loop. If you set a breakpoint in the loop and watch the variable x, you may find that instead of producing a sequence like

9.996
9.997
9.998
9.999
10.000

as you may expect, it actually produces

9.9960000000001
9.9970000000001
9.9980000000001
9.9990000000001
10.0000000000001
10.0010000000001
10.0020000000001

showing why the loop did not finish; i.e. the variable never actually **equalled** 10. The solution is to write `until (x>=10);`, then it will terminate properly. Table 4.11 is the **trace table** for this.

Table 4.11 *Trace table*

Variable x	Expected	Actual
	9.996	9.9960000000001
	9.997	9.9970000000001
	9.998	9.9980000000001
	9.999	9.9990000000001
	10.000	10.0000000000001
	10.001	10.0010000000001
	10.002	10.0020000000001
	etc.	

4.9 Prototyping

In terms of, say, a car or an aircraft, the word **prototype** means a finished product that is used to test the complete design. In programming, the word is used in a different sense. It usually means that the user interface is designed so that the customer can see what the finished product will look like, but the software will not perform every aspect of its specification. In the case of the small tax calculator described above, this could be used as a prototype for a more complete tax calculator; the program 'works', but does not take into account many of the real-life income tax details.

If you consider software designed to run under Microsoft Windows, the language of choice for many people would be C++ as it is very powerful and can generate fast and efficient code. One trouble with C++ is the effort required to produce the 'windows' that make up the user interface. In this case, it is quite possible to use a different language to make the prototype. Visual Basic has strengths in this area; it is known as a Rapid Application Development (RAD) language. The prototypes for customer approval would be made using Visual Basic, but once approved, the same user interface would be built using C++ or another more powerful language.

4.10 Program documentation

When software is developed, this is usually carried out by a team of people. This implies that there must be adequate documentation and communication between the team members, their customers and outside consultants etc. Documentation is especially important when a team member leaves the team, as others will now have to maintain code that they did not write themselves.

As a minimum, this documentation should include the following

- customer specification
- technical specification
- details of algorithms and heuristics used
- version history
- bug reports
- user guide.

Details of algorithms and heuristics used

An **algorithm** is a set of rules that defines how a problem may be solved. It is a set of 'do this, then this, then this' rules that allow either a satisfactory answer or a report that such an answer is not possible. An **heuristic** is different; some problems are not solvable using algorithms, i.e. no set of rules exist to solve the problem. There are some classes of problem where 'an educated guess' is made at the answer, and this answer is then tested for accuracy. If it is not sufficiently accurate, an updated guess is made and the process is repeated either until a satisfactory answer is obtained or until it is clear that such an answer is not possible.

Version history

The version history is where changes to the software are noted. It is usual to have two version numbers, for example 'version 6.3' where the 6 refers to the sixth major revision of the software and the .3 refers to the third bug fix or minor improvement made in the software. The full version history will record exactly what has been changed and why the change was made.

Bug reports

A bug report is where a user will report a fault found in the software. To be really useful, all reports should include exactly how the bug

was found and list any other factors that may affect the software, such as the version of the operating system in use, hardware details etc.

User guide

The user guide should tell the user all that is required to use the software to its fullest extent. It must be written with the user and not the programmer in mind; i.e. it should not assume prior knowledge of the software. Really good application software such as a wordprocessor should be usable without reading the user guide, but this is rarely achieved.

Unit 5 Communications technology

Networks are computers that are connected to allow communication. This introduces a whole set of new problems that must be resolved. The components are designed and made by different manufacturers but must still work together, and the software, both at the operating system level and at the applications level, must also be compatible. This is achieved by use of a **layered architecture**, explained later in this unit.

One of the problems with computing, and especially with networks, is the number of technical words that are used. The most important ones will each be explained here. You will find that you must read some of the sections several times as the subject of networks is perhaps more 'interconnected' than others in computing, i.e. one idea depends on the understanding of another. For example, the section on network architecture will refer to **Ethernet** or **token ring** protocols, but the explanations of these protocols are elsewhere. The idea of a protocol is also explained elsewhere. There is no 'best order' in which to study networks, so re-read these sections until you have a proper understanding of this important subject.

5.1 Network architectures

There are many network architectures, all with their own benefits. The descriptions below are the most common. When networks are called 'small' or 'large', remember the old problem: 'what is the difference between a ship and a boat?'. There is no definition!

Small networks with a few users normally generally use **Ethernet** or **token ring** networks with one or two servers. If **peer to peer** is in operation, there will be no **server**.

Medium-sized networks, with a few hundred users, will have the need to segment the network into logical parts. The client server model is common with medium-sized networks (see below). There may be ten or more servers, and hardware such as **routers** or **switches** to provide the segmentation. Ethernet or token ring is still common with this size of network.

Large networks usually involve many floors or areas in a building, and serve a large organization with diverse needs. This results in a network that must be segmented into logical parts for security, to share the load on servers and the need to balance **bandwidth** for best performance. High speed **backbones** are used, possibly **FDDI**, **ATM** or **Gigabit Ethernet**.

Critical aspects when considering the specification of a network are the level of traffic, where the traffic is heavy, and how can it be reduced. Factors to consider include:

- is the application software on a **server** or on local PCs?
- is part of the PC **operating system** on the server or local PCs (e.g. the Windows swap file)?
- in the business of the organization, do users need to access large, centrally stored databases?
- is there a requirement for bandwidth-hungry applications such as video conferencing?

If software is held locally the network traffic is likely to come from transfer of whole files, so the total load on the network will vary a fair amount but still be quite light. Most of the time, only small demands are made on the available bandwidth. The IT Support department now has a larger job; the maintenance of the system will require visits to each machine on the site. This is one reason for centralizing application software; to reduce this workload.

If software is held centrally or there is a need to access large central databases, or to use video conferencing etc., the traffic rises and therefore you must either provide higher bandwidth or take care in the architecture of the network to maximize the available bandwidth.

Networks

Peer to peer means that each machine is treated as a 'peer', or equal. On a peer to peer system you will be able to see devices on other machines, such a disks, printers etc. This type of network is very good for small organizations. Microsoft Windows from version 3.11 onwards is capable of providing a peer to peer network with no additional network operating system (see http://www.peer-to-peerwg.org/).

The term **server** in computing has several meanings. In one sense, a server is a dedicated piece of **hardware** that provides a **service**; you can buy a 'server' for a network. It is usually a computer with a high performance specification. A second meaning of the term is to describe a piece of **software** that provides a service. A typical piece of such software is 'Apache Server', software that provides the **http protocol** that is used for the world-wide web. Apache can run on a desktop PC to act as a server for other PCs on the network.

A client-server means the PC is (usually) a **client** to services provided by the **server**. If everything is provided by the server, traffic is high; if some functions are locally based, traffic is reduced. The decision is how to split local and server-based services – do you have all network-based printing so all print jobs travel via the network, or do you have some local printing? Most but not all medium or large networks use the client-server model (see http://www.sei.cmu.edu/str/descriptions/clientserver_body.html, or http://www.webopedia.com/TERM/C/client_server_architecture.html, or http://searchnetworking.techtarget.com/sDefinition/0,,sid7_gci211796,00.html).

> **http**
>
> http is the **h**ypertext **t**ransport **p**rotocol. When you look at the web address in a web browser, it may look something like http://www.bbc.co.uk, i.e. the domain of the site you are looking at and the protocol you are using. Browsers (and the Internet) support other protocols, such as ftp (the **f**ile **t**ransfer **p**rotocol) or smtp (the **s**imple **m**ail **t**ransfer **p**rotocol).

Small networks

Possible **topologies** for small networks are illustrated in Figures 5.1–5.3.

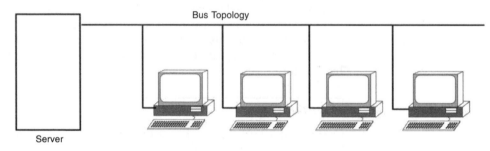

Figure 5.1   *Bus topology with a single server*

Figure 5.2   *Ring topology*

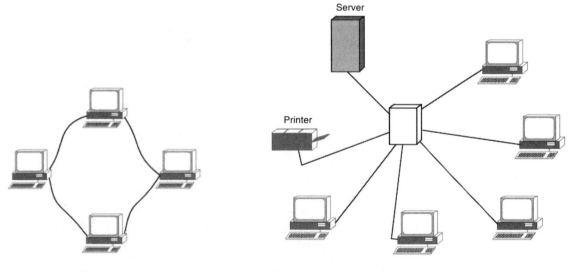

Figure 5.3   *Star topology*

The device in the centre of the star topology of Figure 5.3 is most likely to be a **switch**. A switch is a kind of multiport bridge, i.e. it treats each arm of the star as a separate network, sharing the available bandwidth. Typical values are 10 Mbit/s per PC.

Medium-sized networks

Figure 5.4 shows a possible topology for a medium-sized network. The figure shows a router, but this could be a switch; the choice depends on how the network is to be segmented:

1. Routers allocate segments by use of individual ports, i.e. it is done by the **hardware**.
2. Switches allocate segments by **software** control, so source and destination addresses can be physically anywhere on the network. This arrangement allows for a VLAN, or Virtual LAN. If the segmentation is being done to suit an organization department by department then routers are fine, but VLANs allow for greater flexibility as the organization changes or as the accommodation changes.

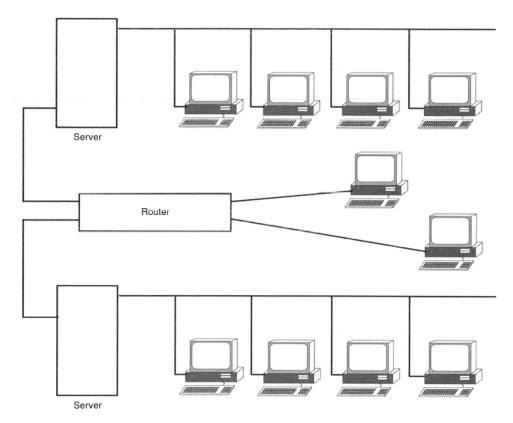

Figure 5.4 *Medium-sized network with collapsed backbone*

A collapsed backbone is a strange name; it simply means there is no longer one single backbone.

Large networks

Figure 5.5 shows a possible topology for a large network. An important difference between medium and large networks is in the management of the bandwidth. It is easy to design a system that has a bottleneck, a part of the system that slows things down because

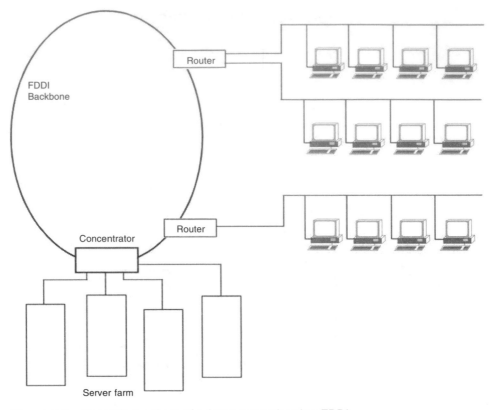

Figure 5.5   *Possible topology of a large network using FDDI*

it is running at full speed, but this speed may not be sufficient to cope with demand. The solution in existing networks is to use traffic analysis software to determine the exact point of the trouble. In the design of a new network, it is important to analyse the bandwidth needs before any design decisions are made. The choice of backbone, between FDDI, ATM, Gigabit Ethernet etc., is not an easy one to make, and there are many factors to consider.

For more information on network topologies, see: http://www.webopedia.com/quick_ref/topologies.html, or http://www.its.bldrdoc.gov/fs-1037/dir-024/_3535.htm, or http://www.cisco.com/univercd/cc/td/doc/product/ismg/policy/ver20/topology/.

5.2 Layering in networks

In the past single companies have tried to dominate the network market so a user is 'locked in' to a single supplier. This situation no longer really exists (although some companies still try!). The way that software and hardware is made to work together is by a 'layered' approach. It is **absolutely vital** that before continuing with your study of networks you understand this idea of layering. The section below is written as an analogy with human communication because many of the problems of network communication are shared by humans.

Analogies

Analogies are used in this book to make thing clear. It is very important that you realize these analogies are not an

> exact match with the subject under consideration, and so should not be taken too far. The idea is to understand the principle rather than the detail.

As with many ideas in computing, there is a published standard that lays down an ideal specification. In the case of networks, this is called the **OSI seven-layer model**. It is an **idealized** layered architecture, but manufacturers generally choose their own (often simpler) layers; for example, the Internet uses a five-layer model.

The reason a layered approach is so effective in network design is that any layer can be changed without changing the overall aim – to communicate.

The seven layers of the OSI model are:

1. Application
2. Presentation
3. Session
4. Transport
5. Network
6. Data link
7. Physical.

What the OSI model means

A set of communication rules between humans is called a **protocol**. You would not, for instance, speak to your family using exactly the same type of language you would use to your friends. People address children differently from the way they speak to old people, etc. Humans have a whole range of (very complex) protocols 'installed' in their brains that are used to communicate. A protocol is a **set of rules** used to manage communication; if you break the rules, communication fails. This means **real communication**, not just the transmission of data. In the human sense, if two people are shouting at each other it is unlikely that one of them is really listening to the other – i.e. they are not communicating, only exchanging words. One of the layers in their protocol stack has failed.

Computer networks use protocols. As these protocols are 'layered', the use of the word **stack** (to refer to layers) has become common – as in **protocol stack**. This is simply language to describe a layered approach.

For more information, see http://www.freesoft.org/CIE/Topics/ 15.htm, or http://www.csie.nctu.edu.tw/document/CIE/Topics/ 15.htm.

OSI seven-layer model: an analogy

Set out below is an analogy between the layered approach to network design, and communication within a group of humans (Table 5.1). As with all analogies, you must not take it too far; it is intended as a guide only.

Imagine a group of people having a discussion, and consider the rules they use to communicate – how they speak, who speaks at any one moment, what language they speak, how loud their voices

Table 5.1   *Approximate meaning of network layers*

Layer	**Approximate** *meaning*
Application	Speak about the subject you wish to communicate – 'Tell me about the weather today', 'Who will win the election?', 'How are you feeling today?'
Presentation	Use of jargon or plain language (does everyone **communicating** know the meaning of the jargon?). Speak in French or English or any other human language
Session	Start or end the conversation, possibly with 'Good morning', 'May I speak now?' or 'That's all for today, thanks and goodbye'. Not concerned with the subject, only the establishment of a communication session. Most people would call this 'starting (or ending) a conversation'
Transport	If the listener has not heard, how do you know this? The listener may send back a message – 'Pardon?', or 'I did not quite catch what you said', indicating that the message has arrived but not been completely received. This is a form of error checking
Network	Look or point at the person to whom you wish to speak, engage eye contact. Establish a **path** to someone you wish to speak to
Data link	Syllables of speech, separate sounds, not speaking if someone else is speaking (collision detection)
Physical	Sound over the air or over a telephone line, megaphone or radio link

are etc. Success or failure to communicate is all that concerns us here. Consider what happens if they break the rules; communication fails to take place.

Consider these points and discuss them with your tutor

1. What happens in one layer between people? For example, at the session layer, what happens to **communication** if you miss these important social points of etiquette? At the network layer, what happens if you do not get a person's attention? The general result is that communication does not take place – at least, not effective communication (remember, do not take this analogy too far!).

2. What happens vertically, i.e. between say the transport and session layers? It is no use saying 'Good Morning' if the hearer does not hear! Each layer 'talks to' or supports the layer above and below it.

3. Can you change the design of one layer without affecting the other layers? Can you, for instance, replace French with English in the presentation layer without affecting communication? In terms of computers, presentation layer software is installed (on the PCs). In terms of humans, as long as French is 'installed' (i.e. learnt) by all the people communicating, it will have no effect; **communication** still takes place.

OSI seven-layered network model and TCP/IP

Each OSI layer has a particular function and set of behaviours. Each layer provides services to the layers above it, and layers communicate directly only with the same layer on other machines. The protocol stack used for the internet is called **TCP/IP, Transmission Control Protocol/Internet protocol**, a five-layer protocol stack that is available across all kinds of computer systems.

Internet resources

Internet protocols from Cisco Systems:
http://www.cisco.com/univercd/cc/td/doc/cisintwk/ito_doc/ip.htm

TCP/IP from Cisco Systems:
http://www.cisco.com/warp/public/535/4.html

Introduction to the Internet protocols:
http://oac3.hsc.uth.tmc.edu/staff/snewton/tcp-tutorial/

NB: Most real-life protocol stacks do not use all seven layers of the OSI model; it is an idealized model and is designed as a guide for future designs. The TCP/IP protocol stack has been included here as a comparison.

Table 5.2 shows the ISO network layer.

Table 5.2 *ISO network layers*

OSI/ISO seven layer model (not every layer is used in every network implementation)	TCP/IP protocol stack
Layer 7, the **application layer**, implements application-specific behaviour, such as the ftp protocol or http (web) session	TCP/IP sockets
Layer 6, the **presentation layer**, controls formatting and data exchange behaviour, such as byte-order conversions, data compression, and encryption. It's in charge of how the data is reformatted for presentation to the application layer, and is often not used	Not used in TCP/IP
Layer 5, the **session layer**, encapsulates network transmissions into 'conversations' and controls synchronization and mode switching between the session's two endpoints. It co-ordinates movement of data from the client to the server	Not used in TCP/IP
Layer 4, the **transport layer**, provides data delivery. It can also split data into packets and reassemble those packets on the receiving side	TCP (transport control protocol) UDP (user datagram protocol)
Layer 3, the **network layer**, provides the services we think of as network services: routing, flow control and so on	IP (Internet protocol) ICMP (Internet control message protocol) IGMP (Internet group message protocol)
Layer 2, the **data link layer**, controls transmission and retransmission of data. The data is formatted in accordance with the physical layer's requirements, and higher layers may reformat or modify it	ARP (address resolution protocol) RARP (reverse address resolution protocol)
Layer 1, the **physical layer**, actually moves bits to and from some kind of network medium, whether it's a 10Base-T cable, a satellite link, or a modem connection	Hardware interface

Common five-layer model: layering in present-day networks

Since the OSI seven-layer model has not been implemented fully, it should be noted that a five-layer model that closely fits the TCP/IP model is becoming very common. It may well be the case that no network ever uses the complete seven-layer model. 'Standards' in the computing business are often defined simply by first becoming popular, and then by being adopted by 'official bodies' later.

The exact descriptions of the layers are different from the ISO model, as are the layer numbers. The key idea to grasp is that of layering itself, rather than the details of each layer. Each layer 'talks' to the one above or below in a way that allows hardware or software from different makers to be used, but the way in which the equipment or software works internally can vary greatly from maker to maker.

The layers in this five-layer model are:

1. Application (Layer 5)
2. Transport (Layer 4)
3. Routing (Layer 3)
4. Switching (Layer 2)
5. Interface (Layer 1).

Layer 1, the **interface layer**, defines the way devices are connected. This is where network standards such as **ATM, Token Ring, FDDI** etc. belong, as do the **Ethernet** standards, more properly called IEEE 802.3, examples being 10Base-T etc.

Layer 2, the **switching layer**, uses hardware to forward **packets** of data according to their MAC address. The MAC address is the **Media Access Control**, a number appended to the packet by the NIC, the Network Interface Card fitted in each PC. The MAC address in each NIC is unique across the world. Data is moved around networks in packets, i.e. the data are split into small pieces, and each packet then 'travels' around the network. Packets can be of different sizes, but 1024 bytes is common.

Layer 3, the **routing layer**, allows the network to be partitioned into logical pieces. With the TCP/IP protocol stack, the IP part of the stack is the layer 3 protocol. Each IP packet contains the source and destination address, so routing decisions can be made. If a network is split into logical parts the routing decisions allow packets only into parts of the network where they 'belong', so saving bandwidth. If a network is not split into logical parts, each packet travel to all parts of the network, wasting bandwidth.

Layer 4, the **transport layer**, is concerned with the way that user applications are handled on the network. This is the TCP part of the TCP/IP protocol stack, and involves things such as the re-transmission of packets that were lost in layers 2 or 3 for any reason. Some layer 4 protocols, such as **Real Time Protocol** (RTP), are concerned with the sequence of packets and their timing – important when packets must arrive in order and in time to support a real-time multimedia application.

Layer 5, the **application layer**, is where applications supply data to layer 4 for transmission. Layer 5 applications are what the users see. Rather than writing the code to communicate directly with layer 4, software such as Microsoft's Winsock is used. A web browser such as Netscape would communicate using Winsock.

5.3 Network protocols

A protocol is a set of rules that define communication and is a term that applies to a wide range of network standards. Each of the protocols are named, and the most widely used are described here.

It is **very important** to refer to the section on **layering in networks** to understand how these protocols relate to the physical network components and the data that travel around the network.

In the early 1970s, a network was designed by the Xerox Corporation to connect their Altos workstations together. After some time, and after joining company with DEC and Intel, the first **Ethernet** specification was published. Since then, the IEEE has published a network standard that is based on Ethernet but is not quite the same. This standard is called IEEE 802.3 and in common language is also called Ethernet, although it is not an accurate description – another example of words slowly changing their meaning. Ethernet is now commonly used to cover any network that uses **CSMA/CD**.

In **Ethernet** networks, the individual standards are known as 10Base-2, 10Base-5 etc. In this coding, the 10 refers to the data rate of 10 Mbits/s, 'base' refers to **baseband** and the number is the cable media type and **approximates** to one hundredth of the segment length in metres. Using this scheme, 10Base-5 is a 10 Mbit/s baseband system with a maximum segment length of 500 metres. Some of the specifications are summarized in Table 5.3. There are many more; 1000Base-LX is just one from a set of specifications that are called **GigaBit Ethernet**.

Table 5.3 *Details of some of the Ethernet physical layer specifications*

	Original Ethernet	*10Base-5*	*10Base-2*	*10Base-T*	*100BaseT*	*1000Base-LX*	*10Broad-36*
Signalling	Baseband	Baseband	Baseband	Baseband	Baseband	Baseband	Broadband
Max. segment length, metres	500	500	185	100	100	5000	1800
Cable	50-ohm coaxial	50-ohm coaxial	50-ohm coaxial	UTP	UTP	Fibre	75-ohm coaxial

You will see references in the marketplace to 10, 100 and 1000 Mbit/s Ethernet. This reflects the enormous rate of progress from the original 10 Mbit/s Ethernet in 1972. To be more precise, Ethernet and IEEE 802.3 run at 10 Mbits/s over coaxial cable; 100Mbits/s Ethernet is known as Fast Ethernet and operates at 100 Mbits/s over UTP, and 1000 Mbits/s Ethernet is known as Gigabit Ethernet and operates at 1000 Mbits/s using fibre and twisted-pair cables.

You should notice that each type has a maximum cable length for each segment of the network. This length restriction is due to the timing required for the particular Ethernet standard. If you were to fit longer cables, the signal timing would no longer conform to the standard and communication would not be reliable.

Internet resources

www.cisco.com/univercd/cc/td/doc/cisintwk/ito_doc/ethernet.htm

www.brother.com/european/networking/

FDDI

This is the **Fibre Distributed Data Interface**, often used to provide a network backbone rather than service to individual PCs.

FDDI is a 100 Mbit/s network standard that runs over a ring topology. It uses token passing rather than the CSMA/CD used in Ethernet, and is designed to run over fibre-optic cables. A related standard called CDDI runs over copper cables; it was introduced to avoid the high cost of fibre cabling.

Fibre-optic cables are more secure than copper because they do not emit an electromagnetic field that can be picked up by unauthorized users. For related reasons, it does not suffer from electrical interference from outside and has a very high bandwidth. Unfortunately, it is expensive to install.

FDDI uses two rings; the primary ring and the secondary ring. This means that if one fibre is broken, communication can continue over the other. Each FDDI has two ports (called A and B) that attach to the primary and secondary rings. Up to 1000 stations can be connected, but a practical limit of 500 exists because if a fibre breaks the 500 stations would become 1000. This is due to the way the signals interact in each station.

Some types of network traffic must have data that arrive in time and in sequence. An example of this is real-time video. Other data can arrive without strict timing, such as e-mail or file transport. FDDI supports both kinds of traffic by providing synchronous and asynchronous transport. Time-critical applications use synchronous transport that can use a fixed part of the 100 Mbit/s bandwidth; asynchronous traffic takes what is left.

ATM

ATM is **Asynchronous Transfer Mode**, a network standard that specifies data packet format and network switching. It was designed for use by telephone companies to provide wide area data transport.

It is characterized by being a high-speed packet switching system that uses very short, fixed-length data packets (48 data bytes + 5 control = 53 bytes). The problem it attempts to solve is the carriage of mixed types of data. The packets for video and other time-critical applications must arrive in time; other data, such as e-mail, does not have this need. ATM can define the quality of service to give constant bit rate (CBR), variable bit rate (VBR) and available bit rate (ABR), depending on the type of traffic to be carried. The speed of ATM varies with the quality of service, but values of 155 Mbits/s over copper and 622 Mbits/s over fibre are common.

Network contention

CSMA/CD

This stands for Collision Sense Multiple Access/Collision Detection. As many network stations are connected to the same wire and this wire uses **baseband** signalling, only one station must be transmitting at once. When a station wishes to transmit over the network, it waits until the line is quiet. If two stations start to transmit data at **exactly** the same time, each waits a random amount of time before re-transmission. This is a system that ensures that one will start before the other, so avoiding collisions.

Humans use this system; imagine you are with a group of people, all having a conversation. Providing you are not arguing, only one person speaks at once; if two start to speak at the same time, both wait for a suitable moment to speak again.

Token passing

On a token ring network, including FDDI, a **token** is sent through the network. The token is used to communicate the **busy** or **free state** of the network. If the previous token indicated that the network was free, a PC that wishes to transmit sends out a 'busy' token, stopping other machines from sending. The data sent out travels around the ring and arrives back at the sending PC, which then responds by sending out a 'not busy' token, allowing access to other machines. Token passing is better than CSMA/CD under heavy traffic conditions.

Error correction and detection

Data errors can and do occur, even in systems that are working correctly. As the data are encoded as 1s and 0s, any physical phenomena that cause a change from 1 to 0 or 0 to 1 will cause an error. Typical causes of such errors are:

- other electrical devices, e.g. fluorescent lighting
- 'dirty' switches, as found in refrigerators and central heating systems, electric motors etc.
- background radio frequencies from space
- random activity of the electrons in the wires and electronic components themselves.

Error correction is simple; once you detect that a 1 should be a 0, you simply change it! The more complex task is to detect the error and the most common way is to use a CRC, Cyclic Redundancy Check.

Internet protocols

Here is a list of the common Internet protocols, followed by further Internet resources.

Telnet Protocol

Telnet programs are a type of terminal emulation program, and allow users to access other computers through the Internet. Once connected via telnet, it is as though the user is directly logged in as a local user.

File Transfer Protocol, FTP

FTP is a client-server protocol. It allows a user on one computer to transfer files to and from another computer over a TCP/IP network. Anonymous FTP allows anyone to download files, but not usually to upload them.

Simple Mail Transfer Protocol, SMTP

This is a protocol that transfers e-mail across the network (see POP below).

Network News Transfer Protocol, NNTP

This refers to the standard protocol used for transferring Usenet news from machine to machine.

Network Time Protocol, NTP

This is a higher level TCP/IP protocol that provides accurate local timekeeping by synchronizing clocks within milliseconds by reference to radio, atomic or other clocks located on the Internet.

Serial Line Internet Protocol, SLIP

SLIP is a standard for connecting to the Internet with a modem over a telephone line. It is not much used now (see PPP).

HyperText Transfer Protocol, HTTP

HTTP is the 'web' protocol; it defines how web pages are formatted and transmitted. When you type a URL into your browser, this results in the sending of an HTTP request to the Web server directing it to fetch and transmit the requested Web page.

Point-to-Point Protocol, PPP

PPP is the Internet standard for serial communications over a modem.

Post Office Protocol, POP

This allows users to access their e-mail from an e-mail server. It must not be confused with SMTP, which transports e-mails across networks.

Internet resources

For more information on protocols, see http://www. techfest.com/networking/prot.htm, or http://www. protocols.com/protoc.shtml.

5.4 The physical communication media

Cabling

The bandwidth of the cable used to transmit data is limited. Several designs are available, but all attempt to obtain the same thing: high bandwidth with low power loss.

Problems to be overcome

1. When you listen to your radio, to improve the reception you may put up an aerial made up of a piece of wire. It may not

work as effectively as a well-designed aerial, but it **will** pick up radio signals. The wire connecting parts of a network is no different; it picks up radio signals as well as electrical interference from common electrical devices. These are known as **Radio Frequency Interference** or **RFI** and **Electromagnetic Interference**, or **EMI**.

2. Cables have a power limitation. The signal to noise ratio can be improved by increasing the power, but this cannot be extended too far.

3. The design of the cable limits the bandwidth. It is no use trying to send a high frequency signal down a cable with low bandwidth, it will not come out the other end! For a simple twisted-wire pair, the bandwidth is limited to approximately 1 MHz.

If a cable is made with two or more conductors or wires, the electrical properties differ depending on:

- whether they are laid side by side or are twisted together
- the distance that separates the wires
- the diameter of the wire
- the purity of the copper conductor
- whether they are contained inside a 'screen' of braided copper
- the length of the wire.

Common cable types

The two commonest cable designs are **Coaxial** and **Unshielded Twisted Pair** (UTP). Coaxial cable has a single copper conductor surrounded by a braided copper sheath. This sheath is connected to ground so that any unwanted signals picked up are run to earth instead of interfering with the signal being transmitted. If you look at the cable that connects your home television to the aerial, you will find that it is coaxial in design.

UTP is simpler and cheaper to make and, being more flexible than coaxial cable, is easier to install. UTP is popular, but ways must be found to make more use of its effective bandwidth. These ways include special signal processing to reduce the effects of noise in the cable so that the bandwidth of UTP is not just a function of the cable itself, it also comes from the devices that connect each end of the cable.

Cabling standards

As is common in the computing industry, cabling is made to conform to standards designed by commercial companies and supported or adopted by official bodies. In the case of networks and cabling in particular, these standards are published by such organizations as the EIA/TIA or the IEEE. The EIA/TIA is the **Electronic Industries Association and Telecommunications Industry Association**, a group founded in the USA. The IEEE (known as the 'I triple E') is **The Institute of Electrical and Electronics Engineers**, a non-profit making technical professional association of more than 350 000 individual members in 150 countries.

Many local area networks (LANs) are cabled with what is called 'cat 5'. This refers to the EIA/TIA category 5 UTP cables. Various categories are shown in Table 5.4.

Table 5.4 *EIA/TIA building cabling standards*

EIA/TIA category	Uses
1	POTS (the Plain Old Telephone System) Analogue voice Digital voice
2	ISDN (Data) 1.44 Mbits/s T1, 1.544 Mbits/s Digital voice
3	10Base-T Ethernet 4 Mbits/s Token Ring ISDN Voice
4	10Base-T Ethernet 16 Mbits/s Token Ring
5	10Base-T Ethernet 100Base-T Ethernet 160 Mbits/s Token Ring 100 Mbits/s distributed data interface 155 Mbits/s asynchronous transfer mode
150-ohm STP	16 Mbits/s Token Ring 100 Mbits/s distributed data interface Full motion video

Fibre-optic cables

Fibre-optic cables have an enormous bandwidth. They are made from glass of extreme purity drawn down into small diameter fibres. It is said that if a block of glass of this purity was made a kilometre thick, it would transmit as much light as a normal window pane. The fibre is constructed as in Figure 5.6. The core is made of glass with a typical refractive index of 1.5 (the amount the air/glass surface 'bends' light), and is clad with a layer of glass with a refractive index that is 99 per cent of 1.5 or $1.5 \times 0.99 = 1.485$. If the fibre was always kept perfectly straight, the light would travel right down the centre. Of course the fibre is never straight, so the two-layer construction is used to cause the light that enters the core to be totally refracted back into the core as shown in Figure 5.7.

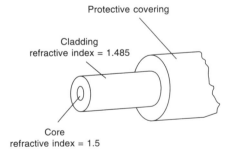

Figure 5.6 *Basic construction of fibre-optic cable*

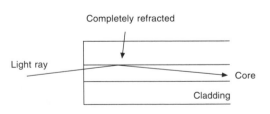
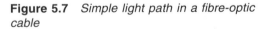

Figure 5.7 *Simple light path in a fibre-optic cable*

It would be a great waste of fibre bandwidth to use baseband signalling unless the signal itself had an enormous bandwidth requirement. Normally this is not the case, so broadband techniques are used. This usually involves **multiplexing**, i.e. sending many signals down the fibre at one time. Fibre cables can carry many simultaneous television channels, data and voice signals all at once.

Fibre-optic cable is quite expensive to install, but the high bandwidth more than offsets this high price. It is generally used to provide the **backbone** of networks, where large amounts of data flow.

Radio or Wireless

Until recently wireless LAN connections have been too slow, but the IEEE have now brought out the standard 802.11b (High Rate) than defines an 11 Mbit/s transmission rate, which will provide performance about equivalent to the original Ethernet 10 Mbit/s. IEEE 802.11b requires two pieces of equipment; a PC with a wireless NIC, and an access point. The access point is wired to the main network via its own bridge. Roaming is possible – just like a mobile telephone, the user can take the PC anywhere in range of the set of access points and remain connected to the network. Use of different protocols will also allow peer to peer connections.

Internet resources

For more information, see 3Com Corporation at http://www.3com.com/corpinfo/en_US/technology/index.jsp, or Intel at www.intel.com.

5.5 Connecting to networks from remote sites

A major problem for Internet or networking companies is the cost of providing connections to large numbers of remote users. There exists a huge investment in the **local loop**; cabling to houses and offices that already carry voice telephone services. ISDN, cable modems and the xDSL standards were developed to use this vast investment without the need to re-cable the world.

The **local loop** is the name given to the last cable run from the telephone company to the buildings supplied with the telephone service. It is sometimes referred to as the 'last mile'.

xDSL is the name given to a range of communication standards designed to carry voice and data traffic. The xDSL standard just coming into use in the UK is ADSL. xDSL can deliver ATM (asynchronous transfer made) services to the home.

Data connections are not the only reason that higher bandwidth is required. Better voice telephone services are also required, so digital systems are being installed that provide added value services to the user, such as caller identification, call waiting etc.

The xDSL standards are:

- ADSL/ADSL-lite – Asymmetric Digital Subscriber Line
- R-ADSL – Rate-Adaptive Digital Subscriber Line
- HDSL – High bit-rate Digital Subscriber Line
- SDSL – Single-line Digital Subscriber Line
- VDSL – Very high bit-rate Digital Subscriber Line.

ADSL, or **Asymmetric Digital Subscriber Line**, is a digital standard that provides an 'always on' service to a remote network. There is no concept of making a call; it behaves to the user more like a LAN connection. It is 'asymmetric' because the upload and download speeds are different. ADSL-lite is a slower version intended for the domestic market; it requires less complex equipment at the user end.

R-ADSL, or **Rate-Adaptive Digital Subscriber Line**, is very similar to ADSL except that the speed can be adjusted to suit cable lengths and conditions.

HDSL, or **High bit-rate Digital Subscriber Line**, is symmetric, it has the same bandwidth for uploads and downloads.

SDSL, or **Single-line Digital Subscriber Line**, is similar to HDSL but will work with single copper wires over restricted distances.

VDSL, or **Very high bit-rate Digital Subscriber Line**, is the fastest of the xDSL standards, and can provide sufficient bandwidth to support video but over shorter distances. The standard can be extended by providing a fibre-optic link from the telephone provider to a local distribution point, but this defeats part of the reason for the xDSL standards – i.e. to use the installed local loop.

Table 5.5 shows the speed in either kbits/s or Mbits/s for up and download of data for various standards, together with approximate maximum distances in km. The abbreviation T1 refers to a US standard for a 1.55 Mbits/s telephone connection, and E1 is the faster European equivalent.

Table 5.5 *Speeds of local loop connection standards*

Standard	Upload	Download	Distance
56 Kbits/s analogue modems	28–33 kbits/s	56 kbits/s	
ISDN	128	128	5.5 km
Cable modem	128 kbits/s to 10 Mbits/s	10–30 Mbits/s (over shared lines)	50 km
ADSL Lite	512 kbits/s	1 Mbits/s	5.5 km
ADSL/R-ADSL	1.544 Mbits/s	1.5–8 Mbits/s	5.5 km
IDSL	144 kbits/s	144 kbits/s	5.5 km
HDSL	1.544 Mbits/s (T1) 2 Mbits/s (E1)	1.544 Mbits/s (T1) 2 Mbits/s (E1)	4.5 km
SDSL	1.544 Mbits/s (T1) 2 Mbits/s (E1)	1.544 Mbits/s (T1) 2 Mbits/s (E1)	3 km
VDSL	1.5 = 2.3 Mbits/s	13–52 Mbits/s	0.3–1.3 km

ADSL modems use a technique that is related to traditional modems, but introduce more complexity. A traditional modem modulates a 'sound' with digital data to make it compatible with the POTS. The POTS was originally designed as a voice-only analogue system, and as such will not transmit digital 1s and 0s. There is an exception to this; in the very oldest POTS, opening and closing the lines was used to dial the number and the 'dial' itself was speed-controlled to open and close the lines at a set rate to match the speed of the switches in the exchange. This was called 'loop disconnect' dialling. For backwards compatibility, some telephones and most modems will still execute loop disconnect dialling. On a phone, you may see a switch marked 'LD' and 'Tone'. LD is loop disconnect, and 'tone' is the system used now to dial numbers – a set of tones of different frequencies. Because of this history the POTS could not transmit 1s and 0s, so modulated sounds were used instead.

The ADSL modems modulate signals of higher frequency resulting in the ability to provide a higher bandwidth. As ADSL is asymmetric, one frequency is used for upload and another for download, with the higher bandwidth being assigned to download. This is called Frequency Division Multiplexing, and means that different signals are carried using different frequencies on the same broadband line. A technique called **echo cancellation** allows the frequency bands to overlap, so using the available bandwidth more efficiently. A filtering device called a POTS splitter is used to split off 4 kHz of bandwidth to provide a simultaneous voice channel that works at the same time as data transmission. As is usual with broadband transmissions, the cost and complexity of the equipment at both ends of the line offsets the saving made by using cheap cabling, but the cost of providing high bandwidth cable to support baseband signalling would be prohibitive. This is the whole purpose of ADSL. The actual system of modulation used is quite complex, but is of no interest here.

ISDN

ISDN means **Integrated Services Digital Network**. It is a switched service designed originally to provide high quality voice telephone connections to PBXs, Private Branch Exchanges. ISDN 30 provides thirty kbits/s 64 lines to support PBXs, but a domestic version is available called ISDN 2 which, as the name implies, provides two 64 kbits/s lines that can be combined to give a bandwidth of 128 kbits/s.

In the UK there has been a slow up-take of ISDN lines, and the newer ADSL lines seem to offer better bandwidth. ISDN requires a call to be set up in a similar manner to a modem used over a voice line, whereas ADSL is always on service; for this reason, ISDN attracts call charges.

Cable modems

Cable modems do not really belong in this section as they do not use the local loop, but must use the cable provided for cable TV services. They do provide a high bandwidth broadband connection. Once connected, cable modems use a LAN protocol to transport data over the network, so issues of security become more of a concern. One of the first cable modem installations had a fault that allowed each user's C: drive to be visible over the network! Download to the user is via the cable modem, but many installations rely on the POTS with a traditional modem to upload data at a much lower bandwidth.

5.6 Virtual circuits in local area networks

Packets

The data that travel through networks do so in small groups of bytes called packets. This happens in both Ethernet and Token Ring networks, and the whole thing is controlled by a set of rules called protocols. Packets contain transport protocol information depending on the network protocol in use, such as Novell's IPX or the Internet protocol stack, TCP/IP. This information is handled by the Network Operating System.

Frames

As the packets must find their way around the network, they must have information attached that gives the addresses of the destination and of the source of the data, together with other information. When packets are wrapped up with this data, the result is called a frame. Frames are made by the Network Interface Card in the PC.

When sending packets over networks the process is called **packet switching**, and this differs from older types of network. The oldfashioned POTS used a **physical circuit**, which was maintained without a break throughout the call. If you telephoned Edinburgh from London, there would have been a single continuous circuit all the way. In these telephone networks, switching equipment established a physical unbroken connection. Modern telephone systems do not use this technique.

Networks use a logical connection between computers. In order to start a communication session, both sender and user exchange information to establish this logical connection. The user does not need to know the physical path taken by the data.

Table 5.6 shows the make-up of two typical frames, shown to illustrate the idea of a packet and of a frame. Different networks

Table 5.6 *Typical frames*

Ethernet frame

Preamble	Destination address	Source address	Type	Data (packet)	FCS
8 bytes	6 bytes	6 bytes	2 bytes	46–1500 bytes	4 bytes

FCS = Frame Check Sequence

IEEE 802.3 frame

Preamble	SOF	Destination address	Source address	Type	802.2 header and data	FCS
7 bytes	1 byte	6 bytes	6 bytes	2 bytes	46 to 1500 bytes	4 bytes

SOF = Start of Frame

Token Ring Data Frame

Start delim	End delim	Frame ctrl	Destination address	Source address	Information	Frame check	End delim	Frame status
1 byte	1 byte	1 byte	6 bytes	6 bytes	0–18000 bytes	4 bytes	1 byte	1 byte

have their own frame design. Each frame contains a single packet of data (see the section on Ethernet for more detail).

The source address and destination address of each frame are often called node addresses but are also called **MAC addresses**, short for Medium Access Control. Every Ethernet card made has a unique MAC address built into the card. These cards, fitted in the computer, are sometimes called Network Interface Cards, often abbreviated to NIC.

Segmentation and reassembly of messages

Unlike physical circuits, packets of data (in their frames) do not follow the same path in an unbroken stream. To send data:

- each message is divided into segments
- each segment is turned into a packet by adding transport protocol information
- each packet is placed in a frame
- each frame is sent over the network
- on receipt, the packet is extracted from the frame
- the packet header is read for protocol instructions
- the data segments are re-assembled into a completed message
- an acknowledgement is sent back to the sender.

The five-layer protocol stack is closely related to TCP/IP, the Transport Control Protocol/Internet Protocol. In order that data can travel over other network types, frames, packets etc. are **encapsulated** – i.e. they become **data** for the next lower layer in the stack. To illustrate this, the TCP/IP system is shown encapsulated into an Ethernet frame (Figure 5.8).

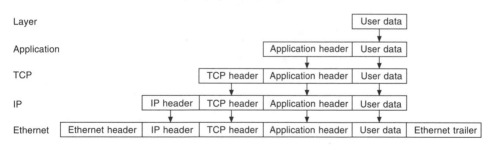

Figure 5.8 *TCP/IP frame encapsulated in Ethernet frame*

Bridges, routers and switching hubs

The maximum distance that data can be sent in a small LAN and the maximum rate at which data can flow are limited by a number of factors. To increase this distance, several different devices are used; **bridges, routers** and **switching hubs**.

Bridging
A bridge is used to join two LANs together. It works by reading the address information in each frame and only sending those frames

that need to be sent, ignoring the others. Overall traffic in the LAN is therefore reduced, making better use of the available bandwidth.

Routing

Routers work in a similar manner to bridges except they work on the packet transport protocol information and not the MAC address. This means that each packet must have this information; packets that do not have this information come from non-routable protocols such as NetBEUI. In a routable protocol such as TCP/IP, the logical address is contained in the packet header. A router is a computer in its own right, and builds a table of logical addresses that map to network cards.

Switching hubs

A switching hub is a kind of multiport bridge. The software running in the hub can make 'intelligent' decisions to make bridges between ports, so making what is in effect even smaller individual LANs. This reduces the traffic flowing all over the LAN, so better use can be made of the bandwidth.

Comparing Bridges with Routers

Table 5.7 compares bridges and routers.

Table 5.7 *Bridges against routers*	
Good points	*Bad points*
Bridges	
Simple to install	Limited configuration options
Need little or no configuration	Lack flexibility
Cheap	Do not work well with routers
Are available from many vendors	Are limited to servicing same type of LANs only
Routers	
Can join dissimilar LANs because they process packets, not frames	Can be expensive
Can create better data paths dynamically	Do not work with non-routable protocols such as NetBIOS or NetBEUI
	Are often more difficult to configure and administer
	Do not make good routing decisions when used with bridges

5.7 Some fundamental ideas

Bandwidth and baud rate

These terms are much used in networking; unfortunately, they are also misused a great deal.

Baud rate

The term **baud rate** is named after a French engineer, Jean-Maurice-Emile Baudot, and was first used to measure the speed of telegraph transmissions before the age of computers. One baud is '**one** electronic state change per second'. This is often confused with **bits per second**, or **bps**. If and only if each electronic state change gives one bit of data, the bits per second will equal the baud rate. Current practice is to encode more that one data bit into each electronic state change, so for most applications bits per second will not equal the baud rate. For this reason, and to avoid confusion, use of baud rates has given way to the more useful measure of bits per second.

Bandwidth

The nature of language is that meanings of words change over time, sometimes developing several meanings. It seems this is happening to the word **bandwidth**. This is a very important concept in networks and data communications, so two definitions are presented here.

The informal definition

Some people use the word bandwidth to refer to the speed at which data can be **downloaded**. This is measured in bytes/second, so a 4 kbyte/s link would be considered a low bandwidth and 100 Mbytes/s would be seen as high bandwidth.

The formal definition

The bandwidth of real communication channels is limited by physics. Some channels can transmit high power signals while others cannot, and most suffer from **noise** – i.e. random signals caused by outside interference. This interference has many causes, such as:

- other electrical devices, e.g. fluorescent lighting, 'dirty' switches as found in refrigerators and central heating systems, electric motors etc.
- background radio frequencies from space
- random activity of the electrons in the wires and electronic components themselves.

In an analogue channel, the bandwidth is the difference between the lowest and highest frequencies that can be transmitted. For example, in the POTS (plain old telephone system) the lowest frequency than could be transmitted was about 300 Hz and the highest was about 3300 Hz, so the bandwidth was 3300 – 300 = 3000 Hz, or 3 kHz. You can experiment with the POTS. If you have a watch that makes a high-pitched alarm, it is quite likely that the frequency is at or above 3300 Hz. If you call a friend and play the alarm down the telephone, it is quite likely that your friend will not hear it – it is not transmitted right through the telephone communication channel. As telephone systems improve so will the bandwidth, so with a modern telephone system your friend may be able to hear it! It still makes the point; a channel has a **physical limit** to the frequencies it will transmit, i.e. it has a limited bandwidth.
   If we use the symbols:

P   for the power of a signal sent through the communication channel, measured in watts

N   for the power of the noise coming out of this channel, also in watts

W   for the bandwidth, measured in Hertz

C for the capacity of the channel in bits/second

then the digital capacity of the channel will be

$C = W Log_2(1 + (P/N))$ bits per second.

This is called **Shannon's Law** after Claude Shannon, who first proved the equation. The ratio P/N is called the **Power to Noise ratio**, and is often used as a measure of quality in data and sound transmissions. If you are listening to the radio and there is a loud background 'hiss' that spoils the music, this is a system with a high P/N ratio; the power of the noise is high compared with the power of the music. If you listen to a music CD on quality equipment, the P/N ratio is low.

Extending the example, with the POTS, the bandwidth is 3 kHz; if we use a signal of 10^{-4} watts and suffer noise of 4×10^{-7} watts then we get a capacity of:

$C = 3000 \times \log_2 (1 + (10^{-4}/4 \times 10^{-7})) = 3000 \times \log_2(251) =$ approx. 25 000 bits per second.

This is the maximum for the channel and is rarely achieved because the equation itself models an ideal channel, and real communication channels suffer all sorts of other problems. To increase the bandwidth you can increase the power P or decrease the noise N; however, unfortunately there is an upper limit to P and noise is very difficult to reduce.

(**NB**: If your calculator does not have a $\log_2$ key you can find $\log_2(x)$ with the formula $\log_2(x) = \log_{10}(x)/\log_{10}(2)$, or more generally for logs of any base, $Log_{baseN}(x) = \log_{10}(x)/\log_{10}(N)$)

Here is the language problem. The POTs has a bandwidth of 3 kHz, yet can transmit 25 000 bits/second. These values are not the same, but in common language the POTS has a 'bandwidth' of 25 kbits/s.

Modem modems are rated at 56 kbits/s but this speed is achieved using data compression; the actual number of 1s and 0s sent is lower than the capacity of 25 kbits/s because this speed is based on an idealized model. You may see modem speeds measured as a **baud rate**, but modern practice is to use bits per second (see above).

In some ways it does not matter if the academically correct meaning of the word bandwidth is misused, as long as people know what you are speaking about – i.e. you still have effective communication. It does matter, however, when ideas of bandwidth are confused between analogue and digital channels.

Decibels

What is a **decibel**? A decibel is ten times a Bel!

What is a **Bel**? A Bel is simply the log of the ratio of two numbers, log(number1/number2), and therefore a decibel is $10 \times$ (log(number1/number2)). For example, suppose Fred can throw a javelin 50 metres but Joe can throw one 75 metres. The ratio of their best efforts is 75/50 = 1.5. If we take the log of this we get log(1.5) = 0.176, so we can say that Joe's best efforts are 0.176 Bels better than Fred's.

The reason we use Bels instead of simple ratios, i.e. we use a log scale and not a linear scale, is that for very large numbers a linear scale becomes unusable. The effect of the log scale is to reduce the size of the numbers. Even so, a Bel is not a useful unit because a difference of 1 Bel means that one value is 10 times the other. It is more common to multiply the ratio given in Bels by 10 to give decibels.

In the javelin example, Joe's throw is $0.176 \times 10 = 1.76$ decibels, or 1.76 dB, better than Fred's.

When you see any measurement given in dB, it is **always** a ratio. If you do not know the 'other number', i.e. the value that is used to calculate the ratio, the measurement is of no use to you. Sound levels are usually quoted in dB, so a sound of 100 dB is loud and one of 30 dB is very quiet. These sound levels are ratios to a fixed standard sound level that can be found in reference works on acoustics. Decibels are **not** a measurement of sound. In the equation given above, the ratio P/N is the **Signal Power to Noise Ratio**. This is usually quoted in dB, as it is just a ratio of two numbers.

Example 5.1

1. A signal has a power of 2.5 watts and the channel has noise on it with a power of 0.005 watts. What is the signal to noise ratio, S, expressed as dB? If the noise could be reduced to 0.00025 watts, what would the signal to noise ratio be then?

Answer

$S = 10 \, \text{Log}(P/N) = 10 \times \log(2.5/0.005) = 26.989$, or 27 dB.
For a noise of power 0.00025 watts
$S = 10 \times \log(2.5/0.00025) = 40$ dB.

2. A communication channel is quoted as having a Signal to noise ratio of 97 dB. Is this a good value?

Answer

97 dB means 9.7 Bels. The number that has a log of 9.7, is the antilog of 9.7, which is 5 011 872 336.273, or approximately 5000 million. This means the power of the signal is 5×10^9 times higher than the power of the noise. Pretty good!

This shows why it is better to use dB for the ratio of large numbers. It is better to quote 97 dB than 5 000 000 000 : 1!

Back to bandwidth

When a signal is transmitted though a communication channel, the level drops off at some point due to the physical nature of the channel. You can see from Figure 5.9 that bandwidth is not a fixed value; it really depends on how you measure it, or at which point on the signal drop-off you choose to measure it.

In Figure 5.9, the complete bandwidth is shown as the point

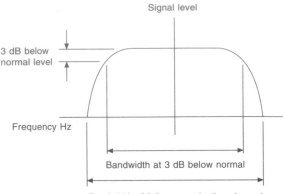

Figure 5.9   *Bandwidth at –3 dB*

when the signal level goes down to zero. At or near this level the signal to noise ratio is unacceptably high, so a point is taken at some arbitrary point below the maximum level and the bandwidth is taken from there. In this example, this point is taken as 3 dB below normal. This results in a narrower bandwidth, but in reality this value is a better guide to bandwidth than if the whole channel width was quoted.

If you see a bandwidth quoted as 100 MHz (3 dB), you will know what it means; the ratio 3 dB is the ratio of the level at which bandwidth is measured against the full signal level.

Baseband and broadband

Baseband is when a cable carries one complete information signal at a time – i.e. the cable is used exclusively for one message at a time, and the whole of the physical bandwidth of the cable is used for that signal. Most computer communication is baseband, i.e. PC to printer and PC to modem. Except for the latest designs, most networks use baseband.

Broadband is where two or more signals are present on the cable at the same time so that the bandwidth is shared between them. This requires more complex equipment at both ends of the cable. The TV signal in the aerial lead to your television is broadband; it contains all the available TV channels at the same time. Circuits in the TV select or tune into just one, discarding the other signals. Broadband signalling can be achieved using frequency division multiplexing. This is where the digital signal is used to modulate a fixed frequency, and this modulated signal is sent down the wire at the same time as other modulated signals of different frequencies. It is often used to mix signals of different types, e.g. voice, data, video etc.

Synchronous and asynchronous communications

Why synchronization is required

Imagine that someone is talking to you very fast, telling you a great deal of detailed information. If you cannot 'keep up', some of the information is lost – i.e. you do not have all the information 'transmitted' to you. Computers have a similar requirement. Data are sent as 1s and 0s at a certain speed, so the speed of the sender must be matched with the speed of the receiver if the data are not to be lost.

There are two common systems used in computing to provide reliable communication; synchronous and asynchronous communication. In this sense, the 'a' of asynchronous means 'not'. This can cause some confusion. Imagine you agree to meet a friend at 11:30 am by the station. To allow this to work, both your watches must run at the same rate and be set to the same time, i.e. be 'synchronized', and success depends on the assumption that both watches remain synchronized. If something goes wrong with either watch, you will miss your meeting. In contrast, if you agree to meet directly after a telephone call, this is 'asynchronous' – your watches do not need to be synchronized, and you act on a 'signal' in this case, a telephone call.

Asynchronous communication

Asynchronous communication is more common than synchronous communication. Data are sent as a series of 1s and 0s, but if the line is already in a '0' state and the next bit is also a '0', the line stays the same (see Figure 5.10). The data byte being sent here is 01101000 (remember, a byte is 8 data bits). You can see that the line only changes when the bits go from either 0 to 1 or 1 to 0. When no data are being sent, the line is quiet; when a byte is to be sent, a start bit will start the communication.

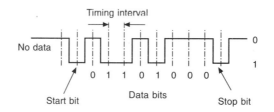

Figure 5.10 *Asynchronous transmission*

A problem with asynchronous communication is that each byte has (usually) 2 bits added, so 2/8 = 0.25 (or 25 per cent) more bits are sent than are required by the data alone.

Synchronous communication

In synchronous communication, data are as sent data blocks or frames. The size of these frames varies from about 1000 to 4096 bytes.

Frames are structured with data plus control information. This information is typically as shown in Figure 5.11, but will vary in detail from system to system. The parts of the frame are as shown in Table 5.8.

In general, synchronous communication is more efficient than asynchronous communication because the number of non-data bits

Flag	Address	Control	Data	CRC	Flag

Figure 5.11   *Data frame for synchronous communication*

Table 5.8   *Parts of a frame*

Flag	8 data bits that indicate the start or end of transmission
Address	is where the frame must be sent
Control	indicates the type of frame
Data	is a varied number of unstructured data bits
CRC	CRC is a Cyclic Redundancy Check. This is where some arithmetic has been performed on the data and the result is stored as the CRC. On receipt of the data, the same arithmetic is carried out; if the result is the same, the assumption is made that the data has arrived uncorrupted. There is only a very small chance of getting the same CRC with corrupted data

is smaller – remember, asynchronous communication typically has 25 per cent more bits added for control. If the total for the flags, address, control and CRC is even as high as 20 and the data take 4096 bytes, the proportion of control bytes = 20/4096 = 0.0048, or just a bit less than 1/2 per cent. The downside is that synchronous communication requires more sophisticated equipment.

For these reasons, synchronous communication is generally used in networks, while asynchronous communication is used to connect simple devices.

5.8 Small computer local communication standards

USB

USB stands for **Universal Serial Bus**, a standard being worked on by Compaq, Hewlett Packard, Intel, Lucent, Microsoft, NEC and Philips. The idea is that peripherals can be plugged in (or removed) whilst the PC is switched on, and do not need to be initialized during the boot-up sequence. When a device is plugged in, the operating system recognizes the event and configures the required device driver software.

Many standard PCs are supplied with two USB ports. Attachment of more than two devices is achieved by USB hubs that allow daisy-chaining, a technique where devices are plugged in one to the next forming a 'chain', thus reducing the amount of cable required. A further reduction in cabling is achieved because USB supplies the power to the devices in the data cable, up to 2.5 watts. Hubs may be cascaded up to five levels deep providing a connection for up to 127 peripheral devices at a transfer rate of either 12 Mbits/s (full-speed) or 1.5 Mbits/s (low-speed). The current USB standard, USB 1.1, is about to be superseded by USB 2.0, which will allow a claimed transfer rate of 480 Mbits/s.

Firewire

Firewire is the common name for a standard called IEEE 1394. This is a serial connection aimed at very high data transfer speeds – at least high for a serial link. Speeds between 100 Mbits/s and

800 Mbits/s are possible, and a speed of 3 200 Mbits/s is promised. Up to sixteen devices can be connected via a single Firewire port. It commonly used to attach digital cameras to PCs, one reason being the very simple cable attachment and set-up that is used.

IrDA

This is an infra-red serial communication standard that is intended to dispense with cables and run at a maximum of 4 Mbits/s. IrDA will also work at standard serial speeds to mimic the old RS-232-C serial standard (see below). Since there is a clear possibility of several devices in one place using IrDA, and the infra-red signal is 'broadcast' around that area, the standard includes techniques similar to those used in networking, to avoid device conflicts and data being sent to the wrong device. It is common to find IrDA on notebook PCs or smaller devices, to allow communication with desktop PCs without cabling.

Serial ports

Serial devices have been around for many years. The earliest machines could be connected to devices such as modems or printers using just three wires; a 'send' wire, a 'receive' wire and a signal return wire. Binary 1s and 0s were sent one after the other, i.e. serially, and the maximum speed was quite low. To improve speed, extra wires were introduced to allow 'handshaking', signals that allowed or disallowed the sending of data depending on the readiness to receive. These data and handshake lines and the associated timings etc. were incorporated into a standard called RS232-C, which used a 25 pin 'D'-shaped connector. Since only a few of these pins were actually used, IBM introduced a similar nine-pin 'D' connector that is now common on modern PCs. Unfortunately, as the standard has 'evolved' over the years, the 25-pin connectors are still common, as are many different arrangements for interconnecting 25-pin, nine-pin old and new devices. Modern PCs with modern serial devices cause little problem, but the use of legacy serial devices with any PC can prove to be problematic. The maximum speed of a serial port is currently 115 200 bits/s. With a simple serial link each 8-bit byte has a 'start' and 'stop' bit added, so using 10 bits/byte; therefore 115 200 bits/s would give 11 520 bytes/s. You may notice that some speeds are given as Mbytes/s and others as Mbits/s. This is because the number of extra bits (i.e. not data bits) is variable, depending on the application and the PC industries' common practice of quoting the largest number to look attractive in advertisements! Also you should be wary of 'standards'.

Serial ports under Microsoft DOS or Windows have names – COM1:, COM2: etc. The set-up for these COM ports quote the speed in bits/s, number of data bits, parity and number of stop bits. A typical set-up may be 9600, 8, none, 1, which means 9600 bits per second, 8 data bits, no parity, and 1 stop bit. Parity is an old error checking system now little used, and is in the set-up to allow connection with legacy devices. You may see 9600 bits/s quoted as 9600 Baud, but the 'baud rate' is not the same as bits per second.

Parallel ports

Most PCs have a single port for the attachment of a local printer. This is a parallel port, i.e. it has control lines and eight data lines, one each for the 8 bits of a byte. Although designed as a single direction port for outputting to printers, some programmers have managed to allow two-way communication. The port is slow by modern standards, but as the printers are even slower, no advantage is gained by using a high-speed link.

Under Microsoft DOS or Windows, the parallel port is called LPT1: (for Line Printer 1). It is possible to add more parallel ports by plugging expansion cards into the ISA bus; they would then be called LPT2: etc.

5.9 The Internet

In some respects, the Internet does not exist! You cannot go to see it, it is not controlled by one governing body, it does not belong to anyone. Saying 'the Internet' is about as vague as saying 'the shops' or 'the roads', in both cases meaning all the shops or roads in the world. The Internet is not a 'thing'; it is simply a large number of machines connected together sharing a common low level protocol, TCP/IP. Over the top of TCP/IP, use is made of a number of higher level protocols.

Sadly, some people seem to think the Internet is the World Wide Web. This is not the case, but the Web (or more accurately the http protocol) is the most popular usage. Using the Web, pages of information are accessed via a URL, a **Uniform Resource Locator**. URLs are made up as follows. Take as an example the URL: http://www.w3.org/Addressing/URL/Overview.html. In this case, the **http://** is the protocol to use; the part that says **www.w3.org** is the **domain** or address of the server where the information is stored; **Addressing/URL/** is the file system directory (called a folder in Windows) where the file is stored; and **Overview.html** is the actual file. The result of typing the URL into a browser is that an http request is submitted to the web server at www.w3.org for the file Overview.html to be transmitted to your machine. If all is well, the web server will 'serve up' the web page to your browser, and the browser software will then **render** the information on the screen according to the **html** content of the page (html is the HyperText Markup Language).

URIs or URLs

You may see mention in some places of a URI instead of a URL. The Internet standards are under constant review and the World Wide Web consortium is discussing the subject of URLs and trying to make them more universal. When implemented, they will then be called Universal Resource Identifiers, or URIs. In general use there is some confusion about what to use, URL or URI. If you would like the most up-to-date information, see http://www.w3.org/Addressing/URL/uri-spec.html.

Searching the Web

Most people use search engines to find what they want on the Internet. Many have a favourite search engine on the grounds that it gives them what they want. The best advice is: **don't have a favourite**. You should realize that there are different kinds of search engine, and each will (may!) find what you want, depending on what that is. It is not unreasonable to use six or more search engines in a particular search.

This difference is not so much in the subject area, but rather how you look and exactly what you want. Broadly, search engine indexes (the things that are actually searched) are either **built** by humans or by 'spider' software. Although the actual picture is a little more complex than this, it is worth remembering when you search. For example, the search engine www.yahoo.com uses indexes built by people, so when someone submits a web address to Yahoo, a real live person decides on where to put it in the index. If you use www.go.com, you will be searching through an index created by software that looks for **keywords** in the Web pages it 'spiders'. Many search engines now use multiple indexes and some even use indexes of different types, but the fact remains that different engines will give different results from the same search. **Use more than one**.

If you search for the words 'History' and 'Computer', you could get references to a file that contains the string '. . . he was playing with his toy computer during the history lesson . . .' simply because it contains the correct words. If you had used a human-categorized search engine, you would have been less likely to come across this problem. On the other hand, if keywords are what you want, a keyword search engine is better. For example, if you want information on colossus and Alan Turing you would be better off with a keyword engine, as neither colossus nor Alan Turing are 'subjects'. As a clear demonstration of the power of keyword search engines, try looking for a single line in a famous (or not so famous) poem. For example, try looking for 'If you can keep your head when all about you' in both www.yahoo.com and www.go.com, making sure you put the string in quotes, you may be surprised at the different hits returned. (This is the first line of a poem called 'If' by Rudyard Kipling, which was voted 'the most popular poem in England'). Even more impressive, look for computer components. On a motherboard, a chip was found with just the number 'ms62256h' printed on it. The Altavista Advanced search engine returned seven hits to data sheets about this SRAM chip, whilst www.google.com returned four.

Another consideration is search syntax. Use **Boolean** expressions, which contain logic symbols or statements like +, −, OR and AND. If you search for the words computer and history, you should enter '+computer +history', the + signs meaning that the word must be present. If you don't use the plus signs, some search engines will do a logical OR operation and search for either computer OR history. It is **well worth your trouble** looking at the search engine tutorial at completeplanet.com/tutorials/index.asp, as this will add much power to your searches. You know when you are getting good at searching the Internet when the number of hits you get from a search is less than 100. A search that gives a million hits is unlikely to be of much use. You can also use the – sign to mean do not include, e.g. +history +computer –mainframe to avoid the word mainframe.

Metasearch engines will search other engines for you and give good results. A problem with this approach is that they do not always pass on the right or full syntax to each client search engine, so carefully constructed Boolean searches do not always work.

If you do not have time to look at the tutorial (or if the Web address has changed since this was printed!), try these ideas:

1. Do **not** use CAPITAL letters in searches. Different engines use different rules about capital letters, but lower case nearly always works.
2. Put strings that contain spaces in quotes, e.g. 'if you can keep your head when all about you'.
3. Use + and – signs **routinely**; some engines use OR and AND, but most take + and –.
4. Use the 'advanced' or 'power' searches. Some search engines only allow Boolean expressions in the advanced search page. You can then search for specific items such as 'stored program' AND electronic AND semiconductor AND silicon AND 'alan turing' AND 'blaise pascal'. On a recent trail with Altavista Advanced, this gave less than 40 hits and some interesting information (note no capital letters in the search string).
5. Use plenty of keywords to narrow down a search. Try +history +computer +microprocessor +intel instead of just +history +computer; the first returned 22 hits, the second over 2000 hits on a recent trial.
6. Try putting the string in a different order. Some engines assume the first word is more important than the second, so +history +computer may give different results from +computer +history.
7. Use the * character as a wildcard – e.g. a search for comput* will find the words computer, computers, computing, computation etc. Some search engines, notably www.google.com, do not allow wildcards.
8. Avoid plurals such as computers, as this will miss the word computer. It is better to use a wildcard like computer*, which will find both.
9. Use either site: or domain: to filter for different countries. In various engines, try +history +computer +pentium +site:uk. It should only give sites in the UK (but will miss those with a .com at the end).

Some subjects are hard to research, and there are several reasons for this. Some commercial information is only available for a payment – for instance, current business performance, stock prices etc. are not generally available free of charge. Other information is swamped by commercial interests – try looking for +pentium +computer and you will find hundreds of companies trying to sell you their oh-so-cheap yet oh-so-fast computers. These are areas that will test your searching skills; often the solution is to use a boolean search that includes a technical term not often found in sales literature. The search string +pentium +computer +silicon returned 90 mainly non-commercial hits, whereas just +pentium +computer returned over 4000 hits that were mainly adverts.

Finally, do a search, using different engines, for the expression

+search +engine*. You will find much information that will aid your use of the fantastic resource called the Internet. Computing is one of the fastest-changing subjects yet known, and it is often difficult to keep up to date. One of the most profitable parts of your study time will be polishing your searching skills.

Unit 6 Systems analysis and design

The aim of this unit is to provide students with the knowledge and understanding of how to analyse systems using a specific information system and appropriate modelling tools and techniques. It will provide coverage of the systems analysis life cycle from feasibility through to analysis, design and implementation. In conjunction to the underlying theory provided within the text, case studies and activities are used to introduce and support the text. Students will learn about fact-finding techniques and the importance of gathering and collating information, identifying problems that exist within an organization, and also how to propose solutions to overcome these problems based on user and system requirements.

This unit will give students an insight into more traditional SSADM concepts and provide adequate coverage of modelling tools such as data flow modelling and logical data modelling, which will support students in fulfilling the requirements of the Systems Analysis unit on the BTEC National qualifications for IT practitioners.

6.1 The role of a systems analyst

Systems analysts have to demonstrate a number of qualities to ensure that they succeed in carrying out their role of examining a system or systems. The examination may be required because an organization is experiencing problems that require somebody external to the organization to resolve them. A systems analyst's role is to provide solutions and recommendations as to why the system is not profitable or efficient, depending on the nature of the systems and the organization.

The tasks that a systems analyst perform comply with a certain framework that includes:

- investigation
- analysis
- proposing
- designing.

Systems analysts need to demonstrate a number of communication skills to enable them to talk to all levels of user within the system. These users might range from management through to technical support and end users, such as data input clerks. Each of these users will expect the systems analyst to identify with them and their given needs and requirements.

The ability to work using a methodological approach is also essential for a systems analyst. The collection and recording of data is crucial to ensure that any recommendations made are a true representation of the user and system requirements. A further quality is the ability to draw upon information and to apply experience and knowledge to each individual investigation. It is a fair assumption that no two systems will be the same, because organizations differ in terms of their core business, culture and resources. Therefore, each system should be investigated uniquely; however, the skill is in reflecting on what has worked well in the past, such as an interviewing technique or the recording of certain information, and in building upon this – the use of good practice.

It is clear that to be a good systems analyst a balance of skills is required (Figure 6.1). An imbalance could result in insufficient collection of information, which might lead to an incomplete investigation. With a lack of business computing or technical knowledge, poor quality recommendations might be made. Finally, the lack of application skills may result in a very static proposal.

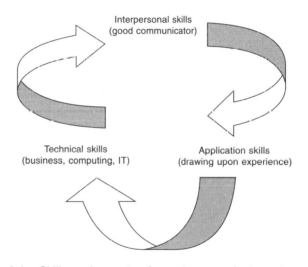

Figure 6.1 *Skill requirements of a systems analyst*

Examination of the skills required of a systems analyst has provided an insight into what is involved in the actual process of examining systems. Systems analysis is, however, a complex procedure that is broken down into quite prescriptive stages. These will now be examined in more detail.

Exercise 6.1

Find two advertisements for a 'Systems analyst', either on the Internet or using a paper or magazine such as *Computer Weekly*, and identify what skills are needed. Match these with the following three areas:

- interpersonal skills
- application skills
- technical skills.

> **Group activity**
>
> Within the class, collate all the information and design a table that maps all of the skills criteria to all of the advertisements. Which skill requirement is most desirable? Why do you think this is?

Why the need for systems analysis?

One of the services that might be provided by a systems analyst is to examine a given problem domain and identify a set of solutions to overcome this. The problem will depend upon the type of organization under investigation.

Organizations fall into two categories; profit making and non-profit making. Profit making organizations include commercial enterprises, industry/manufacturing, and financial institutes. Non-profit making organizations include service industries such as education and health care (although some are deemed to be profit-making), as well as charity organizations. Systems analysis might be required to examine a range of issues associated with money and profits, i.e. a cost reason or an efficiency reason.

Reasons for analysis

1. Cost reason – organizations might require analysis to identify why they are not making a profit, where they can reduce overheads, and how they can increase productivity.
2. Efficiency reason – analysis might be needed to enable an organization to compete better in the market, to improve communication, or resolve resource issues.

Exercise 6.2: Classifying the need for systems analysis

As already described, there are two main reasons for carrying out systems analysis. Complete the table below, giving examples of both cost and efficiency problems associated with each scenario that would require a systems analyst – for example, 'buying items of stock in bulk', cost issues (profitability, cash flow, poor debtor payments), and efficiency issues (storage of stock, personnel to supervise stock provisions, impact upon existing working practices).

Scenario	*Cost reason*	*Efficiency reason*
Launching a new product onto the market		
Installing a new network system		
Examination of a payroll system		
Identifying whether a new branch should be opened		
Deciding whether to set up a commercial website		

Problems that exist within an organization will vary, with some focusing on cost, others on efficiency, and a proportion on both cost and efficiency. Whatever and however varied the problem domain, one aspect that will remain constant throughout the investigation is the implementation of the systems analysis process.

The systems analysis process

Systems analysis derives from SSADM (structured systems analysis and design methodology), which uses a very structured and formal framework consisting of stages, steps, tools and techniques. Prior to any investigation there has to be a need for systems analysis, and somebody will need to initiate the requirement.

The request for carrying out systems analysis can be made by a range of people, including company directors, department managers, functional supervisors, or proprietors of a business. Systems analysis is rarely initiated by end users, although they might be consulted as part of the process. The person who requests the need for systems analysis can be referred to as the 'project sponsor'.

The role of the project sponsor is to provide information to the systems analyst, thus allowing the initial investigation to start.

Figure 6.2 provides an overview of the types of information required, either from a project sponsor or from an initial investigation. A project sponsor may be unfamiliar with the systems analysis process, and will therefore not know what information is sought. Standard documentation that might be provided includes:

1. An organization chart
2. A brief of the requirements (outlining problems, expectations, proposals, constraints of the project such as money or time)
3. A list of personnel – users of the system (outlining what job roles there are etc.)
4. An overview of the system – what the systems does, how it does it, inputs, processing and outputs, constraints etc.

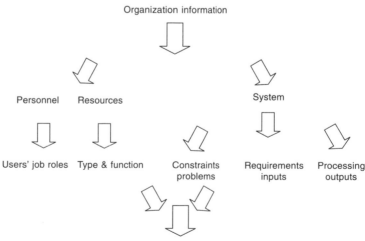

Figure 6.2   *Information required to carry out a systems investigation*

5. A resource list
6. Documentation used to support the system.

Depending upon the size or type of organization under investigation, some, all or none of the above might be provided. If there is insufficient information, the first step in the systems analysis process is to carry out an initial investigation to gather all the information required.

Initial investigation

An initial investigation should be carried out, regardless of how much information the project sponsor provides. The reason for this is first to confirm all of the facts and information already given, and secondly to gather up any missing information that has not been given.

An initial investigation can take up a lot of the project time because the systems analyst is dependent upon other people (i.e. the users of the system) to provide the information. Even if a very tight deadline has been given for completing the systems analysis project, at least a third of the time must be spent gathering the information. Errors made at this time, in the collection of the data, might result in misinformation, leading to incorrect assumptions and proposals.

As information is collected, it should be recorded for future reference. It is important that the systems analyst adopts a methodical approach to the collection and recording of information. There may be insufficient time to go back and gather information at a later stage in the investigation, and therefore all facts should be documented and clearly referenced for the future.

One method of recording the information is to use a table that clearly sets out the details criteria of the information. Table 6.1, for example, provides an overview of information collected from users of an IT department.

An identifier has been used to allow easier cross-referencing to other tables of information that may be set up. The user name is recorded in case there is more than one user doing the same job, which is very probable in most organizations. The role is also given followed by a brief description outlining what the user does.

Although it is clearer using this format who the users are and what they do, the table still does not provide all the information needed to carry out a full investigation into the IT department.

Exercise 6.3

For each of the users identified in Table 6.1, write down a list of questions that would need to be asked to ensure that a more detailed investigation can take place. For example, to Carol Dye: Who are the ten people within the IT department, and what do they do?

When you are satisfied that sufficient and detailed information has been collected and recorded, you can then move on to the next stage of the initial investigation. This involves:

Table 6.1 *Recording user information in an IT department*

ID	User name	Role	Description
1	Carol Dye	IT Director	• manages a department of ten people • looks after the day-to-day running of the IT department • sets IT targets with the Company Director • delegates weekly tasks to the IT staff
2	Jason Kirk	Network manager	• in charge of three network staff • looks after the day-to-day running of the networks • oversees networking installations • liaises with Carol Dye on future networking projects
3	Adam Fuller	Software manager	• in charge of the programming team • looks after and oversees all of the programming projects • liaises with Carol Dye and Jenny Francis, Internet team leader
4	Paul Jacobs	Programmer	• reports to Mark Cornish, Software manager • works on developing new programs to support the organization • Uses C++, Java, Oracle and SQL • currently working with the Internet team to design a new client website

- documenting the findings
- providing initial recommendations to the system requirements
- providing feedback to the project sponsor
- seeking approval from the project sponsor
- continuing with the remainder of the project.

All the activities that have been described in the initial investigation stage represent the first stage of the systems analysis life cycle, that of 'feasibility'.

6.2 Systems analysis life cycle

All projects go through a number of stages before they are completed, and this project development can be referred to as a 'life cycle'. Within the context of systems analysis, the life cycle follows a traditional framework common to other information systems.

The systems analysis life cycle has evolved from the structure set out in SSADM (structured systems and design methodology). Systems analysis and design fit into this structure, but the cycle is less prescriptive and the stages involved are more informal in terms of identification of specific steps and tasks.

Within the SSADM structure there are three main stages: feasibility, analysis and design (Figure 6.3).

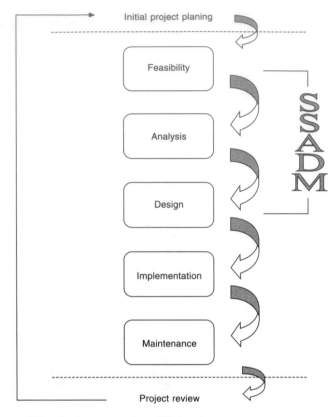

Figure 6.3   *Systems analysis life cycle*

The life cycle is a continuous loop, with each stage feeding into the next. Each stage has a dependency on the stages above and below, which sometimes creates an overlap and integration of tasks between the stages. The initial project planning cascades into the main part of the life cycle where the project development takes place.

At the end of the project development and implementation a review should take place, which will then trigger further action. This action might include:

- further upgrading and development
- adjustment to the project
- closure and signing off of the project.

The review therefore feeds back into the initial project planning stage. If further adjustments or upgrades are required, this will instigate another feasibility study and the launch of further projects.

Initial project planning

This initial stage of the life cycle is almost assumed, and in some cases is not indicated on the traditional life cycle model because it is incorporated within the feasibility study. However, it is worth referring to this initial study to emphasize the fact that the analyst needs to be prepared for the main investigation and the fact-finding exercise. This preparation might include investigation into the

---

Question 6.1

1. What three main stages make up SSADM?
2. Why is the maintenance stage required?
3. Why should each stage be carried out in order?

organization and the system for which the investigation will take place. Clarifying the project brief (if given at this stage), understanding the given problem domain, and establishing the resources required to carry out the investigation are important.

Feasibility study

Within the feasibility stage of systems analysis, an investigation takes place. This investigation is referred to as a 'feasibility study', and can be broken down into three areas (Figure 6.4).

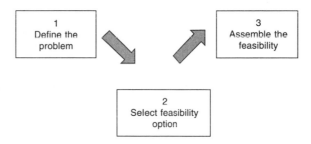

Figure 6.4 *Components of a feasibility study*

In conjunction with the components of the feasibility study, an input source, the initial investigation, feeds into this process. The physical output is the actual feasibility report, and this feeds into the next stage of the systems analysis life cycle.

The function of the feasibility study is to determine the viability of the project proposal and its implementation. During this stage a number of questions may be asked, these include:

1. Can the project be carried out within the set constraints, for example in the allocated time and budget, and will the resources be adequate to support the complete life cycle of the project?
2. What will the impact be on the system and the user?
3. Can the proposal be fully justified?
4. Will the proposal have the necessary resources to ensure that it is successfully implemented?

The answer to these questions should be yes, we do have the time, money and resources, and yes, the impact will be positive, bringing new benefits to both the systems and the users. These benefits include:

- greater efficiency in terms of processing activities within the system
- reduced cost and overheads
- a more standardized way of working and a sharing of good practice across the organization
- improved user and customer satisfaction.

The proposal must be fully justified and quantified, and the necessary resources should be in place.

Once the feasibility of the project has been addressed and the questions answered, the next stage is to examine and establish the actual area of investigation. Defining the system boundaries is

Question 6.2

1. What is the purpose of the feasibility study?
2. Why is the feasibility stage so important?
3. What is the purpose of setting the system boundary?

crucial to the success of the project, and to ensuring that the most appropriate information is being collected within the system boundary. The system boundary can be defined in a number of ways, as set out in Figure 6.5.

Figure 6.5   *Establishing the system boundary*

Setting the boundary can also be referred to in terms of setting the 'scope' – identifying the area(s) of investigation. It is recognized that defining the systems boundary can be very difficult because of the way organizations are structured. Not all organizations have clear boundaries as in Figure 6.3. Most have central functional departments such as marketing, finance and IT for example, the specialist systems being integrated within these as shown in Figure 6.6.

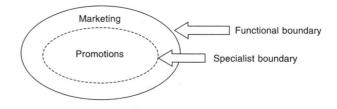

Figure 6.6   *Integration of systems*

Another difficulty in establishing the boundary is when two or more functional departments have dual or multiple or roles, causing an overlap in the system boundaries (see Figure 6.7).

To establish the correct system boundary or the extent of the boundary, information must be collected for verification. The information required can be obtained from a number of sources, including:

Figure 6.7 *Overlap in system boundaries*

- the project brief
- the project sponsor
- users

} outlining and defining the system boundary

- documentation

defining the structure of the organization or identifying functional roles and responsibilities.

Exercise 6.4

1. Identify two documents within an organization that will help an analyst to establish the system boundary for a department such as 'sales'.
2. Describe why these documents are important to this process.

After the boundaries have been clearly defined, the main part of the investigation can begin in terms of identifying the complexity of the problem. Although the problem may be clearly defined within the initial project brief, the investigation that takes place may reveal secondary problems or inaccuracies in the information given and these could distort any proposals put forward. To overcome this situation, and to ensure that all problems have been identified accurately, a fact-finding investigation should be undertaken.

Fact-finding investigation

A fact-finding investigation involves the use of a number of tools and techniques that are applied in order to gather information. The tools and techniques available to the analyst include:

- interviewing
- questionnaires
- investigation of documentation
- observation.

These are the four major recognized methods for gathering information within the fact-finding investigation, although others do exist – e.g. brainstorming sessions, focus groups and workshops.

Interviews

Interviewing users of a system is one of the first stages in the investigation. The objectives of interviewing are shown in Figure 6.8.

Through interviewing users, an analyst can ensure that the information already received is correct. Furthermore, interviewing

Figure 6.8   *Interview objectives*

might uncover new information, and gives the analyst an opportunity to understand the system better through the eyes of the user.

There are a number of factors to be considered when interviewing users, including (Figure 6.9):

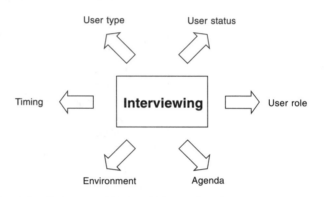

Figure 6.9   *Factors to be considered when interviewing users*

1. **User type** – senior management, head of a department, team leader, data entry clerk, administration staff etc.
2. **User status** – the higher the users are in the hierarchy of the organization, the more limited the time might be to assist with an interview.
3. **User role** – what position do users have within the organization, and what impact do they have on the system investigation?
4. **Agenda** – users within the system might have their own reservations about changes to their system, and may therefore be biased in their interview answers. For example, users might feel threatened during an interview and in fear of losing their job if they feel that the analyst has been called in to cut costs or identify inefficiencies within the system. It is therefore the role of the analyst to decide what is fact and what is fiction, and this can be achieved by validating information with a third party.
5. **Environment** – this will influence the quality of information given by a user; users will feel more comfortable in certain environments in which they feel safe and are sure that they can talk in privacy. For example, managers will feel more comfortable being interviewed in their office as opposed to a staff common room, which is public and more informal.
6. **Timing** – this is crucial in terms of the qualitative aspect of the interview. If the interviewee is prepared and has made an effort to set time aside for questioning without interruptions, the information given will be of a better quality and more detailed.

Other factors that will have an impact upon the interview are the analyst's skill in communicating with all levels of user, and in ensuring that the user feels at ease with the questioning.

Exercise 6.5

1. Working in pairs, set up a fact-finding interview to identify what your interview partner did at the weekend. One person should provide the information about the weekend, and the second should ask a series of questions to extract as much information as possible.
2. To ensure that both people have an interviewing role, once the first interview has been conducted the roles should be reversed so that the interviewee becomes the interviewer.
3. At the end of the exercise, information should be fed back to each interviewee. During the feedback stage the interviewee should say how he or she felt during the interview process, and what information was not uncovered. The interviewer should then feedback and confirm that the information extracted was correct.

Questionnaires

Questionnaires are an excellent way of gathering and consolidating information, providing:

- the questionnaire is structured appropriately
- a control mechanism is in place for gathering up the questionnaires
- the correct user group has been targeted.

Questionnaires should be set out clearly to provide opportunities for short answers based on facts and figures (giving the quantitative aspect), and descriptive answers (providing the qualitative aspect). A balance of questions will ensure that the analyst collects all the information required to continue with the investigation.

It is always best to provide a time constraint for the return of questionnaires – e.g. please return within three working days. Another way to ensure that questionnaires are returned is to get users to fill them in and collect them at the end of the session, if this is feasible.

When designing a questionnaire, it is an important to consider who the questionnaire is aimed at. The target audience is significant because users can interpret a question very differently, depending upon their status and the role they play within the system.

Exercise 6.6

1. Design a questionnaire that could be given to one of the following users:

   - the manager of a new company that sells records and CDs on-line over the Internet
   - a check-out operative at a supermarket
   - a teacher/lecturer working in a school or college.

2. The aim of the questionnaire is to identify what the

Question 6.3

1. What are the four main fact-finding techniques?
2. Identify two other techniques that could also be used.
3. What factors should be considered when interviewing users of a system?

user does within the system and how, who the user communicates with, and what pressures or constraints exist within his or her system.

Group activity

1. Set up small groups based on a mix of users for whom the questionnaire was designed. Each group should have at least two of the chosen user types, i.e. manager, check out operative or teacher/lecturer.
2. Within the group, identify which questions are common to the range of users and which are unique to a specific user. Discuss why these similarities and differences occur.

Figure 6.10 shows a sample questionnaire template.

ID number:	001	System objective:	**Upgrade computers in the Finance and IT departments**
Name: Robert Smith		Department: Networking	Job title: IT support Administrator

Tasks undertaken each day:

- Remove back-up disks and take them off-site
- Set up new users on the system
- Set up security on the file systems
- Produce system documentation and procedures manuals
- First line support – help desk
- Assist with installations and upgrades.

Communicates with: Network manager, other IT support staff in the department, users at all levels, software and hardware manufacturers.

Documents used:

- New user set-up forms
- Internet access forms
- Back-up schedules
- Support call log.

Constraints and problems:	User solutions:
1. Too much documentation 2. Users sometimes have to make multiple requests for passwords because there is no tracking system of who applied when, and sometimes the 'set-up' forms get mislaid.	Automate the support call log, using a database Better storage system and introduce a tracking system

Please tick the following if you agree:

Problems exist with the following

Network ☐   Operating system ☐   Other software ☐   Inexperienced users ☐

Please identify how the above have contributed to the problems with the IT system:

Any other information:

User complaints about the time it takes to attend a call-out. Network keeps crashing, especially between 8:00 and 9:00 in the morning.

Figure 6.10   *Sample questionnaire template*

Investigation of documentation

Examination of documentation is a very good way of understanding the way in which a system operates and the processing activities that take place. Through investigation of documents an analyst can authenticate user statements as to what happens within the system and how, and also trace the source and recipient of certain information.

Examining physical data and information will also ensure that the facts are correct because they have been documented formally. Documents that might be examined in an investigation include:

- invoices
- purchase orders
- goods received notes
- receipts
- customer records.

Exercise 6.7

For each of the following systems, identify five documents that could be examined and describe how important this information would be to an analyst.

1. Travel agents
2. Doctor's surgery
3. School or college
4. Supermarket
5. Football club.

Examination of documents will reveal how information flows internally and externally through the system, the quality and frequency of the information, and also the data capture and storage mechanisms.

Observation

Depending upon the type of system under investigation, observation might be the primary tool for gathering information. Observation is especially effective in dynamic environments where lots of activities are taking place. These activities may not rely on masses of documentation and, because of the nature of the activity, interviewing or questionnaires may not be appropriate. In this scenario an analyst can observe the users and then record what is being achieved and how.

An example of this is the observation of a waiter or waitress in a restaurant who is under pressure to serve the customer quickly and efficiently. Time might be limited for conducting an interview, the balance of qualitative questions on a questionnaire may be inadequate for drawing conclusions, and the only document in use might be a food order pad.

When all of the information required as part of the fact-finding exercise has been gathered, the next stage is to prepare a document that can be given to the project sponsor to ensure that investigation to date meets the required expectations. This document is referred to as a 'feasibility report'. The contents of the feasibility report include:

- an overview of the current system and current system environment
- identification of the problem/problems

Question 6.4

1. What are the benefits of investigating documents in a system?
2. What problems might arise during an investigation of documentation?
3. What document is used to present the findings of the feasibility study?

- details of documentation used to gather or collate information
- a list of options outlined in the business and technical system options
- a selected option
- an action plan for the remainder of the project.

Following the collection of information from the fact-finding exercise, the analyst then has to collate the information and assimilate this into a structured framework from which conclusions can be drawn. To assist in this task a number of formal SSADM documents exist to allow for a more manageable analysis of the information collected. These documents allow the analyst to track roles and responsibilities, and also the requirements of both the system and the users within the current system environment.

6.3 Investigation of the current environment

The fact-finding stage provides the analyst with the information required to examine the current system and put forward a number of options to overcome the problems identified.

In analysing the current system, the following areas should have been examined or identified:

- what happens in the current system
- who is involved, i.e. the users
- the scope of the system under investigation
- the problem(s)
- an overview of solutions as provided by the users.

With this vast amount of information, the analyst has to ensure that documents are not mislaid or information overlooked. To do this the information collected can be transferred onto templates that specifically identify with aspects of the system, such as user information or system requirements. Two of the documents that can assist in this process of standardizing information are:

- user catalogues
- requirements catalogues.

User catalogues

A user catalogue records specific information about a user within a standard template format. The type of information that is recorded includes the job title, responsibilities, and a description of the job role (see Table 6.2).

A user catalogue can be completed at the time of the fact-finding investigation or afterwards, once all the user information has been collected. The user catalogue can be a single-user or a multi-user document. If a user has varied job roles, it might be more practical to use a single document. If there are a number of users with limited job roles, they could all appear on a single template.

Table 6.2 *Sample user catalogue*

User catalogue	
Job title	*Job role/responsibility*
Check-out operative	**Serving customers at the till** • Scans food, drink and household consumables • Deals with cash, cheque, debit and credit card transactions • Assists with bag packing if required
Shelf-packer	**Stacking shelves** • Checks off stock items on the stock sheet • Confirms stock quantities • stacks shelves • Alerts supervisor if re-order required
Stock supervisor	**Authorizing stock orders** • Checks re-order details given by shelf-packer • Fills in an order request form • Gets request authorized by stock manager • Contacts head office, who process the order **Preparing staff rotas** • Liaises with stock and shelf-packing staff • Prepares weekly staff rotas • Authorizes overtime payments

Requirements catalogues

Requirement definition

The main objectives of systems analysis are to identify what problems exist within a system, to define them and to provide solutions to the problems. Identification of problems can come from users, or from the examination of documentation during the fact-finding investigation. A list of requirements may also be stipulated in the original project brief.

Problems that exist within a system might include:

• slow or inefficient processing activities
• poor response times
• restricted or limited systems
• inadequate resources
• lack of quality
• lack of security
• use of obsolete processing.

As each problem is identified it should be recorded, and the function of documenting the problem is referred to as 'requirements definition'. The document in which requirements are recorded is a 'requirements catalogue'.

The types of requirements proposed by users fall into two categories:

• functional
• non-functional.

Functional requirements

Functional requirements are specific to the operation and processing of the system – i.e what the system should do. Examples include:

- displaying how many items of canned vegetables are in stock
- the ability to update the stock items
- the ability to adjust stock item promotions on a weekly basis
- producing a report to show how many cans of processed peas have been sold in a week
- Informing the supervisor when an item has reached the minimum stock level.

Non-functional requirements

Non-functional requirements identify the constraints of the system, for example:

- stock items should be updated within a specific response time
- the new automatic stock system will need to interact with other systems within the organization
- the new system will need to be compatible with existing software in use
- security and access restrictions will need to be in place for different users.

Once requirements have been identified and classified as functional or non-functional, the next step is to document them using a requirements catalogue.

The requirements catalogue

The requirements catalogue is the second document that assists the analyst in formalizing findings. Like the user catalogue, it can be prepared at the time of carrying out the fact-finding investigation, or once the information has been gathered.

The requirements catalogue is an important document because the requirements identified feed into the 'business systems options' and the final feasibility report.

The entries in the requirements catalogue can include information such as:

- the user's identity
- identification of the requirement type (functional or non-functional)
- a description of the requirement
- quantification of the requirement, i.e. target values and acceptable ranges etc. For example, 'to be processed within five minutes of the request'
- overview of the projected benefits
- identification of other dependencies such as further requirements.

To assist the analyst further a standard template can be used for the requirements identified (see Figure 6.11).

To complement the requirement catalogue entries a summary table can be set up (see Table 6.3) that provides an overview of the functional or non-functional requirements by identifying:

- requirement identification number
- requirement
- status (desirable or essential).

The majority of requirements may be functional requirements. However, there will be elements that will have non-functional

---

Question 6.5

1. What is the function of:
   - a user catalogue?
   - a requirements catalogue?
2. List the two types of requirements, and give an example of each.
3. What is a 'requirements definition'?

Requirements catalogue for Store-line Supermarket system			
Requirement ID: 004	Status: Essential	Source: Stock Manager – Pete Jefferson	User involved: Stock Manager, supervisor and stock control team
Functional requirement ☐ Non-functional requirement ☐		Requirement: To provide reports of stock reaching minimum ordering level	
Benefits to the system:		• More accurate ordering system • Ensure that over and under ordering of stock is reduced • Reduce time spent on stock administration • Faster ordering direct to supplier.	

Non-functional considerations:	Access Report should only be accessed by supervisor status or above	Action Set-up a password system

Comments:

Dependency on other requirements:	Requirement ID 001 002 003	Status Essential Desirable Desirable

Proposed solution/s:

1. Transfer stock data onto a database system
2. Set up a reports function
3. Set-up a password system
4 Link new system with 'point of sale' data system

Figure 6.11 *Example of a requirements catalogue entry*

Table 6.3 *Summary requirements list*

Requirement ID	Description	Status
001	Integrate stock control and point of sale systems	Essential
002	Automatic supplier ordering	Essential
003	Use existing hardware	Desirable
004	Reports of stock reaching minimum order level	Essential

considerations as shown in Figure 6.11 with the requirement 'to provide reports of stock reaching minimum ordering level'.

Information taken from the requirements catalogue will be used as the basis for preparing the **business system options** (BSOs) and **technical system options** (TSOs), this collective information then feeding into the final feasibility report.

6.4 Modelling tools

Data flow modelling

Data flow modelling is an established SSADM tool that is used to examine the environment of the system under investigation through the use of data flow diagrams (DFDs) and associated descriptors that are used to identify and establish:

- the flow of information within a system
- the processing activities that take place
- the storage mechanisms used.

Together, the diagrams and the descriptors provide a top-down approach to understanding the system (Figure 6.12).

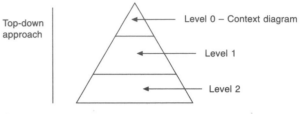

Figure 6.12 *Top-down approach of DFD*

1. External entities

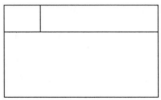

2. Process boxes

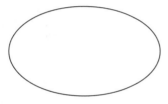

3. Data flows

4. Data stores

Figure 6.13 *Data flow diagram tools*

The top-down approach adopted in data flow modelling is designed to provide a more in-depth analysis of the system the further down the levels. At level 0, which is also referred to as a context diagram, a single process is used to identify the flows of information between the system in its entirety and any external entities.

Level 1 data flow diagrams use a number of processes to represent what is happening in the entire system under investigation. The level 1 diagram provides an insight into the processing of information, sources and recipients of information, types of information, and the storage mechanisms used. The diagram provides a visual insight into the system.

Level 2 diagrams are specific to certain processes that have already been identified at level 1. Level 2 diagrams use a single process, which is a detailed expansion of the version represented at level 1. Within the single process more specific information is detailed, which provides a true and more accurate representation of the system.

Data flow diagrams are very subjective in that analysts examining the same system might interpret some information very differently. The actual framework and tools that are used in data flow modelling are standard, but the way in which the data flow diagram is constructed may be unique to the analyst. The only way to ensure consistency when designing a data flow diagram is to check back with the users, and seek approval from the project sponsor that the data flow diagram is a true reflection of the system.

Tools used in data flow diagrams

There are four tools that are used in the preparation of a data flow diagram, as shown in Figure 6.13.

Each of the tools is used in conjunction with the others to create a data flow diagram. Closer examination of the tools reveals that each has an equally important role in examining different aspects of the system:

- external entities identify people and organizations outside of the system under investigation
- processes represent the activities that take place within the system
- data flows provide the physical link between data sources that flow to, from and within the system

- data stores detail the type of storage mechanism used to hold the data/information within the system.

External entities

External entities are used to represent people or organizations that have a role in the system but are not necessarily part of it.

Example 6.1

Royal Saints Hospital has called in a systems analyst to identify any areas within the hospital that are running inefficiently. The hospital is due to have inspectors in to examine the hospital's procedures and also their spending to enable new targets to be set for the next financial year. The areas of the hospital that are under investigation are X-rays, and accident and emergency. The first system that you have been asked to investigate is X-rays.

Typical external entities for X-rays might include:

- patients coming into the X-ray department
- other hospital departments, such as accident and emergency, or surgery
- doctors and medical staff from other departments
- inspectors.

External entities can appear in a system more than once. In the example given here, a patient would be part of a number of processes within the X-ray system in terms of providing patient details, having a consultation with the doctor, and having the actual X ray. To indicate that a patient appears more than once in the system, the corner of the external entity is crossed as shown in Figure 6.14.

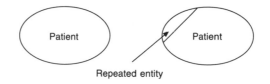

Repeated entity

Figure 6.14 *Sample external entities*

Exercise 6.8

1. Identify a range of external entities for each of the following systems:

    - airline company
    - mail order catalogue company
    - wages department.

2   Identify one external entity for each of the systems which could be repeated, and describe why.

Process boxes

Process boxes represent activities that take place within the system and also activities that are linked to the system.

All activities have a process attached to them; something triggers the process, and an action might become the output of the process. Figure 6.15 illustrates the activity of sending and receiving e-mail.

Figure 6.15 *Sending and receiving e-mail*

The process box has three distinct sections, each with its own identifier in Figure 6.16.

- (1) identifies the process box with a unique number
- (Stock room) provides details of the location where the activity is taking place
- (Check items in stock) identifies the activity that is taking place.

Figure 6.17 provides an example using process boxes.

Figure 6.16 *Sample process box*

> ### Exercise 6.9
>
> Think about an activity that you did at the weekend and record the activity using a set of processes, labelling each accordingly.

Data flows

Data flows indicate the direction or flow of information within the system:

$\longrightarrow$ Feeding out to an output

$\longleftarrow$ Feeding in to an input.

Data flows provide the link to other data flow tools within a system. These links are shown in Table 6.4.

Figure 6.17 *Example of processes to identify a trip to the supermarket*

Table 6.4 *Data flow links*

Data flow links	Data store	External entity	Process
Data store	X	X	✓
External entity	X	X	✓
Process	✓	✓	X

The matrix clearly defines that the flow of information within a system must always evolve around a process. The direct flow of information from process to process indicates that two activities can take place without the intervention of an input such as a data entry clerk. This is true in terms of automatic processing, where a program could receive a set of information and collate or process it, which could then automatically trigger a second process, for example running off a report. Without the use of automated systems direct links from process to process would rarely exist, and they should therefore not be linked on a data flow diagram.

All data flows should be labelled clearly to identify the type of data or information that is being passed to and from sources and recipients, e.g.

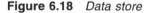

A source is somebody or something that is the source of information (i.e. information flows from it); a recipient is somebody or something that receives information (i.e. information flows to it).

Data stores

Data stores represent different types of storage mechanisms, and there are four different types:

1. D: digitized or computerized storage mechanisms such as files on a database
2. M: manual storage mechanisms such as a filing cabinet
3. T (M): manual transient data stores, which are temporary manual storage mechanisms such as an in-tray on a desk
4. T: computerized data stores that is temporary, for example e-mail (which may be read once and then moved to a permanent storage file, or deleted).

There are two components to a data store, as identified in Figure 6.18.

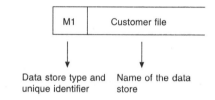

Figure 6.18 *Data store*

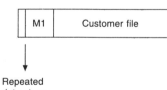

Figure 6.19 *Repeated data store*

In this figure, the information provided tells us that the data store type is manual and the identifier (1) associates to the data store mechanism, which is a customer file. If the customer file was accessed again within the system, it would then become a repeated data store. All of the information remains the same, but we identify the repeated aspect by inserting a second line (see Figure 6.19).

Exercise 6.10

Identify four typical manual and one typical computerized data store for each of the following systems:

- hotel reservation system
- buying a ticket for a concert
- organizing a holiday.

Designing data flow diagrams

The four data flow diagram tools identified complement each other in providing an accurate, diagrammatic overview of the system under investigation. As previously mentioned, data flow diagrams

Question 6.6

1. Name the four tools used in the preparation of data flow diagrams and describe the purpose of each.
2. Which two tools can be identified as being repeated?
3. What does the notation (D), (M) and (T) mean?

provide a top-down approach to modelling. This allows the analyst to interpret the system through three representations, the context diagram, Level 1 DFD and Level 2 DFD. To provide a more realistic and, more importantly, consistent overview of data flow diagrams, Store-line Supermarkets provides as a case study system.

Case study 6.1: Store-line Supermarkets

Store-line Supermarkets is an established chain of supermarkets that are located across the country. Over the past six months the Managing Director of the chain, Mr Thomas North, has discovered that they are losing their proportion of the market to another competitor. Since the beginning of the year their market share has fallen from 16 per cent to 12 per cent.

Store-line Supermarkets has fifteen stores across the region, all located in major towns or cities. The structure of the company is very hierarchical, with the lines of command as shown in Figures 6.20 and 6.21. The structure is generic across all branches.

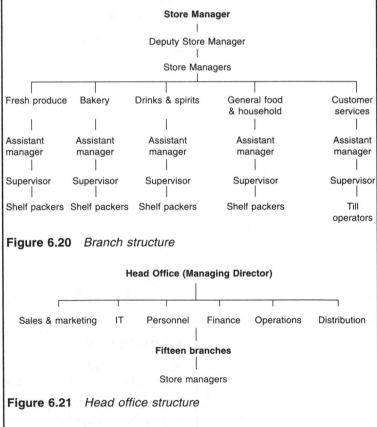

Figure 6.20   *Branch structure*

Figure 6.21   *Head office structure*

All of the functional departments are located at the head office, which has the following implications:

- all recruitment is done through head office for each of the branches, which means that all the application forms have to be sent either by post or on-line (if the application was filled in on-line)

- all stock ordering is done through head office, which has negotiated local supplier contracts for each of the branches
- all of the promotions, for example 'buy one get one free', and all of the price reductions or special offers are filtered through from sales at head office
- all salaries are paid via the finance department at head office
- all deliveries and distribution are made through local suppliers in conjunction with head office instructions.

All the branches communicate on a regular basis, and branches distribute surplus stock items to other branches if they are running low, to reduce supplier ordering costs.

Thomas North has asked for an investigation to take place based on a branch in East Anglia. You have been given some general information about the organizational structure, but Mr North is keen for you to carry out an investigation at the branch. You have been given four weeks to carry out the analysis and then feed back to Mr North.

Fact-finding

Using a variety of fact-finding techniques, you have managed to collect the following information:

1. There are 150 employees at the branch:

    - Store Manager – Mr Johnston
    - Deputy Manager – Miss Keyton
    - five store managers, five assistant managers and five supervisors
    - fifty full-time and part-time check-out staff
    - forty full-time and part-time shelf stackers
    - ten stock clerks
    - ten trolley personnel
    - three car park attendants
    - twenty cleaners, gardeners, drivers, and other store staff.

2. The store managers control their own areas, with their own shelf-stackers and stock personnel.
3. All stock ordering is batch processed overnight to head office on a daily basis by each of the store managers in consultation with the deputy branch manager.
4. All fresh produce is delivered on a daily basis, and non-perishable goods are delivered three times a week by local suppliers.
5. All bakery items are baked on-site each morning.

As each department seems to operate on an individual basis, the first part of the investigation for week one will focus on the fresh produce department.

Fresh produce system

Ann Prior and her assistant manager Mary Granger manage the fresh produce department. Within the department their supervisor, John Humphries, oversees six display/shelf stackers and four stock personnel.

After consultation with a range of employees, the following account of day-to-day activities has been given.

Each day Ann holds a staff meeting within the department to provide information about new promotions, special discounts or stock display arrangements. Any information regarding new promotions comes through from head office. All information received regarding promotions etc. is filed in the branch promotions file. If any price adjustments need to be made that day, the stock personnel are informed so they can check the daily stock sheets.

After the meeting the stock personnel liaise with the shelf/display personnel with regard to new stock that needs to go out onto the shop floor. The information about new stock items and changes to stock items comes from the daily stock sheet. When new items have been put out or stock price adjustments made, they are crossed off the daily stock sheet.

Items that have arrived that day are delivered from the local fresh produce supplier; when the items come in the stock personnel check the daily stock sheet for quantities and authorize the delivery. If items have not arrived or there is an error in the order, a stock adjustment sheet is filled in; this is kept in the stock office. At the end of the day John will then inform Mary of the stock adjustments. Mary then sends off a top copy of the adjustment sheet to head office, and files a copy in the stock cabinet.

Information about stock items running low comes from the daily stock sheet. If an item is low, a stock order form is completed. A top copy is sent to head office and a copy is filed in the stock cabinet. Orders should be made five days prior to the actual requirement of the stock, as head office then processes the information and contacts the local supplier. In an emergency, local supplier information is held by Ann, who can ring direct to get items delivered. However, this costs the company more money because a bulk order has not been placed. Authorization also has to be given by the operations manager at head office and information filled in on the computerized stock request form, which is e-mailed to head office each day, which sends back confirmation.

Head office dictates that all documents filled in on-line also need to have a manual counterpart, one which is sent off while the other is filed with the branch.

Problems with the system include the following:

1. Sometimes the network at head office is down, which means that stock items are not received within five days.
2. The promotions are not always appropriate because of a lack of certain stock. Sometimes it works out that the stock that the branch has a surplus of is wasted because branches cannot set their own promotions in-store

3. The stock cabinet is filled to capacity, and because everything is in date order it is difficult to collate information about certain stock items
4. If there is an error in the stock delivery, nothing can be supplied until the paperwork has been sent off to head office or authorization has been given, even if the supplier has the stock requirement on his lorry.
5. There is too much paperwork.
6. There is little communication with other departments.
7. Targets, which are set by head office, cannot always be met due to the stock ordering problem.
8. Some stock items that come in are not bar-coded.

Context diagram

The context diagram provides a complete general overview of the system and its relationship with external bodies and entities that are outside of the system boundary (Figure 6.22). The relationship between the system and external bodies is represented through data flows of information between the two.

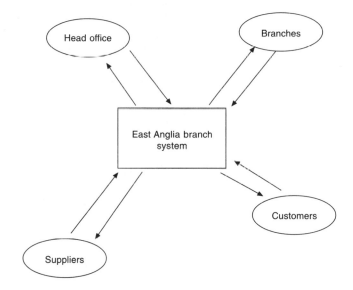

Figure 6.22 *Context diagram for Store-line Supermarkets*

If a context diagram were needed to illustrate just the fresh produce system, fresh produce would appear in the centre of the diagram and other departments within the branch would be added around it as external systems. These would include:

- bakery
- general food and household
- drinks and spirits
- customer services.

Level 1 data flow diagram

Level 1 DFDs provide a general overview of what is happening with the system. The overview will include types of information being passed within the system, documents, storage mechanisms, people, activities, and anything that has an impact on processing activities.

The initial system to be examined at Store-line Supermarkets is 'fresh produce,' and therefore the data flow diagram will be based on this specific system.

Ten-step plan for preparing a level 1 data flow diagram

Step 1   Read through the information collected from:

- the project brief
- the fact-finding investigation
- the user catalogues.

Step 2   Sort the information into clear sections, identifying the following:

- the users external to the system (sources and recipients of information)
- the documents used in the system
- the activities that take place in the system.

Step 3   Produce a 'systems information table'.

Step 4   Convert external users to external entities.

Step 5   Convert documentation to data stores.

Step 6   Convert activities to processes, and identify where the activity takes place and who is involved.

Step 7   Start on a small scale by looking at the input(s) and output(s) to a single process, using data flows to represent the link(s) of data and information.

Step 8   Position the other processes in the diagram.

Step 9   Connect the remainder of the processes with their attributed input(s) and output(s).

Step 10   Check for consistency (examine the initial documentation to ensure that all the information has been represented, and check back with the users or project sponsor that the diagram is correct).

The following is the ten-step plan as used at Store-line Supermarkets.

Step 1 Information is collected from the project brief and the fact-finding investigation carried out at Store-line Supermarkets. The systems boundary is fresh produce

Steps 2 & 3 The information is sorted and a systems information table drawn up (Table 6.5).

Table 6.5   *Systems information table*

External entities	Data stores (documents)	Processes (activities)
Head office	Promotions file	Daily meeting
Supplier	Daily stock sheet	Put out and adjust stock
	Stock adjustment sheet	Check deliveries
	Stock cabinet	Order stock
	Stock order forms	
	Stock request forms	

Steps 4, 5 & 6 Conversion of information into DFD tools (Figure 6.23).

Figure 6.23   *Converting information into DFD tools*

Step 7 Single process DFD (Figure 6.24).

Figure 6.24   *Single process DFD*

Steps 8 & 9 Connection of the remainder of the processes (Figure 6.25).

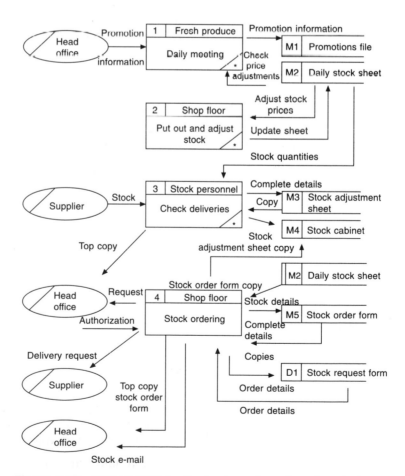

Figure 6.25   *Level 1 DFD for the fresh produce department of Store-Line Supermarket*

Step 10 Ensure that information is accurate and complete; check it against information provided by the personnel within the fresh produce department.

Exercise 6.11

Identify the system that you use for getting up in the morning and coming into College. Identify the activities that take place, who is involved with your system and any documents that you might use to get you to College, ready for your first lesson.

Level 2 DFD

A level 2 DFD provides a more detailed view of a specific process that has been represented at level 1 (Figure 6.26).

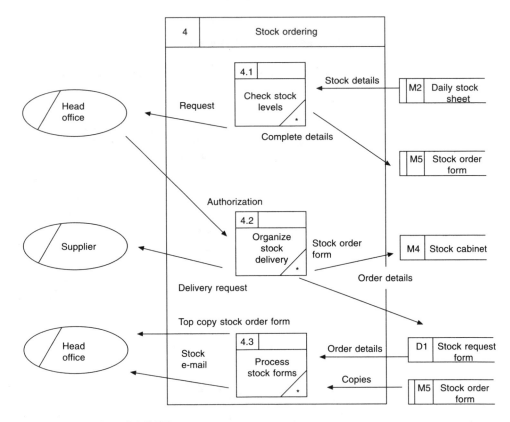

Figure 6.26 *Level 2 DFD*

Exercise 6.12

1. Within the class, identify somebody who has a part-time job or hobby. Get that person to talk through and explain what they do as part of their job/hobby. Record all the information with regard to:

   - what tasks they do
   - who they communicate with
   - what documents they use

> - where information comes from and what happens to the information.
>
> 2. From the information given, produce a context diagram and Level 1 and Level 2 data flow diagrams (if appropriate) for the system.
> 3. One person should then draw up the diagram on the board so that everybody can contribute to the representation of the system. At each stage, checks should be made with the user to ensure that all the information is correct.

Documentation

The second element of data flow modelling is the documentation that accompanies the actual diagrams. The documentation is used to support and clarify areas of the diagram that may be ambiguous.

Documentation that can be used in data flow modelling includes:

- elementary process descriptions (EPDs)
- external entity descriptions
- input/output descriptions.

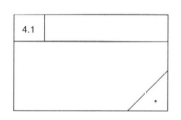

Figure 6.27 *Example of an elementary process*

The different levels of data flow diagram contain different types of processes. Processes at level 1 may be broken down further to a level 2. If a process cannot be broken down any further, this is indicated by putting an asterisk notation in the bottom right-hand corner of the process box (see Figure 6.27). This notation states that there is no further composition of the process. Each elementary process will then have an associated elementary process description, and the descriptions identify the activities or operations that take place.

External entity descriptions detail the status of the external entity in terms of identification of the role and responsibilities it has as part of the system. Table 6.6 provides an example.

Table 6.6 *Example of an external entity description for the Head office at Store-line Supermarkets*

Entity name	Description
Head office	Central functional branch that provides all of the information regarding: - promotions and special discounts - daily price adjustments - stock delivery details - authorization of emergency supplier stock deliveries. All top copies of documentation are forwarded to the head office each day.

Input/output provide textual descriptions of the data flows that extend across the system boundary providing links to external entities.

Data flow modelling provides the analyst with a visual tool from which accurate representations of the system can be drawn. Data flow diagrams assist in identifying the activities and the data that is used within the system, and the textual descriptions provide the support and clarity.

Logical data modelling

Another tool that is used to identify and represent the activities of the system is logical data modelling. This tool provides a detailed graphical representation of the information used within the system and identifies the relationships that exist between data items.

Similarly to data flow modelling, logical data modelling uses a set of tools and associated textual descriptions.

The diagrammatic aspect of logical data modelling is referred to as 'logical data structures'. These structures have four main components (Figure 6.28):

1. Entities
2. Relationships
3. Degree
4. Optionality.

Entities

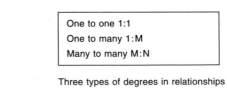

Typical entity types

Relationships

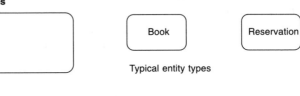

Relationship identified by a linked line between entities

Degree

One to one 1:1
One to many 1:M
Many to many M:N

Three types of degrees in relationships

Optionality

Does the relationship definitely exist, or is it an optional relationship?

Figure 6.28   *Logical data structure notations*

Table 6.7 *Systems and entities*	
System	*Entities*
Library	Book
	Lender
	Reservation
	Issue
	Edition
Hotel	Booking
	Guest
	Room
	Tab
	Enquiry
Airline	Flight
	Ticket
	Seat
	Booking
	Destination

Entities

Entities provide the source, recipient and storage mechanism for information that is held on the system. Examples of typical entities for the following systems are illustrated in Table 6.7.

Each entity has a set of attributes that make up the information occurrences, for example:

Entity:	Book
Attributes:	ISBN number
	Title
	Author
	Publisher
	Publication date.

Each set of attributes within an entity should have a unique field that provides easy identification to the entity type. In the case of the entity type 'book', the unique key field is that of 'ISBN number'. The unique field or 'primary key' will ensure that although two books may have the same title or author, no two books will have the same ISBN number.

Relationships

To illustrate how information is used within the system, entities need to be linked together to form a relationship. The relationship between two entities could be misinterpreted, so labels are attached at the beginning and the end of the relationship link to inform parties exactly what the nature of the relationship is.

Figure 6.29 *Example of entity relationships*

For example, in Figure 6.29 the nature of the relationship could be any of the following:

- an author can write a book, therefore the book belongs to an author
- an author can refer to a book, therefore the book is in reference by an author
- an author can buy a book, therefore the book is bought by an author
- an author can review a book, therefore the book is reviewed by an author (Figure 6.30).

Figure 6.30 *Identifying entity relationships*

The actual relationship that exists in this scenario is that an author updates a book, therefore the book has been updated by an author.

Degree

There are three possible degrees of any entity relationship:

1. One to one, 1:1, denotes that only one occurrence of each entity is used by the adjoining entity (Figure 6.31).

A single author writes a single book

Figure 6.31   *A one-to-one relationship*

2. One to many, 1:M, denotes that a single occurrence of one entity is linked to more than one occurrence of the adjoining entity (Figure 6.32).

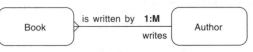

A single author writes a number of books

Figure 6.32   *A one-to-many relationship*

3. Many to many, M:N, denotes that many occurrences of one entity are linked to more than one occurrence of the adjoining entity (Figure 6.33).

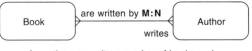

An author can write a number of books and
books can have more than one author

Figure 6.33   *A many-to-many relationship*

Although M:N relationships are common, the notation of linking two entities directly is adjusted and a link entity is used to connect the two (Figure 6.34).

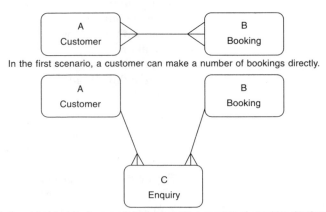

In the first scenario, a customer can make a number of bookings directly.

In the second scenario, a customer can make a number of enquiries that lead to a booking, while bookings result from a number of enquiries made by customers.

Figure 6.34   *Adding a link entity*

Optionality

There are two status types given to a relationship; first, those that definitely happen or exist, and secondly, those that may happen or exist. The second status is referred to as 'optional'.

A dashed rather than a solid link denotes optionality in a relationship (Figure 6.35).

In this scenario a customer may or may not decide to make a booking. If they do the booking will definitely belong to/ be made by a customer.

Figure 6.35   *Optionality*

Logical data modelling documentation

The second component of logical data modelling is the documentation that supports the logical data structure. The documentation used includes:

Question 6.8

1. What should an entity description include?
2. Why should entity relationships be labelled?
3. Provide sample attribute lists for the following entities:
   - appointment
   - invoice
   - menu
   - supplier.
4. What would the primary key be in each case?

- Entity descriptions
- Attribute lists.

Every entity should have an associated 'entity description' that details items such as:

- entity name and description
- attributes
- relationship types and links.

Every entity has a set of attributes. If a large system is being investigated, a number of entities and their associated attributes will need to be defined and therefore an 'attribute list' can be prepared.

Attribute lists identify and describe all of the attributes. The primary key attribute, which is normally made up of numerical data (e.g. supplier number, National Insurance number, examination number), is referred to first, followed by the remainder of the attribute items.

Decision tables

Decision tables provide a simple way of displaying certain actions that occur under certain conditions. They provide a visual representation of this by clearly defining sections devoted to stubs and entries (Table 6.8).

Table 6.8   *Decision table*

	Rules			
	1	*2*	*3*	*4*
Conditions stub	———————→		Conditions entries	
Actions Stub		Action entries	←———————	

The advantages of preparing a decision table are that all combinations of conditions will be considered, and there is a clear overview of what conditions have been met or not met. The standard layout also ensures that information is clearly understood and can be used by a number of end users.

6.5 Business system options

Business system options provide support and justification to the proposals given in the feasibility study. The main objective is to use the BSOs to overcome problems and provide a solution for the requirements of the new system. The BSO will be based on the information given by users outlined in the requirements catalogue. Business system options should be justified in terms of:

1. Are the proposals financially viable and achievable?
2. Will the impact upon the organization be positive and beneficial to the system?
3. How will users benefit from the changes?

Question 6.9

1. Describe what is meant by a tangible cost.
2. Give three examples of a tangible cost.
3. Describe what is meant by an intangible cost.
4. Give three examples of an intangible cost.
5. What factors need to be considered when developing business system options (BSOs)?

4. Will the proposal cause minimal disturbance in terms of implementation to the systems environment?

These areas can be assessed and quantified by carrying out two further types of analysis; 'cost-benefit analysis' and 'impact analysis'. **Cost–benefit analysis** provides an overview of the costs involved with a certain project and maps these against the attributed benefits. In theory every cost listed should have a benefit marked against it in order to justify the expense. The costs can be broken down into two areas: tangible and intangible.

Tangible costs are costs that can be assigned to physical items such as new hardware, software, or additional office equipment. **Intangible costs** are costs for non-physical items such as installation of the hardware, or training to use the new software.

The information in a cost–benefit analysis can be presented in a matrix or a table as shown in Table 6.9.

Table 6.9   *Example of a cost–benefit analysis*

Tangible costs	£	Intangible costs	£	Benefit/s
Three new PCs	4700.00	Installation of PCs	160.00	Wider access to the system by users Reduction in processing activities Improved customer service due to faster response time
New desk-top publishing software	400.00	Training with the software	350.00 35.00 an hour	Ability to create company documents in-house such as letterheads and logos Saving of £650.00 per quarter by producing promotional material in-house and not via a marketing agency
	5100.00		510.00	

Exercise 6.15

Providing business solutions

John Graham is the owner of a small IT recruitment agency, 'IT Works'. Mr Graham currently employs two recruitment consultants who have access to a single computer in the office. There are two telephone lines, one for calls and one for the data connection. The consultants do all of the administration following the temporary or permanent placement of somebody on their books, or the chasing of employers for placements. This takes on average two hours each day. Each consultant has a target to place five people each week, but this target has not been met for the last month by either consultant.

Mr Graham has asked you as a close friend, and also with your skills as an analyst, to put forward some solutions as to how business practice can be improved. To assist you in making recommendations and also in drawing up a cost–benefit analysis, the following information has been provided:

- IT Works provides placements to six large and four small organizations in the area (the company does not have the capacity to provide to any more)
- three new organizations have moved to the area recently and are looking for reputable agencies to provide them with permanent and temporary staff (potentially offering £6000 in introductory fees alone)
- IT Works has thirty people on their books waiting to be placed
- there are periods in the week when no matches between the people on their books and the placements available can be made
- there are only a few hours a week when new contacts can be made
- each consultant spends at least half of their time out of the office with clients
- administration is done ad-hoc when time permits.

Impact analysis

An impact analysis examines the impact of a proposal on the systems environment. The degree of the impact is then quantified in terms of positive and negative, the aim being to introduce a proposal that has a majority of positive aspects and minimal negative aspects. It would be unrealistic to have a new system proposal with no negative impacts because of the constraints imposed – for example, costs, limited time and resources etc. A change to the existing system could also be seen as a negative impact initially for some users, who are familiar with current processing activities and cannot see the advantages of change.

To carry out an impact analysis a number of areas should be examined, as shown in Figure 6.36, and the impact on each considered. A table can then be drawn up as shown in Table 6.10 identifying the subject of the analysis – for example, a user of the

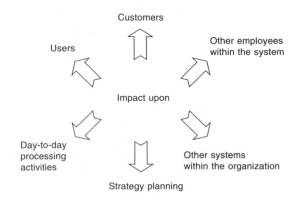

Figure 6.36   *Areas to be considered in an impact analysis*

Table 6.10   *Example of an impact analysis table*

Introduction of a new stock control system		
Areas examined	Impact (+ve or –ve)	Rationale
Customers	+ve	More items in stock and a wider range of items in stock
Users	+ve	Easy access to stock information
	–ve	Time taken to familiarize with new system
Other employees within the system	+ve	Shared and better communication Information readily available
Day-to-day processing activities	+ve	Reduced stock paperwork Automated procedures
Other systems within the organization	+ve	Compatibility with other systems, such as 'point of sale'
Strategy planning	+ve	More competitive for the future

system, a customer or a specific processing activity and the degree of the impact in terms of positive, negative or both.

6.6 Technical system options

Technical system options (TSOs) examine a range of technical, developmental, organizational and functional aspects of the newly proposed system (Figure 6.37).

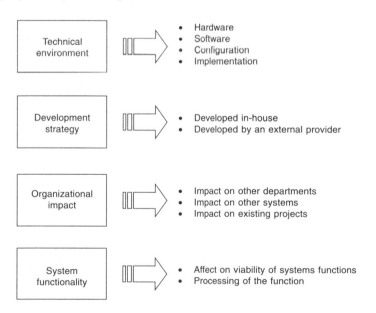

Technical environment	⇒	• Hardware • Software • Configuration • Implementation
Development strategy	⇒	• Developed in-house • Developed by an external provider
Organizational impact	⇒	• Impact on other departments • Impact on other systems • Impact on existing projects
System functionality	⇒	• Affect on viability of systems functions • Processing of the function

Figure 6.37   *Main areas of TSO development*

An analyst is not expected to have expertise in every stage of the project development. Although one of the skills of an analyst is to have technical expertise, in the majority of cases a third party would be called in to advise and, later in the project development, to implement the technical requirements of the new system.

As with the BSO, there are steps involved with the development of TSOs. The first step is actually to identify or define the TSO, and the second is to select the TSO.

Defining the TSO

To assist the analyst in defining the technical requirements of the system, information will be taken from the requirements definition and information provided by the users in the requirements catalogue. Knowing what the system requires technically will provide the analyst with the foundation on which the following can be examined and expanded upon:

- identification of internal and external constraints
- overview of TSO options
- detailed breakdown of TSO option.

Identification of internal and external constraints

Identification and application of the requirements put forward should be analysed from a business (BSO) and a technical (TSO) viewpoint. From a business viewpoint, a number of financial, social and ethical factors are considered to check that the support is in place to implement the systems proposals. From a technical viewpoint, other factors present themselves that are more specifically orientated to the technical implementation of the systems proposals. These factors could also be regarded as constraints of the system requirements (Figure 6.38).

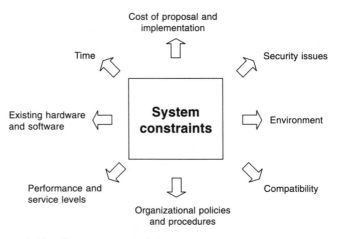

Figure 6.38 *System constraints*

Each of the factors need to be addressed:

1. Is there enough money within the budget to cover a range of tangible and intangible costs to support every aspect of the technical proposal?
2. Will there be adequate time to ensure:

    - acquisition of required system components
    - implementation
    - transferral and updating of procedures, data and information
    - testing?

3. How will the new system fit in with any existing hardware and software?
4. Will the new system be compatible and operate across the required platforms?
5. Will the technical environment be sufficient in terms of storage, cabling, mains sockets etc.?
6. Will the new system meet the required performance and service levels?
7. Will the new system meet the required standards and adhere to the company's policies and procedures?
8. What security will be required, how will user security be set up, and what security procedures will need to be enforced?

Overview of TSO

At least three TSOs should be presented that meet all (or some) of the specified criteria. The sample TSOs should also take into consideration the factors mentioned. The sample TSOs should provide an outline of:

- technical aspects of the system – outline of hardware, software, connectivity, security, maintenance, compatibility issues etc.
- functionality – how the proposal meets the specified requirements
- impact analysis – how the TSO will affect the users, existing procedures and documentation, future developments etc. (the impact analysis should be modelled on a framework similar to that of Figure 6.37)
- cost–benefit analysis (see Table 6.9).

All of the TSO options should be presented in a plan outlining the technical developments and research to date. The plan should also include proposals for the remainder of the project once an actual TSO has been decided upon.

Detailed TSO

The chosen TSO should be developed further to ensure that all the costings previously carried out are valid and current (this is especially important with the changing prices of hardware components, if applicable). A full breakdown of how the system will be implemented and maintained should also be included. Other information that should be expanded upon includes:

- a breakdown and full costings of the system
- a proposed strategy for implementing the system, to include who it will affect internally and who will be involved externally, when the system installation will take place, and how it will be installed
- security requirements and set-up of firewalls, passwords, monitoring software etc.
- proposed input and output screen designs if the software is customized
- limitations in terms of storage, upgrades, compatibility etc.
- a full breakdown of the benefits of the TSO, to include current and future projections and also how each specified requirement is met.

Question 6.10

1. How do TSOs differ from BSOs?
2. What factors are considered when developing TSOs?
3. Why should the inclusion of security issues be of importance at this stage?
4. What costs would need to considered if an organization wanted to install a network system into a department with no existing computers?

6.7 Systems design

Once new system proposals have been agreed, the next stage in the process is to design suitable user interfaces, input screens and menu systems. The introduction of a new system can cause many problems for an organization and these can include:

- compatibility with existing systems
- transference of data between systems
- lack of understanding of the new system by current users.

Compatibility with existing systems

If an organization is introducing a new system into a single department or functional area such as 'accounts', one factor to be considered is compatibility with existing systems in other areas of the organization. Compatibility issues can be a problem due to an incorrect combination of hardware or software. The only ways to overcome this are to upgrade or to find a way to integrate the two systems.

Transference of data between systems

Although issues of hardware and software incompatibility may have been addressed at an early stage, another problem is based on the transfer of data from the existing system to the new system. Problems relating to this include:

- the expertise available to transfer data
- the time taken to transfer data
- the tangible and intangible costs associated with the transfer.

Access to historical data is essential in order for an organization to function efficiently. With a new system installed, current data can be added, but access to records containing customer or supplier information is also needed. To do this, existing data need to be transferred and readily available as soon as the new system goes on-line.

Lack of understanding of the new system by current users

Users may have been content with an existing system, so the introduction of a new system may cause problems, especially with differences in hardware, software or processing methods. Ways to overcome these problems include:

- involvement of users at the design stage
- training.

If users feel confident with the new system, they will feel less threatened by its function and capabilities.

One way to overcome the problems of implementing a new system and end user reluctance to accept it is to prototype a smaller version or part of the system in preparation for the final design.

Prototyping

Prototyping provides the opportunity to design an experimental system or part of the actual system design to test whether or not it meets the specified user or system requirements. By building an actual working system, refinements can be made. This makes it a flexible approach to system design.

Question 6.11

1. What issues would you need to consider when implementing a new system?
2. There are many different ways of implementing a system, such as:

    - parallel
    - Big Bang.

    Explain the main characteristics of each of these two implementation processes.
3. What would you do to ensure that an end user felt confident in using a new system?
4. Research the benefits of prototyping.

Appendix 1: Mapping of outcomes

Unit 1	
Review interpersonal communication skills in a variety of contexts	1.2
Produce written and graphical material to meet a range of end user needs	1.1
Respond to written materials	1.3–1.5
Undertake and evaluate relevant research	1.6
Unit 2	
Explain the internal operations of a model microprocessor	2.1 to 2.6
Evaluate modern computer systems hardware	2.12 to 2
Produce simple low level programs	2.7
Install and use modern operating systems	2.8
Unit 3	
Examine the need for information and its role in organizations of various class, size and structure	3.1, 3.3, 3.5
Investigate the functional areas within organizations and the information flows between them	3.2–3.4
Examine the methods for data handling and processing of information within organizations	3.6–3.7
Understand the physical and operational requirements of a business system	3.8
Unit 4	
Apply simple analysis and design techniques to the software development process	4.9 to 4
Develop basic high-level code using an appropriate procedural programming language	4.2 to 4.8
Produce appropriate documentation for a given program application	4
Use suitable testing methods to ascertain the correctness of a working piece of code	4

Unit 5

Explore the main elements in a data communications system	5.1, 5.4, 5.5
Describe hardware and software used in data communications	5.4 to 5.6, 5.8
Investigate computer networks and their development	5.2
Explain the importance of the Internet and World Wide Web	5.9

Unit 6

Demonstrate an understanding of the principles of systems analysis and design and their part in the development process	6.1–6.2
Investigate and analyse an information system problem and document the results of your analysis	6.2–6.4
Produce and document a design solution to the problem	6.4–6.5
Produce a test plan for the completed design	6.6

Index